This is the first book to explore the complex relationship between theatre, fashion, and society in the late Victorian and early modern era. Beginning with Oscar Wilde's subversive use of modishness in the 1890s, Kaplan and Stowell consider the reception of the "sex problem" play, stage images of the seamstress and shop assistant, the rise of the theatricalized fashion show, and attempts by Edwardian feminists to use both haute couture and the stage to challenge gender stereotypes and aesthetic conventions. Examining such diverse topics as the emergence of the society playhouse, fashion journalism, the role of the couturière-costumier, department store marketing, and the establishment of "dress codes" by militant suffragettes, the study provides a new context for assessing plays by established writers like Wilde, Bernard Shaw, Arthur Pinero, and Harley Granville Barker, as well as lesser-known figures such as Edith Lyttelton, Emily Symonds, and Cicely Hamilton. The book, with numerous illustrations from the period, will be of interest to students and scholars of theatre and fashion history, cultural studies, English literature, and women's studies, as well as to playgoers and general readers.

THEATRE AND FASHION

Pygmalion. Act v ensemble for Mrs. Patrick Campbell. Design by Handley Seymour. Reproduced by courtesy of the Trustees of the Victoria and Albert Museum from *Theatre Costume Designs* published by Emmett Publishing Ltd.

THEATRE
AND FASHION

Oscar Wilde to the Suffragettes

JOEL H. KAPLAN

AND

SHEILA STOWELL

CAMBRIDGE
UNIVERSITY PRESS

Published by the Press Syndicate of the University of Cambridge
The Pitt Building, Trumpington Street, Cambridge, CB2 1RP
40 West 20th Street, New York, NY 10011-4211, USA
10 Stamford Road, Oakleigh, Melbourne 3166, Australia

First published 1994

Printed in Great Britain at the University Press, Cambridge

A catalogue record for this book is available from the British Library

Library of Congress cataloguing in publication data
Kaplan, Joel H.
Theatre and fashion: Oscar Wilde to the suffragettes / Joel H.
Kaplan and Sheila Stowell.
p.   cm.
Includes bibliographical references and index.
ISBN 0 521 41510 1
1. Theater – Great Britain – History – 19th century.   2. Theater –
Great Britain – History – 20th century.   3. Costume – Great Britain –
History – 19th century.   4. Costume – Great Britain – History – 20th
century.   5. Theater and society – Great Britain.   6. Feminism and
theater – Great Britain.   7. Fashion – Great Britain – History – 20th
century.   I. Stowell, Sheila, 1954– .   II. Title.
PN2594.K36   1994
792'.0941'09034 – dc20   93-3664   CIP

ISBN 0 521 41510 1 *hardback*

For our daughters
Jordan
Philippa
Isabel

Contents

Illustrations

Acknowledgments

The research for this study was carried out over a period of four years in a number of libraries and archives in North America and the United Kingdom. We would like to thank the following institutions for extending to us the courtesy of their facilities: the British Library, the British Library Newspaper Library (Colindale), the Mander and Mitchenson Theatre Collection, the Fawcett Library, the Garrick Club, the Arts Club, the Theatre Museum, the Museum of London, the Victoria and Albert Museum, the Guildhall Library, Selfridges Archive, Harrods Archive, the University of London (Senate House), the University of Glasgow (Special Collections), the University of Bristol (Theatre Collection), the New York Public Library at Lincoln Center (Billy Rose Theatre Collection), the Forbes Magazine Collection, and the Harry Ransom Humanities Research Center (HRHRC) at the University of Texas at Austin.

We are indebted to the following individuals for a variety of kindnesses, including assistance with research material, responses to queries, and comments upon earlier drafts of our work: Diane Atkinson, J. Conway, John Dawick, Anthony B. Dawson, Joseph Donohue, Bernard Dukore, Meredith Etherington-Smith, Richard Foulkes, Viv Gardner, Mara Gottler, Cathy Henderson, Claire Hudson, Russell Jackson, Dennis Kennedy, F. J. Lewis, David Mayer, Jan McDonald, Valerie Mendes, Margery Morgan, Robert Newman, Barry Norman, Kerry Powell, F. J. Redding, Eric Salmon, Ivan Sayer, Kay Staniland, Christian and Zita Viola, Peter Whitebrook, Jim Winter, and Jon Wisenthal. We are particularly grateful for the encouragement and support provided by Victoria Cooper and Sarah Stanton at Cambridge University Press, and for the services of copy-editor Christine Lyall Grant.

We would like to thank the following associations and institutions for allowing us to present work in progress under their auspices: the

Edinburgh International Festival, the Museum of London, the International Federation for Theatre Research, the American Society for Theatre Research, the Mid-America Theatre Conference, and the Universities of Glasgow, Leicester, London, and Manchester.

Plates 1–5, 10, 13, 16–19, 25, and 26 are reproduced by courtesy of the British Library and British Library Newspaper Library (Colindale); plates 11, 15, 20, and 21 by courtesy of the Theatre Museum and the Trustees of the Victoria and Albert Museum; plates 22–24 by courtesy of the Museum of London, and plate 12 by courtesy of the Forbes Magazine Collection, New York. Plates 6–9 and 14 are from the authors' own collection. Quotations from the works of Bernard Shaw and Harley Granville Barker appear through the courtesy of the Society of Authors as literary representatives of the Estates of Bernard Shaw and Harley Granville Barker.

Material from this study has appeared in earlier form in *Modern Drama, Theatre History Studies, British Theatre in the 1890s*, ed. Richard Foulkes (Cambridge University Press, 1992), and *Harley Granville Barker: An Edinburgh Retrospective*, ed. Jan McDonald and Leslie Hill (Glasgow: Theatre Studies Publications, 1993).

Our research has been generously supported by the Social Sciences and Humanities Research Council of Canada.

Introduction

Writing for the *Dramatic Review* in the winter of 1885 William Archer predicted that "the fashion-play" would become "*the* art-form of the late nineteenth century." Replying to dramatist Dion Boucicault, who had condemned works in which leading ladies wore "six or seven new dresses" the same night, Archer insisted, tongue-in-cheek, that comedy and melodrama, the principal genres of the previous century, were spent forces. What was wanted, in a new age, was rather "the courage to do openly what many have surreptitiously attempted, namely, to dramatize a fashion plate." The benefits of such a drama were readily apparent, from the befuddlement of the Lord Chamberlain's Office, which did not generally "meddle with ... dress," to the prospect of a large, paying public on both sides of the Atlantic. Indeed, so timely was the venture that, if approached in the proper spirit, it promised to "become a national solemnity, uniting all classes and parties, like the trilogies of Athens or the circus sports of Rome" (8 February 1885, 20–21). In the event, Archer spoke more prophetically than he knew. Over the next quarter-century the vexed relationship between fashion and the stage would intrude itself into the center of late Victorian and Edwardian social life, helping to shape phenomena as seemingly disparate as the emergence of the society playhouse, the coming of Ibsen, the rise of the modern fashion show, and the adoption of "dress codes" by militant suffragettes. It would also affect, more specifically, the production and reception of dramatic texts by writers both canonical and now marginalized, from Oscar Wilde, Arthur Pinero, Bernard Shaw, and Harley Granville Barker, to Cicely Hamilton, Elizabeth Baker, Emily Symonds, and Edward Knoblock. The broad interplay between theatre and community in which these events participated included, besides playscripts and their presenters, a privileged audience unsure of its own boundaries, and an enterprising group of West End modistes eager to exploit theatre connections to compete with established rivals. Both the stage traffic that resulted, in women's bodies as well as gowns, and the uses to which such traffic was put by playwrights intent upon anatomizing fashion products and gender roles, offer a unique opportunity to reassess a self-conscious employment of stage dress Roland Barthes, in "The Diseases of Costume," has condemned as "pathological" (pp. 41–50). If couture house clothes are, in Barthes's terminology, too "hypertrophied" to assist in the arduous tasks of argument or signification, what happens when fashion itself becomes the subject as well as a means of dramatic discourse?

The five chapters that comprise the present volume explore from a range of complementary viewpoints the shifting relationship between theatre, fashion, and society, in the period that separates *Lady Windermere's Fan* from the outbreak of the Great War. In attempting to bring to bear upon some quarter-century of theatre history recent work in fashion studies, social history, and dramatic literature, we have drawn freely (and eclectically) upon a variety of approaches, from performance phenomenology and reception theory to feminist historiography and theatre semiotics. We have, in the process, tried to listen to voices speaking from the period itself, consulting a wide range of published and unpublished materials, including theatre prompt books, rehearsal notes, costumes and costume renderings, fashion house and department store records, personal correspondence, and, above all, some sixty periodicals addressing, for diverse publics, contemporary issues of dress, theatre, and fashion politics. An initial chapter attempts to reclaim a cultural matrix for the society comedies of the *fin de siècle*. Its starting-point is the convergence in the early 1890s of an aggressive fashion press, innovative merchandising by a new breed of independent dressmakers, and the transformation of a select group of West End theatres into an essential part of the London Season. Upon stages like the Haymarket, the Criterion, and the St. James's, we argue, leading ladies not only served as living mannequins, displaying for their more affluent patrons a selection of couture house goods, but in so doing completed within the playhouses themselves a voyeuristic triangle between stage, stalls, and gallery that echoed the arrangement of semi-public society events like Ascot, Henley, and the Derby. It was a dynamic exploited by Oscar Wilde and Henry Arthur Jones, who in a series of comedies that replicated the minutiae of fashionable life enabled the stage to gaze back at its viewers. Wilde's complaint in 1891 that Victorian sobriety had turned men's formal wear into a "frame" or dark border used "to isolate and separate women's dresses" articulated a tactical problem. How to create precise but expansive visual texts out of the male restraint and female display that had come to characterize late Victorian fashion? Wilde's response was to challenge his dandies with the task of expressing themselves through a dwindling vocabulary of visual forms. Hence the importance attached to the well-made tie and carefully thought-out buttonhole. Women's costume offered, in contrast, a broad field for sartorial play, enabling icons of mid-century melodrama to be turned, through the efforts of firms like Lewis and Allenby, Mary Elizabeth Humble, and Mesdames Savage and Purdue, into fashion "statements" that challenged moral and aesthetic orthodoxies. Jones's more frontal assault upon the objects of good society is best seen in *The Liars* (Criterion 1897). The bleakest of the decade's comedies of modern life, the rot beneath its glittering surface was signaled by the engagement of the couturière Lucile, whose risqué ensembles enabled Jones to argue, through the language of dress, a moral bankruptcy his producer had been loath to let him put into words.

Our second chapter, a study in performance phenomenology, focuses upon the body and wardrobes of a single actress, suggesting how both were used to create, and ultimately dismantle a peculiarly English form of drama. Through the 1890s, Mrs. Patrick Campbell was virtually synonymous with what contemporaries called the "sex problem play," a dark counterpart to that decade's increasingly troubled society comedies. An attempt to dress Ibsen to Mayfair standards, the form, whose most considerable practitioner was Arthur Wing Pinero, substituted for intellectual debate a sensuous materiality Shaw dubbed "Pineroticism." We take as our initial text Harley Granville Barker's observation that through the late eighties and early nineties the suburbanity of Ibsen's worlds created real barriers for West End audiences weaned on a diet of Scribe, Sardou, Dumas, and Augier. Elizabeth Robins's 1891 production of *Hedda Gabler* became for such playgoers the acceptable face of "progressive" theatre. The most up-market of Ibsen's works, it suggested ways in which problem playmaking might be reconciled with smart gowns and chic accessories. The production of Pinero's *Second Mrs. Tanqueray* at the St. James's in 1893 was an attempt to move such drama from the fringes to the center of smart society. In so doing both Pinero and his producer, George Alexander, relied upon the anorexic eroticism of the young "Mrs. Pat" to steer a perilous middle course between melodrama and modernity. Outfitted by Mesdames Savage and Purdue in a sequence of gowns meant to chart her progress from demi-mondaine to the legal chattel of a West End gentleman, the actress helped to create a disturbing image of a bony lady in fashionable wraps, a death's head in the drawing room that folded the play (and genre) in a spectral morbidity. Two years later, in *The Notorious Mrs. Ebbsmith*, Pinero used his performer's disconcerting slenderness to mediate between the like somatotypes of the shabbily dressed spinster and tight-laced provocatress. Shifted mid-play into a *décolleté* evening gown of Italian cut, Mrs. Pat took issue with both the scope and nature of Pinero's text. Her response was to make her own body a site of rebellion, inviting viewers to rewrite the play's conclusion. In *Pygmalion*, some two decades after, Shaw sought to deliver a death-blow to a "wicked" but remarkably resilient "Pinerotic theatre," re-dressing that drama's most redoubtable icon as sham duchess and Covent Garden flower-girl. Yet if, through a tangle of conflicting motives, we can discern an attempt to bring Mrs. Pat within the orbit of disquisitory playwriting, Shaw's attacks upon the actress as a "dressmaker-made woman of fashion" were countered by Mrs. Pat's own determination to reconcile free-thinking with couture house gowns. Operating through ensembles built by her personal dressmaker, Madame Handley Seymour, and, as it turned out, at some cost to her professional career, she conducted a counter-argument that resisted Shaw's text as effectively as she had resisted Pinero's some twenty years earlier.

Mrs. Patrick Campbell's 1904 production of Edith Lyttelton's *Warp and Woof* is our point of departure for two chapters that examine an Edwardian preoccupation with the processes as well as the products of haute couture. In the first we consider the work of three feminist playwrights who sought to place upon West End stages the abuses of an exploitative dress trade. In *Warp and Woof*, Lyttelton, wife of Colonial Secretary Alfred Lyttelton and a member of the exclusive Souls, confronted an audience of society peers with damning images of their own making. Drawing upon a rich tradition of seamstress iconography, as well as a literary heritage that reached back to Thomas Hood's "Song of the Shirt" (1843), she dramatized, in concert with Mrs. Pat, not only the ills of a West End dressmaking emporium, but the ways in which its products oppressed both their

makers and purchasers. The point was underscored by the metamorphosis, over an evening, by society costumier Otto Viola, of three
fashionable ladies into emblems of unleashed and predatory sexuality. Mrs. Pat, casting herself against type as Lyttelton's seamstress,
Theodosia Hemming, concluded the play with a thundering *j'accuse*,
denouncing, before an audience of smart admirers, the "canni-
balism" of haute couture. What Lyttelton did for the sweated
seamstress, Cicely Hamilton and Elizabeth Baker attempted to do for
the related figure of the drapery shop assistant. Building upon union
organizer Margaret Bondfield's accounts of the hard lot of retail
workers, including their victimization by a much despised "living
in" system, both playwrights offered correctives to the escapism of
"shop-girl" musicals like *The Shop Girl* (Gaiety 1894) and *The Girl
Behind the Counter* (Wyndham's 1906). Responding to the fancy-dress
transformations characteristic of that genre, each playwright introduced to her work dressing or undressing episodes, designed to
demonstrate what Hamilton, in *Marriage as a Trade* (1909), called a
woman's "professional" interest in adornment. In Baker's *Miss
Tassey* (Royal Court 1910), the harlequin oufitting of a young shop
assistant is juxtaposed with the suicide of a middle-aged co-worker no
longer able to sell herself behind a counter. The much discussed
dormitory undressing scene that opens Hamilton's *Diana of Dobson's*
(Kingsway 1908) was, likewise, calculated to replace "romance"
with a gritty matter-of-factness. Indeed, critics were surprised at the
way in which the disrobing of five shop girls making ready for bed
could be made so mechanically unarousing. Each author, in lobbying
for legislative relief, while insisting upon the need for new myths by
which to live, appealed to both society and working-class spectators,
taking as her provenance not merely trade abuse, but the spectacle
and meaning of women dressed.

In or about 1900 the couturière Lucile theatricalized fashion
marketing by building a ramp and curtained recess at one end of her
shop in Hanover Square. Here, to the accompaniment of music and
flashes of limelight played from the wings, a succession of "glorious,
goddess-like girls" paraded gowns for coteries of invited guests. Our
fourth chapter begins with such attempts to carry stage experience
back to the world of commercial dressmaking, and the consequent
replacement of the seamstress and shop assistant by the mannequin
or couture house model as the millinery trade's most conspicuous
object of male desire. Lucile, together with her Parisian counterpart

Paul Poiret, encouraged male attendance at what she termed her mannequin parades, using techniques of theatrical display to both arouse and contain her viewers. The complex eroticism that resulted – working-class women dressed as society ladies promenading silently for middle- and upper-class men – was augmented by a decision to substitute for the numbers by which gowns had hitherto been identified names that flirted with open prurience. The full hothouse effect of the Edwardian fashion show is preserved in a column by novelist Marie Corelli, who complained in 1904 of the "remarkably offensive" way in which male viewers were "invited to stare and smile." Such occasions provided, in turn, a resonant language for those who wished to explore, on commercial and repertory stages, the fraught relationship between clothes, consumption, and the objectification of women. In *The Madras House*, presented to avant-garde playgoers as part of Charles Frohman's 1910 repertory season, Granville Barker offered a Lucile-style mannequin parade as the culmination of a comprehensive indictment of a trade and ideology that had consigned women to lives of buying and being bought. Dressed by Madame Hayward, a rival of Lucile's who used the occasion to mock the house styles of her competitors, the episode commented upon the human costs of erotic advertising, as well as attempts by department store moguls like Gordon Selfridge and Richard Burbidge to seek new markets in an emerging women's movement. While applauded through its brief run by the labor and suffrage press, *The Madras House* must be set alongside the commercial success of West End musicals like *The Girl Behind the Counter* and *Our Miss Gibbs* (Gaiety 1909) which openly celebrated both Edwardian consumerism and what they called the independence of "the shopping woman." On the legitimate stage, the fashion industry found its most adept apologist in popular playwright Edward Knoblock, whose 1914 success *My Lady's Dress* used former Gaiety Girl Gladys Cooper, Bond Street milliners Ospovat and Zac, and a parodic view of a Poiret "private show," to argue in melodramatic terms the innocence of couture house art.

The larger questions raised by such works, especially as they affected the production and consumption of images of women, are the subject of our final chapter, which turns from the theatre proper to the reactions of Edwardian feminists to theatricality, fashionability, and gender stereotypes. Taking as our starting-point an emblematic meeting between Lucile and militant suffragette Emmeline Pankhurst, we begin by looking at the ways in which suffrage supporters embraced haute couture as a means of combating anti-suffrage propaganda. Dressing well, as a retort to caricatures of the dowdy spinster or "would-be man," became, under the circumstances, a political act, as women fought for their rights *as women* to occupy space previously occupied by men alone. Public response to the appearance of fashionable feminists is approached through an examination of attitudes towards suffrage street theatre and Elizabeth Robins's 1907 "dramatic tract" *Votes for Women!* (Royal Court). As one contemporary complained, with some justification, suffrage sympathizers faced the prospect of either being dismissed as failed women or patronized as pretty ones. The formation of the Actresses' Franchise League in 1908, with a playwriting division under the directorship of Inez Bensusan, is seen as part of a larger attempt to grapple with such issues. So too are the commercially successful "sartorial" dramas of Emily Morse Symonds, a suffrage supporter who, in pieces like *Clothes and the Woman* (Imperial 1907) and *Tilda's New Hat* (Royal Court 1908), sought to identify women's finery with independence and female camaraderie. Such works are considered within the context of a volatile alliance between suffrage consumers and fashion producers, a troubled but mutually profitable arrangement that allowed fashion advertising in prohibited publications and the marketing of suffrage gowns in West End department stores. The fruits of this rapprochement are apparent in stage plays and street processions in which suffrage feminists were able to turn the tables upon their opponents, presenting anti-suffrage supporters as unmodish or overdressed. A final section considers the special case of entrepreneur Gordon Selfridge, whose attempts to appropriate the women's movement for commercial ends had been pilloried in Granville Barker's 1910 *Madras House.* We focus upon both Selfridge's support for the suffrage cause, as well as the dangers inherent in his self-serving boosterism. The chapter, and study, concludes with a brief examination of *Selfrich's* [sic] *Annual Sale* (Savoy 1910) and *The Suffrage Girl* (Royal Court 1911), two plays presented under Selfridge's own auspices, in which Selfridge, conflating modern consumerism and female emancipation, attempted to return the stage, after two decades of dress debate, to the uncritical merchandising that had characterized it in the pre-Wilde nineties.

CHAPTER I

The glass of fashion

On 25 February 1892, the *Lady*, a gentlewoman's magazine that had begun publication some seven years earlier, introduced a column dealing with "Dress on the London Stage." In a brief preamble, Thespis, the column's pseudonymous author, set out its rationale. Hitherto, we are told, London fashion was fed by the couture houses of Paris, especially the great Maison Worth. Now, however, even the most casual observer might note "another source from which costumiers and others interested in dress draw largely – namely, the London stage." In a handful of West End theatres, especially in plays of modern life, audiences regularly encountered novelties of cut, color, and silhouette that offered alternatives to the formalism of the Parisian Houses. Playgoers, moreover, were beginning to incorporate such items into their own wardrobes, initiating, in the process, a pragmatic if sobering form of theatre criticism. Can any play really be bad, Thespis asks, if we gain from it "a new idea for a bonnet, hat, or other feminine trifle?" Recording debts of gratitude to actresses Marion Terry, Maude Millet, and Mary Moore, all identified with particular fads or fashions, Thespis concludes by promising, in future issues, parallel coverage of French couturiers and English stage gowns (225–227). In the end, the *Lady*'s theatre column proved short-lived. Its promise, however, was fulfilled in a variety of sister publications. Florence in the *Sketch*, Virginia in *Black and White*, Miss Aria in the *Queen*, Thalia in the *Players*, Player Queen in the *Lady's Pictorial*, and Diana and Flower-o'-the-May in the *Illustrated Sporting and Dramatic News* offered readers, through the nineties, elaborately detailed accounts of women's stage dress, supplementing their texts with lavishly executed fashion plates. In focusing upon the London stage as a platform for marketable commodities such writers not only identified dressmakers unnamed in theatre programs, but supplied trade information and street addresses. Virginia, catering to the widest public, sold paper patterns for costumes described in her column. From the far side of the footlights the phenomenon is best summed up by Florence Alexander, who, as wife to actor-manager George Alexander, oversaw women's costumes at the exclusive St. James's Theatre: "I was rather 'extreme' [i.e. meticulous] with clothes on stage, for in those days people went to see the St. James's plays *before* ordering a new gown" (Mason, p. 233). The suggestion, once again, is of a stage not merely reflecting but anticipating and creating fashion.

If such merchandising represented, as novelist Marie Corelli would later charge, a cynical collusion of stage, shop, and society press (*Bystander*, 27 July 1904, 436–439), it was facilitated in the nineties by a new wave of independent designers determined to break the monopoly of established houses. Through the previous decade male modistes such as Worth and Redfern had dressed female actors for a variety of West End roles. The pattern had been set in Paris some thirty years earlier, when Charles Frederick Worth, a transplanted Englishman, overwhelmed the French fashion world with the products of a single couture firm organized upon modern industrial lines.[1] Between 1860 and 1890, Europe's first "man-milliner" reshaped the look as well as the methods of luxury dressmaking, abolishing the bonnet and cage-crinoline, while championing, in rapid succession, the shoulder train, walking skirt, tunic dress, and cuirass bodice.[2] On Parisian stages Worth's passion for dress reform made possible a rapprochement between classical detail and contemporary cut. For period drama he drew upon an encyclopedic knowledge of fashion history to create modish variations upon seventeenth- and eighteenth-century styles. In plays of modern life – which inevitably meant society life – Worth brought to theatre costumes the same fabrics, embellishments, and precision tailoring that had come to distinguish his off-stage work. It was a practice that received royal assent when the Empress Eugénie commanded Worth to copy for her personal use a stage gown he had made for actress Marie Delaporte. Such methods established a two-way traffic between stage and salon that prepared the way for the marketing strategies noted by Thespis and Corelli. They also enabled Worth to achieve a control over theatre fashion so absolute he was able to dictate to dramatists like Scribe and Sardou what his clients would wear in their plays.[3] By the mid-eighties Londoners could read about Worth's theatre gowns in the fashion pages of the *Queen* or Oscar Wilde's *Woman's World*. They could also see them at first hand in the stage wardrobes of Lillie Langtry, and the melodramas of "sporting life" presented at Drury Lane by impresario Augustus Harris (Booth, p. 71).

Dresses by Worth continued to be worn in West End plays through the nineties. The decade also saw, however, the first real challenge to Worth's monopoly of on- and off-stage fashion. In Paris the attack was led by Madame Paquin, who sought to replace the "dignity" for which Worth was most often noted with a more openly theatrical glamor. She was seconded in this by Mesdames Gerber and Vertran, whose House of *Callot Sœurs* offered clients more heavily decorated alternatives to Worth's drawing-room gowns. In London, where Worth's influence had been felt at one remove, the stage became the principal marketplace in which his authority was tested by rivals who had neither the prestige nor resources of their Parisian counterparts. Mesdames Savage and Purdue, Mary Elizabeth Humble, Madame Eroom, and Mrs. James Wallace, later known as Lucile and, later still, Lady Duff Gordon, all made their first appearances in *Trades* and *Commercial Directories* between 1891 and 1895, identifying themselves as "Dressmakers" rather than "Costume Makers" or "Theatrical Costumiers." When they worked for the stage, as each in turn did, they attempted to form exclusive alliances. Mesdames Savage and Purdue became, in effect, house dressmakers to the St. James's, where their chiffons, silks, and leg-of-mutton sleeves helped to establish the look and feel of George Alexander's society drama. Between 1892 and 1897 they built costumes for thirteen productions, including *Lady Windermere's Fan*, *The Second Mrs. Tanqueray*, *The Masqueraders*, and *Liberty Hall*. Madame Eroom performed a like service for Charles Wyndham at the Criterion, where over a two-year period, between 1894 and 1895, she dressed actresses in some half-dozen pieces, including *The Home Secretary* and *The Case of Rebellious Susan*. Neither seems to have worked for other managements, each regarding herself not as a theatre professional but a society dressmaker using the stage for promotional purposes. With the exception of Lucile each of these figures curtailed stage work after receiving the Drawing Room commissions that enabled her to call herself "Court Dressmaker."[4] In the interim, playhouses became second showrooms, with London's leading ladies serving as living mannequins. Indeed, if we note that the fashion model was herself a relatively recent invention, the widespread use of actors for advertising ends may be seen as a calculated response to the wood and wax lay figures still used to display clothes in more conservative establishments.

Before considering how such events were appropriated by playwrights and their producers, it might be well to recall the manner in which, by the century's end, a select group of West End theatres had themselves become part of the London Season, perpetuating in their very architecture some of the tension between public space and privileged enclosure that helped to define late Victorian society. Not only Alexander's St. James's and Wyndham's Criterion, but the Garrick under John Hare, and the Haymarket under Lewis Waller and Herbert Beerbohm Tree attracted to their stalls and boxes playgoers whose mere presence would be noted in the society papers and clubland press the following day, spectators for whom the mirror up to nature was invariably stuck full of visiting cards. For such coteries, intent (in the language of commodity theorists) upon consuming images of their own wealth and power, the costumes and accessories of society drama held a special significance (Gagnier, pp. 105–106). The most obvious of obtainable goods, they could not only be admired on stage, but literally bought, carried back through the looking-glass, and made to participate in a world of social intercourse, a triumphant vindication of Wilde's quip about life, in the end, mimicking art. From the pit and gallery, such acts of up-market consumerism were observed by a wider public of journalists, middle-class householders, clergymen, and laborers, many of whom queued for hours to obtain seats in the theatres' upper reaches. Indeed, in the creation of a triangular and voyeuristic relationship between stage, stalls, and gallery, London's more fashionable theatres reproduced a dynamic familiar to those who attended Ascot, Henley, or the Derby, where a working- and middle-class public divided its time between scheduled events and the watching of well-heeled fellow spectators "sometimes literally behind bars" in private cages (Davidoff, p. 32). The difference was that regattas, horse races, and the like, were "passive" texts, incapable of looking back at their readers. With the introduction of potentially critical playscripts, viewers in all parts of the house were encouraged to look anew at the commercial interplay of stage and stalls, and to reassess a kind of drama Shaw would later dismiss as "a tailor's advertisement making sentimental remarks to a milliner's advertisement in the middle of an upholsterer's and decorator's advertisement" (*Saturday Review*, 27 February 1897, 219).[5]

It was within this context that society comedy was reinvented by two playwrights peculiarly alive to the nuances of modern dress. For Oscar Wilde, at the St. James's and Haymarket, the form offered opportunities to comment upon the smart circles to which he himself had recently gained entrance. A proponent of multiplying personalities through dress, Wilde had, in the eighties, experimented with aesthetic, bohemian, and "rational" clothes as vehicles for individual expression and pragmatic self-marketing. His sartorial transformations were abrupt and public enough to draw the fire of London's satiric press. On 31 March 1883 *Punch* had marked Wilde's passage from his "aesthetic" to his "French bohemian" phase by running a mock advertisement presenting for sale "the whole of the Stock-in-Trade, Appliances, and Inventions of a Successful Aesthete, who is retiring from business" (155). The following year, in a comprehensive lecture on dress, Wilde defined fashion, by which he meant the compulsory garments of England's upper ten thousand, as "a form of ugliness so unbearable that we are compelled to alter it every six months" (Ellmann, p. 246). A half-decade later, as a writer of society plays, he had himself adopted the uniform. It was an about-face that had its parallel in the comedies themselves, from which aesthetic, "rational," and even legitimate fancy dress were rigorously excluded. Society would be reproduced only in its *grande toilettes* as Wilde (like his stage dandies) revealed his virtuosity by working within limitations. The decision had implications for both male and female costume, as well as for the larger issues of gender raised in Wilde's plays. Victorian sobriety, Wilde had argued in an 1891 letter to the *Daily Telegraph*, had turned the well-made tie and carefully thought out buttonhole into last stands of masculine self-fashioning. It had also reduced the decorative function of men in groups to that of a "frame" or dark border used "to isolate and separate women's dresses" (*Selected Letters*, pp. 90–92).[6] Operating almost entirely through ties, waistcoats, and those all-important buttonholes, Wilde's dandies would taunt his sober gentlemen with "frivolous" options to late Victorian earnestness. Indeed their obsession with buttonholes – Lord Goring changes his three times a day – is a visual embodiment of their attempts to substitute for the manly culture of club and playing-field a world seen in purely aesthetic terms. Women's wardrobes, in sharp contrast, offered a broad arena for sartorial play, allowing icons of mid-century melodrama, including

the magdalen, the adventuress, and the puritan wife, to be turned
into "fashion statements" that cut provocatively across moral and
generic boundaries. What resulted were new if troubling stage fables,
bred from a self-conscious yoking of theatrical cliché and haute
couture.[7]

Wilde's first "drama of modern life," *Lady Windermere's Fan* (1892)
is best seen as a negotiated compromise between the playwright and
his producer. George Alexander, who bought the work in 1890 while
arranging his initial lease for the St. James's Theatre, confessed in a
private note to critic Clement Scott that the piece was intended to
"draw a class of people to the St. James's with whom I am not at
present in touch" (Kaplan, "Puppet's Power," 62). The "class" to
which Alexander alludes has been anatomized in recent studies by
Leonore Davidoff and Regenia Gagnier. An aristocratic elite
preoccupied with rituals of access, London Society had by the
nineties found its integrity threatened by new money, fresh claimants,
and corresponding doubts about its own perimeters. Its response was
to place increased emphasis upon the display ceremonies by which it
regulated its pleasures, relying upon shifting subtleties of behavior
and dress to shut the door upon interlopers and parvenus. The
segregation of political from social life, the emergence of a "smart
set" with a penchant for hedonistic consumption, and new roles for
women as arbiters of taste and "custodians of the turnstile" all
contributed to what Davidoff has termed the "theatricalization" of
Society itself, a phenomenon that shaded imperceptibly into the
literal theatrics of the Social Season. Wilde, whose name Alexander
hoped would lure this coterie to his playhouse, moved confidently at
its center, his presence a tribute to his own skills at self-making. *Lady
Windermere's Fan*, however, would be more than a device for stroking
the sensibilities of Alexander's public. The glass of fashion, as Wilde
held it, might dazzle society with the opulent textures of its own
surfaces. Yet the precise codes of dress and manners through which
privilege was asserted and power flowed would be anchored in stage
worlds that queried the very values they enacted. The demographics
of West End playgoing, moreover, assured a wide context for such
efforts. The image of smart society catching its likeness in Wilde's
carefully set mirrors would itself be entertainment for pit and gallery
patrons, able to watch with voyeuristic relish an intimacy between
stage and stalls Artaud would liken, in another context, to "the

encounter of one epidermis with another in a timeless debauchery" (Gagnier, p. 8).

The subject of *Lady Windermere's Fan*, as working drafts of the play make progressively clear, is the uneasy relationship between morals and manners in contemporary Mayfair. Wilde's vehicles are the stock types of domestic drama, including the social-climbing adventuress and long-suffering wife. Mrs. Erlynne, the play's unconventionally "bad" woman, is a complex figure with a long pedigree. In *Stage-land*, Jerome K. Jerome's 1889 lampoon of theatre types, her ancestors are characterized as unprincipled creatures "generally of foreign extraction" who smoke, overdress, and have good heads for business (pp. 33–39). It was a line that stretched back to the "dark women" of Gothic melodrama, although it had moved spectacularly up-scale in the 1860s with stage versions of Mary Elizabeth Braddon's *Lady Audley's Secret*. Mrs. Erlynne had begun, in Wilde's earliest drafts, as Mrs. Alwynne, a grasping hypocrite attempting to blackmail her way into London Society. In the act of composition, however, Wilde claimed to have transformed her into "a character as yet untouched by literature" (*Selected Letters*, p. 103). Not only was his villainess "toned down" to Mayfair standards – she dressed well without overdoing it – her refusal to participate in what Nina Auerbach has called the "conventional abasement" of her type (p. 163) queried the manner in which such figures were traditionally written and read. On opening night, Mrs. Erlynne's mid-play attempt to save Lady Windermere from an adulterous affair was made especially uncomfortable by Wilde's decision to keep from his audience until Act IV the knowledge that his adventuress and puritan wife were mother and daughter. Wilde's purpose, as he maintained in a letter to Alexander, was to avoid accusations of sentimentality while upending the expectations of West End viewers smug in their knowledge of social and stage conventions.[8] In the end both play and production would work to this purpose, engaging spectators in a discourse of clothes in which, to cite Davidoff once again, "every cap, bow, streamer, ruffle, fringe, bustle, glove and other elaboration symbolized some status category for the female wearer" (p. 93).

In the absence of documentation it is hard to parcel out precise responsibilities for stage dress at the St. James's. If we can argue by analogy from practices in place at the equally fashionable Criterion Theatre, Wilde as playwright would have made "costume suggestions" to the ranking female member of his troupe – at the

Criterion this was Mary Moore, at the St. James's Florence Alexander. Acting on the company's behalf she would then have recommended appropriate dressmakers, herself overseeing the construction of individual items. For *The Physician*, for example, staged at the Criterion in 1897, Henry Arthur Jones informed Mary Moore that he wanted for an essential effect a mourning gown "very much smarter than the ordinary widow's garb." It was Moore who then selected Maison Lucile, visiting that company's workrooms on several occasions to offer specific advice about fabrics and decorations. The outcome, in Moore's own words, was "that, instead of wearing the conventional widow's dress, Miss [Marion] Terry appeared in a beautiful coat of black charmeuse covered with sequins, and lined with ermine (imitation) which showed when she moved" (Moore, p. 242). For *Lady Windermere's Fan*, the St. James's management approached the recently established firm of Savage and Purdue, couturières who, largely because of their success with this play, became Alexander's resident design team. The gowns had to be built on short notice as the piece had been put hurriedly into the St. James's bill. But for a new fashion house making its debut in London's *Trades Directory* that same year, the prospect of dressing both Marion Terry (Mrs. Erlynne) and Lily Hanbury (Lady Windermere) for a much publicized Wilde première had obvious advantages. The timing, as well, was propitious. Not only would work fall during the relatively "dead" dressmaking month of February, it allowed Mesdames Savage and Purdue to place upon the St. James's stage some twelve weeks before the opening of the Season what amounted to a mid-summer wardrobe, not merely imitating but generating styles (and sales) for the coming year (plate 1).[9]

The result was a production that, for advertising as well as thematic ends, sought to open sartorial middle ground upon which the opposing emblems of old melodrama might meet. Indeed, the very fact that costumes would be seen as commodities in their own right – committing in Barthes's "ethic of dress" the sins of "formal beauty" and "illusory sumptuousity" (p. 44) – became crucial to Wilde's plot. The five outfits worn by Mrs. Erlynne and Lady Windermere offer numerous instances. When Mrs. Erlynne makes her first appearance, as an equivocal guest at Lady Windermere's birthday ball, Wilde calls for her to be both "*very beautifully dressed and very dignified*" (p. 35).[10] The combination, itself a departure from the

1. "*Lady Windermere's Fan* at the St. James's Theatre" (*Lady*, 10 March 1892).
Mesdames Savage and Purdue's ensembles for Mrs. Erlynne (Act IV, center) and
Lady Windermere (Acts II and III, left; Act IV, right).

brash overdoing of her predecessors, suggested for Mrs. Erlynne a respectability at odds with her sense of erotic mystery. The range of desired responses is signaled in Wilde's dialogue. To the fashionable Lady Plymdale, Mrs. Erlynne is "that well-dressed woman," while the male gaze of the knowing Mr. Dumby reduces her to "an *édition de luxe* of a wicked French novel, meant specially for the English market" (p. 38).[11] The ballgown of iridescent white satin created for the occasion by Savage and Purdue provided Wilde with a suitably ambiguous text. First night critics, at any rate, found it formally decorous while remarking upon the snake-like sheen it seemed to acquire as it moved under Alexander's stage lights (*Echo*, 22 February 1892, 1). The floor-length opera cloak that covered the gown through Act III was, likewise, an attempt to reconcile Mrs. Erlynne's acceptability with her troubling sexuality. Made of black satin brocaded with gold feathers and lined with pink bengaline the garment was, in itself, luxurious to a fault. Yet the very use of a full-length cloak, in a year in which efforts to introduce short Parisian capes were being snubbed by London's fashion critics, helped Wilde to sever his adventuress from her continental roots.[12] It was, however, in Mrs. Erlynne's extended scenes with Lady Windermere that Wilde's dramatic design and the commercial instincts of Savage and Purdue worked most handily together. In the first of these, set in Lord Darlington's rooms after midnight, the play's selfless villainess attempts to save the reputation of its compromised wife. Through the episode Lady Windermere, like Mrs. Erlynne, wears over her ballgown of the previous act a richly brocaded satin cloak lined with identical pink bengaline. Mrs. Erlynne, anxious to depart, remains covered through the scene, while the skittish Lady Windermere registers her doubts by twice removing her cloak. The result was a mocking of visual expectations that helped to realize the play's controlling paradox. In what Peter Raby has described as the "male preserve" of Lord Darlington's chambers (p. 90), dressed alike in brocade and pink bengaline, Wilde's bare-armed and *décolleté* heroine confronts a villainess firmly wrapped in a garment of sound English manufacture.[13]

A like scrambling of visual codes occurs in Act IV. It was in the play's final exchanges, Wilde claimed, that the novelty of his piece would be made plain: his good woman would repudiate her puritan past, and his adventuress, for ultimately selfless motives, decline to reveal her identity to her daughter. Once again, the distance that separated traditional types was narrowed by Savage and Purdue, who attributed to both women a seasonable craving for muted browns and Eastern motifs. Lady Windermere played the scene in a short Russian coat of mushroom velvet, Mrs. Erlynne in what was described as an equally smart mushroom-brown overdress and Russian jacket braided in the Hussar manner. The effect, as in Lord Darlington's chambers, was to query through sartorial "jumbling" the moral dichotomies out of which domestic melodrama had been built. The device, moreover, was narrative as well as iconic. As erring parent and abandoned child, Mrs. Erlynne and Lady Windermere participated in a sub-genre of "reprobate mother" plays popular through the previous decade. Wilde's immediate source was Pierre Leclerq's *Illusion*, presented at the Strand in July 1890 (Powell, pp. 22–26). Leclerq's wayward mother, Blanche Faneuse, is, like Mrs. Erlynne, a high-toned adventuress who observes from a distance the society daughter she has deserted. At the play's close, however, La Faneuse seeks forgiveness from her child. After a teary scene of reconciliation, she makes her final appearance in an outfit of "severe black," helpfully identified as "My costume till I die!" Wilde's response was to turn Mrs. Erlynne into a mask for exuberant survival, enabling her to dismiss with cavalier insouciance the posturing and gown-shifting of Leclerq's protagonist. Both points are made in a passage in which Mrs. Erlynne, after declaring that "heart" does not "go" with "modern dress," lectures her son-in-law, the sober-minded Lord Windermere, on the ways of smart society:

I suppose, Windermere, you would like me to retire into a convent or become a hospital nurse, or something of that kind, as people do in silly English novels and silly French plays. That is stupid of you, Arthur; in real life we don't do such things – not as long as we have any good looks left, at any rate. No – what consoles one nowadays is not repentance but pleasure. Repentance is quite out of date. And besides, if a woman really repents, she has to go to a bad dressmaker, otherwise no one believes in her. (pp. 80–81)

When the play was printed the following year Wilde added to the speech an emphatic tag "and nothing in the world would induce me to do that." It was an attempt to recreate for his reading public something of the force Mrs. Erlynne's phrase first had when delivered to a St. James's audience in what was praised as the evening's most sophisticated gown.

The comic leave-taking of Wilde's adventuress was marked by two further fashion arguments, both noted in the society press. Through the play's final act Mrs. Erlynne wore an especially handsome bonnet, the creation of Madame Yorke of Conduit Street, a West End milliner who often worked in concert with Madame Savage. Of "ivy leaf" shape, made of black velvet, tightly covered with lace and transfixed with diamond ornaments, the piece was described in Thalia's "Wardrobe Wrinkles" column as "a positive poem" (*Players*, 8 March 1892, 268). Virginia, in *Black and White*, confessed that the object "induced [her] to transgress the tenth commandment without a moment's hesitation" (27 February 1892, 288). What drew particular attention was the manner in which the hat incorporated a spray of pale pink roses that seemed to "just rest" upon Mrs. Erlynne's hair. To place the effect, we must know that 1892 was marked by what Virginia spoke of as a renewed "passion for wearing real flowers" rather than the artificial or exotically dyed specimens popular through the previous season (287–288). Indeed, Thalia praised Mrs. Erlynne's pink roses at the expense of the "wonderfully ugly" green carnations worn on stage by Wilde's dandy, Mr. Cecil Graham, and, afterwards, by Wilde himself, when delivering a controversial curtain-call speech.[14] Such items, she complained, resembled "nothing but those imitation wooden trees which invariably accompany the child's box of farmyard toys." Mrs. Erlynne, in her stylish bonnet with "real" roses, was read (ironically enough) as more modish and more "natural" than either her forebears or creator. The second point in Mrs. Erlynne's leave-taking sprang directly from Wilde's script. When she departs, Mrs. Erlynne takes with her the play's all-important titular property, Lady Windermere's fan. A Scribean piece of stage furniture used with impressive ingenuity, the fan's progress through the work enables us to trace not only Wilde's plot but the shifting relationships between his characters and their adopted masks or attitudes.[15] Yet beyond – or rather before – such applications we should note the fan's irreducible status as fashion object, coveted by many of Alexander's consumer spectators. Fashion critics described it to such ends. We know, for example, that it sported sixteen white ostrich feathers fixed to a handle of yellow tortoiseshell, upon which "Margaret" (the Christian name shared by both Mrs. Erlynne and Lady Windermere) was traced in diamonds. The *Lady* illustrated it in an elaborate multi-block plate (10 March 1892, 290), while the *Queen*, speculating about where "real life" Lord Windermeres might purchase similar items, directed readers to Duvelleroy's of Regent Street (7 May 1892, 766).[16] The point was that the fan itself, an ostentatiously chic wardrobe addition, could, like the name displayed so prominently on its handle, complement with equal facility the play's "good" or "bad" woman. Mrs. Erlynne's appropriation of it at the close of Act IV, as memento, symbol, and fashion accessory, sums up the manner in which Wilde, in his first play of London life, worked subversively through the market forces of luxury dress-making.

If the homogeneity imposed by Mesdames Savage and Purdue proved central to the meaning of *Lady Windermere's Fan*, Wilde's remaining society plays, *A Woman of No Importance* (1893) and *An Ideal Husband* (1895) achieved their effects through sartorial contrast and diversity. This too, however, was a function of their modes of production and reception. Both plays were performed at Beerbohm Tree's Haymarket Theatre, under the respective auspices of Tree himself and matinée idol Lewis Waller. Although enjoying a privileged position among West End venues as a second home for fashionable comedy, the Haymarket, unlike the St. James's, seems never to have used the services of an in-house dressmaker.[17] While Savage and Purdue went on to assume responsibility for the costuming of society plays at Alexander's theatre, preparing for the 1893 season both *The Masqueraders* and *The Second Mrs. Tanqueray*, Tree preferred an older system of farming out garments to a variety of firms, often for use within the same work. As the Haymarket did not routinely credit dressmakers in its programs, nor record in its account books payments to individual designers, it is not always possible to identify gowns worn in any given production. A perusal of first-run notices, however, reveals an intriguing split between the attention paid to Haymarket costumes in the fashion and non-fashion press. For St. James's productions, whose modernity was vouched for by Mesdames Savage and Purdue, virtually all garments were noted by fashion columnists, with most illustrated in full-page fashion plates. For society plays staged at the Haymarket, drama critics and graphic artists continue to document a broad range of costume effects. Fashion writers and their illustrators, however, restrict attention to a handful of items, usually products of the better-known couture houses. Considering differences of aim and audience such divergence should not surprise us. Reviewers and artists commissioned to record plays for the general public were invariably drawn to moral and sentimental tableaux. Confrontations of vice and virtue, such as Gerald's defiance of Lord Illingworth in the third act of *A Woman of No Importance*, were particularly popular. Costumes caught up in such actions were reproduced, as a matter of course, in a richly charged iconic context. Fashion critics, advising clients on wardrobes for the coming season, had other priorities. For Virginia to describe or Etincelle to illustrate a stage gown was tantamount to affirming its social status and sales potential. In their reception of a play, characters of major importance whose dress was not likely to be emulated by readers disappear entirely. Others, virtuous and vicious alike, appear side by side in elegantly posed fashion groups, especially if their outfits are of common manufacture. As a result, readers encountered in adjacent columns of publications like the *Queen*, *Black and White*, the *Sketch*, and the *Lady's Pictorial* some of the same garments participating in emotionally heightened moral debate and morally "blind" advertising copy. The dichotomy was not lost upon Wilde or his producers.

A Woman of No Importance, which opened at the Haymarket in April 1893, is generally regarded as Wilde's most schizophrenic comedy. It is certainly the one in which he was least willing to accommodate his critics. Responding to doubts about the uneasy mix of theatrical posing and witty dialogue that had characterized *Lady Windermere's Fan*, Wilde perversely but characteristically cranked up both his melodramatic and epigrammatic machinery. His fable, he boasted, was taken from the pages of the *Family Herald*, while his leisurely first act, set on the lawns of Hunstanton Chase, was a "perfect" episode in that it contained "absolutely no action at all" (*Sketch*, 9 January 1895, 495). The play's attitudinizing is associated largely with the figure of Mrs. Arbuthnot, who years earlier had been seduced, if not quite abandoned, by the sophisticated dandy who has since become Lord Illingworth. As the plot unfolds, Gerald, their illegitimate son, wavers between the competing worlds (and styles) of his parents, finally forging a curious *ménage à trois* with his mother and Hester Worsley, a puritan heiress from New England. The work closes with the departure of all three for "better, wiser, and less unjust lands." Cutting across this action Wilde intrudes a stagnant, cynical world of modish exquisites, the play's "butterfly women" as Florence called them in the *Sketch* (26 April 1893, 740). In addition to Lady Hunstanton, the group includes Mrs. Allonby, a smart exemplar of *fin de siècle* sexuality, the promiscuous Lady Stutfield, and Lady

Caroline Pontefract, a comic grande dame, played by Roma Le Thière, who off-stage instructed debutantes in drawing-room deportment (*Dramatic Peerage*, pp. 136–137). Structurally the play consists of a series of symmetrical reversals of value, language, and situation, as Mrs. Arbuthnot and Lord Illingworth, against Wilde's society backcloth, bid for the affections of their son. Act II concludes quietly with the apparent triumph of the urbane Lord Illingworth. Act III, played to a rousing traditional "strong close," ends with the victory of Mrs. Arbuthnot, registered in a tableau so howlingly outsized, Noël Coward would recycle it to comic effect as the second act curtain of *Hayfever*. In its own day, William Archer proposed chastising Wilde by having the scene reproduced "in all the horrors of chromolithography" with great "crinkly letters" advertising the moment when Gerald, his hand raised against Lord Illingworth in defense of the puritan Hester, learns from his mother the secret of his birth: "Stop Gerald stop, he is your own father!" (*World*, 26 April 1893, 26).

In *Idylls of the Marketplace* Regenia Gagnier has proposed that the play's dual appeal was Wilde's response to a divided Haymarket audience. Spectators in the stalls and boxes, she argues, paid lip service to the conventional morality embodied in figures like Gerald, Hester, and Mrs. Arbuthnot, while sympathizing with the worldly Lord Illingworth. At the same time, middle-class viewers in the pit and gallery could read both Tree's production and its engagement of upper-class patrons as a thumping attack upon society itself (pp. 122–125). The point is well taken. Yet while social reformers like Sysinnius of the *Illustrated Church News* talked of "a living sermon preached nightly on the hollowness of the *fin de siècle* society code" (27 May 1893, 556), reaction in the clubland and fashion press was neither simple nor untroubled. Indeed, for those who had come to bask in the kind of spectacle Gagnier characterizes as "the existing order's uninterrupted discourse about itself" (p. 9) the evening's entertainment proved remarkably tough-minded. Not only had playwright and producer set melodrama and wit at loggerheads, they had done so in a manner that pried apart the work's visual and fashion centers. Their chief, if unwitting, agent was the London firm of Lewis and Allenby, a distinguished company of Regent Street silk mercers engaged by Tree to dress three of his leading ladies. Contracted to provide wardrobes for Blanche Horlock (Lady Stutfield), Julia Neilson (Hester Worsley), and Maud Tree (Mrs.

Allonby), the establishment steered a safe middle course between the antique and ultra-modish. Following the lead of Charles Worth, whom they had at one time employed, Messrs. Lewis and Allenby harped upon an 1890s vogue for all things early Victorian, creating garments praised in the fashion press as belonging simultaneously to "yesterday" and "the day after tomorrow" (plate 2).[18] Mrs. Tree's first-act dress was, the *Sketch* proclaimed, "pure Louis XV," its white silk chiné calling to mind "old fashioned chintz" (26 April 1893, 740). *Black and White* described her as "*jolie à croquer* in her 1830 gowns" (29 April 1893, 524), while Florence, invoking a convention of fashion-plate prose Wilde would himself borrow for the published text of *An Ideal Husband*, likened her to "a dainty figure sketched by Lancret." Julia Neilson appeared in an Act IV outfit of pink and yellow glacé silk, identified by Florence as "1830 in style," while Blanche Horlock, in lace-trimmed flounces and full cape, seemed to the *Queen*'s fashion critic "quaint and old-fashioned" (13 May 1893, 773).[19] The profusion of 1830s detail in the costumes of all three prompted Virginia to despair at the prospect of taking in the play at one sitting. Promising a return visit to do the work justice, she had to substitute for *Black and White*'s expected theatre plate a drawing of a dress she had bought for her own wardrobe (13 May 1893, 571). The outcome, in each case, was to fix the play's fashion interest in its Lewis and Allenby gowns, the only items (literally) marketed in society circles.

Yet as initial notices make clear, the play's status as fashion plate was undermined by its moral organization and affective power. Even society critics noted the incongruity of the three smartly dressed women set before them. Viewed as a collection of couture house mannequins the gathering was unambiguous. But as the dandiacal Mrs. Allonby, the vacuous Lady Stutfield, and the puritan Hester Worsley, the trio invited a degree of scrutiny foreign to fashion-plate art. As odd-woman-out, the censorious Hester proved the most problematic. The appearance in the role of the leggy, statuesque Julia Neilson contributed to the effect. During the 1891 Haymarket season the actress, who in her autobiography would celebrate Wilde's comedies as "dress parades," appeared as Drusilla Ives, the Quaker sensualist of Jones's *The Dancing Girl*. Described in the *Players* as "more concerned with her mirror than a quiet Quakeress should be" (3 June 1892, 84), Neilson's Drusilla had, by 1893, become a byword for the nonconformist conscience trapped by a conventional love of

2. "Dresses Worn in *A Woman of No Importance*" (*Queen*, 13 May 1893). Lewis and Allenby's gowns for Mrs. Allonby (upper left), Lady Stutfield (upper right), and Hester Worsley (lower left and right).

finery.[20] By mid-play she had yielded to Jones's wicked Duke of
Guisebury, a part taken, like Lord Illingworth, by Tree himself. Such
associations bled through to Wilde's comedy, in which Hester's
formal denunciation of drawing-room society – "a dead thing
smeared with gold" (p. 52) – was delivered in a sensuous gown of
white satin, entirely veiled by silver-spangled tulle. Florence pronounced the outfit "in itself... pretty, but somehow ... hardly suited
to the stately, puritanical Hester Worsley" (*Sketch*, 26 April 1893,
740). Objections were made to the manner in which the fabric,
"glistening and shimmering with every movement," jarred awk-
wardly with Hester's repressed sexuality.[21] Player Queen in the
Lady's Pictorial made a desperate stab at justification, wondering
whether the costume's star-spangled satin might refer to Hester's
New World origins (29 April 1893, 642). That such "indecorum"
was, however, part of Wilde's design is indicated by scripted
references to Americans buying their clothes in Paris (p. 25), as well
as pointed allusions to Hester as "that pretty prude" (p. 112) and
"the Puritan in white muslin" (p. 113). It is also underscored by the
manner in which Hester's attack upon Mayfair mores is immediately
deflated by her hostess, Lady Hunstanton: "My dear young lady,
there was a great deal of truth, I dare say, in what you said, and you
looked very pretty while you said it, which is much more important"
(pp. 54–55). Once more the world of fashion was used to destabilize
dramatic types and moral expectations, here transforming a puritan
homilist into a figure the *Echo* would liken to "a superb Juno dressed
by Worth" (20 April 1893, 1).

It was, however, in its handling of the melodramatic Mrs.
Arbuthnot that the play conducted its most telling clothes debate.
The "two severe looking gowns, both black," worn by Wilde's
penitent, were, as Florence reminded *Sketch* readers, "appropriate to
a betrayed woman" – or, at least, appropriate to the manner in
which such figures were presented on popular stages (26 April 1893,
740).[22] Yet while the satiric press fastened upon the obvious, likening
Mrs. Arbuthnot to both a magpie in velvet and "Hamlet's aunt"
(*Punch*, 6 May 1893, 213), more fashionably astute critics noted the
degree of smartness that had been negotiated within the type.
Indeed, early references to Mrs. Arbuthnot as a shabby or unbecom-
ingly dressed ex-seamstress were deleted by Wilde who came to
substitute for mere sobriety what fashion historian Anne Hollander
has called "conspicuously consumed 'emotional' black" (p. 380).[23]

The result was an elegant form of anti-fashion that borrowed from the codified chic of Victorian mourning as well as the self-conscious theatricality of mid-century dandies and bohemians.[24] It also incorporated a smart eroticism noted by both Lord Illingworth and Mrs. Allonby. Mrs. Arbuthnot's plunging neckline and form-fitting bodice are clearly visible in engravings of the play's Act III tableau prepared for the *Illustrated London News* (29 April 1893, 516) and *Black and White* (29 April 1893, 522) by graphic artists Ray Potter and Stewart Browne. In performance the impression was enhanced by Tree's engagement for the role of Mrs. Bernard Beere, a smoky-voiced contralto billed as "the English Bernhardt." As often found at Monte Carlo gaming tables as on the London stage, Mrs. Beere, who had made her reputation as Tosca, Fedora, and Adrienne Lecouvreur, was noted for her ability to "carry … off, as to the manner born, costumes which would perhaps appear bizarre on ordinary women" (*Dramatic Peerage*, pp. 23–24). In an interview granted the *Sketch* a week after the opening of Wilde's play, the actress volunteered that she "rather like[d] the sombre plainness of [her] gowns" (26 April 1893, 739). She appreciated, at any rate, the visual – as distinct from fashion – advantage they gave her over her Lewis and Allenby rivals. Her instincts were vindicated by society critics, who, on the whole, found her a powerful alternative to the play's showy amoralists. The *Queen* observed the "distinction and classic grace" with which Mrs. Beere carried "her plain black velvet gown … and trailing black alpaca robe" (22 April 1893, 623). To *Modern Society* she "looked superb" (29 April 1893, 759), to the *Lady's Pictorial* "exceedingly handsome" (29 April 1893, 661), to the *Lady's World* "pale and interesting in [her] close-fitting black velvet dress" (26 April 1893, 4). Even Florence conceded the manner in which her uncredited, unsaleable gowns enabled her to "stand … out strongly in grim, sombre majesty against the brilliant dresses of the butterfly women of the play" (*Sketch* 26 April 1893, 740). What Wilde had done, in effect, was to reverse the roles of figure and ground set forth in his *Daily Telegraph* letter, creating in *A Woman of No Importance* an "unplaceable" elegance framed by the frivolities of an established West End designer. His final point would be made by the social invisibility of Mrs. Arbuthnot's wardrobe, demonstrated by its absence from fashion-plate illustrations. On stage Mrs. Arbuthnot's gowns might present viewers with "handsome," "graceful," "majestical" correctives to the tulles and satins of Lewis and Allenby, but, like Mrs. Arbuthnot herself, they were ultimately inadmissible to good society.

Wilde's last excursion into society drama was a product of mixed auspices. Rejected in mid-composition by actor-manager John Hare who had commissioned it for his Garrick Theatre, *An Ideal Husband* was presented at the Haymarket in January 1895, during the joint tenancy of Lewis Waller and Henry Morell. The play's published text, brought out by John Smithers in 1899, after Wilde's release from prison, presents a script reshaped by an author who must have realized that he would no longer be in a position to influence his works in performance. While all of Wilde's published plays depart significantly from extant acting and licensing copies, *An Ideal Husband* is unique in the extent to which it attempts to create for a reading public a sense of visual immediacy. In revising, Wilde not only adjusted contemporary references – fashionable colors, sums of money, and the like – but added lengthy stage directions ensuring that thematic points would be made by stylistic and sartorial means. Lord Goring, the play's dandy hero, is recast as a variant upon Wilde's own prelapsarian self. Described on his Act I entrance as "*A flawless dandy ... [who] plays with life, and is on perfectly good terms with the world*" (p. 146), he becomes by Act III "*the first well-dressed philosopher in the history of thought,*" his qualifications displayed in "*evening dress with a buttonhole ... a silk hat and Inverness cape ... White glove[s and] ... a Louis Seize cane*" (p. 212) – identical, in fact, to one Wilde himself was known to carry. An insistence that Goring "*stands in immediate relation to modern life*" likewise echoes Wilde's claim, in *De Profundis*, to have "stood in symbolic relation to the art and culture of my age."[25] Similar additions evoke for readers the brilliance of the play's social milieu. Not only is Wilde precise about Lord Goring's "*Adam room*" (p. 212), Lady Chiltern's "*Louis Seize sofa,*" and Sir Robert's "*large eighteenth-century French tapestry – representing the Triumph of Love, from a design by Boucher*" (p. 133), he adopts a self-conscious form of fashion prose to find painterly, or at least period, equivalents for each of his major characters: "*Watteau would have loved to paint ...* MRS MARCH-MONT and LADY BASILDON" (p. 133), Lord Caversham is "*Rather like a portrait by Lawrence*" (p. 135), "*Vandyck would have liked to have painted* [SIR ROBERT CHILTERN'S] *head*" (p. 140), Lady Chiltern is "*a woman of grave Greek beauty*" (p. 133), her sister-in-law, Mabel "*like a Tanagra statuette*" (p. 135), and Mrs. Cheveley, the adventuress of the piece, "*A work of art, on the whole, but showing the influence of too many schools*"

(p. 137). By restricting himself to generic and period tags, Wilde ensured that his text would not be outdated by too local a knowledge of contemporary fads or fashions. Nevertheless, in asserting literary control over what had been, in performance, a collaborative and often accidental art, an attempt was made to transfer to the printed page the dress logic of the drama's 1895 debut.

Sartorially the interest of Waller's production lay in its triangle of principal women (plate 3). One, at least, was constructed on familiar lines. Lady Chiltern, wife to the play's ironically titled hero, was a puritan of the Lady Windermere–Hester Worsley stamp. Yet in fashioning her Wilde tipped the balance from "pretty prude" to moral monitress. The result was a character who seemed to forfeit the sympathy of most of the play's first critics. To the radical Shaw and liberal Archer she appeared "stupidly good" (*Saturday Review*, 12 January 1895, 45) and "rather trying" (Archer, *Theatrical World* 1895, p. 19), to the reactionary Clement Scott "abnormally moral" and (above all) "unwomanly" in her quickness to judge her erring husband (*Daily Telegraph*, 4 January 1895, 3). Her reception by the society press was equally vexed. "Monocle" of the *Sketch* found her "a heartless, dull person of no quality at all... a petticoat Torvald Helmer" (9 January 1895, 496). It was a verdict in which the role's creator Julia Neilson concurred, condemning the character as "an impossible prig... pitiless in her perfection, cold and stern and without mercy" (p. 139). On stage, however, Lady Chiltern's severity was mitigated by a wardrobe of silks, diamonds, and rich brocades. We do not know who designed or made any of her three Haymarket gowns. Each, however, indulged in what Hollander has termed a nineteenth-century tendency to see fashionable women's dress as "an extensive complicated system... separately conceived and embellished" (p. 152). With the hindsight of some fifty years, Neilson would later characterize Lady Chiltern's outfits as "astonishing" testimonies to "the dressmakers of that period [who] used yards of material, and piled things in every nook and cranny" (p. 140). They were also, she might have added, calculated to display to best advantage her limbs, throat, and bared shoulders. An Act I ballgown of cream brocaded silk featured a remarkably low-cut bodice, decked with chiffon and strewn with Neapolitan violets. A second act white satin walking-dress, in which we are given to understand Lady Chiltern has been attending a meeting of the Women's Liberal Association, was brocaded with a Pompadour

3. "Dresses Sketched in *An Ideal Husband*" (*Queen*, 12 January 1895). Mabel Chiltern (far left) in one of Madame Humble's "perfectly plain" pleated skirts; Mrs. Cheveley (lower right) in her Act I ball gown with three of its offending swallows visible on its back and hem.

design of shadowy pink roses. Innocent of a collar, it left neck and throat "perfectly free," an effect complemented by full sleeves with "deep transparent cuffs" (*Sketch*, 9 January 1895, 541). The disparity between appearance and professed values was noted by the *Queen*, which categorized Wilde's heroine as "a paragon of correct principle, [who] nevertheless dresses enchantingly" (12 January 1895, 55). The observation, made without prejudice, reassured viewers that beneath Lady Chiltern's stern morals and progressive politics beat a "womanly" heart after all. It is a paradox Wilde plays with in an early debate between Lord Goring and Lady Chiltern over the proper relationship of smart bonnets to feminist causes (pp. 187–188). Its resolution took the form of an Act IV turn-about, in which Lady Chiltern, parroting Lord Goring's view that "a man's life is of more value than a woman's" (pp. 264–265), forgives her tainted husband, enabling him to accept a Cabinet post. The episode may be read as that of a hard woman instructed in the quality of mercy, or a thinking one reduced to her wardrobe.

Parallel clothes wars were waged in the play's subsidiary action. Mabel Chiltern is Wilde's attempt to reconcile what he called the "*tyranny of youth*" and "*courage of innocence*" with the crack and sparkle of *fin de siècle* wit. Derived ultimately from a tradition that included Shakespeare's Beatrice and Congreve's Millamant, Mabel's quick tongue but unquestionable virtue set her apart from both the "clever" Mrs. Erlynne and sexually knowing Mrs. Allonby. In Waller's production the role went to Maude Millet, the period's most persistent ingenue. A stage direction added for Wilde's 1899 readers looked to capture something of Millet's "*English type of prettiness, the apple-blossom type*" (p. 135). At the Haymarket, playgoers applauded Mabel's chaste forwardness, finding in her mix of "contemporary damsel" and "girlish grace" a refreshing alternative to the un-approachable Lady Chiltern (*Lady's Pictorial*, 12 January 1895, 43). Yet while Mabel complains of having to labor under dress codes imposed by her puritanical sister-in-law – "Gertrude won't let me wear anything but pearls, and I am thoroughly sick of pearls. They make one look so plain, so good and so intellectual" (p. 167) – the fashion press declared her the most stylish of the play's women. The divided response is explained by the engagement of the exclusive Mary Elizabeth Humble to dress Millet for the production's Haymarket run. Madame Humble, whose "master hand" was immediately recognized by Florence (*Sketch*, 9 January 1895, 541),

was the most distinguished couturière to design costumes for any of
Wilde's premières. By 1895 she had been a court dressmaker for three
seasons, her "pretty showrooms" in Conduit Street being especially
busy during Ascot week. Notable, in an age of excess, for the relative
repose and restraint of her designs, Madame Humble, three months
before the opening of Wilde's play, had received "special con-
gratulation" from the *Lady's Pictorial* for offering readers "the most
advanced fashions of the season" (6 October 1894, 451). In Mabel's
wardrobe her touch appears most distinctively in an Act IV ensemble
of "perfectly plain skirt" and full-sleeved, box-pleated blouse, a
combination Madame Humble had championed through the winter
of 1894–1895.[26] Enabling "Miss Millet's dresses [to] stand out well
from all the others," such chic understatement proved a ready
vehicle for Mabel's own modish simplicity (*Sketch*, 9 January 1895,
541). It, too, was an effect Wilde sought to translate to his published
text, adding in page proofs an exchange in which the brazen Mrs.
Cheveley foolishly condescends to Mabel's "simple...suitable"
frocks. Mabel's reply, "I must tell my dressmaker. It will be such a
surprise to her," firmly resituates both women (p. 197).

An adventuress of the old school, Mrs. Cheveley was herself placed
by the work's most equivocal wardrobe. Played by the comparatively
inexperienced Florence West (Mrs. Lewis Waller), Wilde's "Adelphi
villainess" was a counterblast to the author's own Mrs. Erlynne.
Stripping her not only of elegance but even the glamor and mystery
traditional to the type, Wilde produced a woman-with-a-past Shaw
praised as "kinetoscopically realistic," by which he meant "selfish,
dishonest, and third rate" (*Saturday Review*, 12 January 1895, 45).
Finding her "overdressed for her part" – in spite of her insistence
that "a woman's first duty in life is to her dressmaker" (p. 232) –
critics wondered whether Mrs. Cheveley possessed the necessary
"polish" to move freely in good society (*Illustrated Sporting and
Dramatic News*, 12 January 1895, 665). In the text proper Lord
Goring condemns her for wearing "far too much rouge...and not
quite enough clothes," a combination he interprets as "a sign of
despair in a woman" (p. 185). From the stalls, the fashion press
pronounced her "vulgar...undignified" (*Lady's Pictorial*, 12 January
1895, 43), "stagy" (*Morning Post*, 4 January 1895, 3) and, once
again, "overdressed" (*Illustrated Sporting and Dramatic News*,
12 January 1895, 665). Ironically, her only garment to win general
applause was an adventuress's cloak of black and red satin, worn

during a late-night visit to the unsuspecting Lord Goring. The *Queen* noted the origins of both item and episode, alluding to "the traditionally embarrassing evening call in the traditionally splendid evening cloak" (12 January 1895, 59). More to the point were the two unattributed gowns in which Mrs. Cheveley made her public appearances. Calling upon Lady Chiltern in Act II – the scene in which she patronizes Mabel's "simple ... suitable" frocks – Wilde's parvenu wore an outfit calculated to sound the base string of gaucherie. The *Sketch*, which condemned its color scheme as "startling, to put it mildly," records a dress "of yellow mirror moiré ... [with] a deep square collar of scarlet velvet ... a collar band of bright-green velvet, with a bunch of violets set at each side ... [sleeves] of cream-coloured chiné glacé, brocaded with pink roses and foliage, and to crown all ... a hat of green straw, [with] masses of orchids in various colours, including purple and red" (9 January 1895, 541). Florence, who asked readers to "imagine the effect," chose not to illustrate it in her column. On stage the garment remained an object lesson in unwomanly push, a foil to set off the more marketable wares of Madame Humble and company. It was a quality Wilde attempted to capture in the 1899 Smithers text, presenting his villainess, in a passage already cited, as "*showing the influence of too many schools.*"

A more brutal lesson was offered by Mrs. Cheveley's Act I ballgown, an evening dress of emerald-green satin decorated with a sextet of dead swallows (*Sketch*, 9 January 1895, 541).[27] Such ornamentation immediately set Mrs. Cheveley at the center of arguments about shooting parties and vanity markets that had occupied West End playgoers through the season of 1894. Precipitated by Mrs. Nettleship's use of bird corpses for a costume in Sydney Grundy's *The New Woman* (Comedy 1894), the uproar culminated in a *Queen* editorial, "Feathers and Fashions" (20 October 1894, 652), repudiating slaughter in the name of style, and a *Sketch* campaign calling upon women of fashion "to make a stand against this veritable massacre of the innocents." The Nettleship dress was specifically cited as "a painful example of the cruel thoughtlessness of some of Fashion's followers" (*Sketch*, 12 September 1894, 386). Set within the broad context of anti-plumage agitation, given new impetus by the founding in 1889 of the Society for the Protection of Birds, and kept before the public through the nineties by the increasingly militant *Punch* cartoons of Linley Sambourne, the subject was one to which Wilde was particularly sensitive.[28] The first number of the *Woman's World* (December 1887) issued under his editorship had featured an illustration of "a hat, covered with the bodies of dead birds" to which exception had been taken by the *Pall Mall Gazette*. In defending his paper's editorial policy, Wilde found it prudent to distance himself from the practice.[29] In the face of continued opposition, much of it within the fashion community, Mrs. Cheveley's gown was a deliberate provocation. *Modern Society* spoke in heated terms of its "six slaughtered swallows poised on the wing" (12 January 1895, 278), while the *Queen* offered readers a patient lecture on the semiotics of stage taxidermy: "We have seen birds worn on this stage before as an insignia of vice, and when we noted that an entire flight of swallows have been disposed upon the newcomer's costume we have little doubt of the lady's character" (12 January 1895, 55). Florence, expressing "nothing but disapproval for [Mrs. Cheveley's] mode of trimming," urged readers to deliver like verdicts "by refraining from imitation." It was an outcome the *Sketch* (once again) hoped to shape by declining to reproduce a gown its fashion critic had judged "barbarous and unpleasant" (9 January 1895, 541).

For a more frontal assault upon the objects of good society we must turn to the Criterion comedies of Henry Arthur Jones. The most insular and provincial of English authors, Jones seems at first glance an odd candidate for society playwright. During the 1880s, when Wilde was editing the *Woman's World*, lecturing on "The House Beautiful," and establishing literary contacts in Paris, the self-educated Jones, a draper's assistant from Ramsgate and Gravesend, was struggling to build a new English theatre upon what he called "the sinewy and vertebrate frame" of native melodrama. While Max Beerbohm would later note the effect of Jones's riding gear in the chintz parlors of the late Victorians, contemporaries were more immediately struck by a new if often bellicose voice raised in journals like the *Nineteenth Century*. In "The Theatre and the Mob" (1883), the first in a series of polemical essays, Jones argued for the drama's need to deal with difficult, controversial issues. The theatre, he insisted, was an "unwieldy Siamese Twin" whose two bodies, "dramatic art" and "popular amusement," fought for common sustenance. It was a playwright's duty to nourish the former, and the task of both critic and public to lend their support. Such conviction, at its most appealing, is caught in Spy's 1892 cartoon of a spurred and booted Jones, hands on hips, chin thrust pugnaciously forward, dressed to ride roughshod over recalcitrant audiences (*Vanity Fair*, 2 April 1892, n.p.). Jones's relentless proselytizing, however, became a running joke in the satiric press. One contributor to *Fun* magazine lampooned the playwright as "Envy Author Groans," a glum philosopher who used the stage to expound moral problems (12 February 1895, 72). Another cast in doggerel verse Jones's call for "purposeful entertainment" (Cordell, p. 156). Even Wilde joined the chorus, although his target was the author's determined solemnity. There were, Wilde liked to tell audiences, three rules for good playmaking: "The first... [was] not to write like Mr. Henry Arthur Jones." "The second, and third rules," he added, were "the same" (Doris Arthur Jones, p. 187). In a letter to Alexander, who in the autumn of 1894 had praised both playwrights before the Birmingham Arts Club, Wilde pretended not to have heard of his fellow dramatist: "Who is Jones? Perhaps the name as reported in the London papers was a misprint for something else. I have never heard of Jones. Have you?" (*Selected Letters*, p. 126). In a similar vein, young "Gilbert," Wilde's mouthpiece in "The Critic as Artist," is allowed to demonstrate the unimportance of subject-matter by affirming that it is possible to talk intelligently even about "the plays of Mr. Henry Arthur Jones" (*Complete Works*, p. 1027).

Yet for all this, by the mid-nineties Jones stood alongside Wilde as London's most accomplished writer of society comedy. Indeed, when *The Liars*, the best of Jones's plays, was produced in 1897, two years after Wilde's disgrace, it was widely rumored to have been Wilde's work presented, for tactical reasons, under his rival's name. The transformation of Jones's style and subject-matter was due largely to his collaboration through the nineties with actor-manager Charles Wyndham, who had made his reputation in "rattling farce" two decades earlier. In 1883–1884 Wyndham had refurbished the small, stuffy Criterion Theatre in Piccadilly Circus, originally built as a basement annex to Spiers and Pond's restaurant complex. Together with leading lady Mary Moore, he turned the venue – to be known by society patrons as the "Cri" – into London's third house for elegant comedy.[30] By the early nineties, when the Criterion's place in the social season seemed as assured as that of the St. James's or Haymarket, the *Era* could speak not only of "Mr. Wyndham's fashionable following," but of "the sets and sub-sets who follow them" (6 October 1894, 11). It was for this enterprise that Jones supplied, between 1893 and 1900, five scripts, each cut to the whims and fancies of Wyndham's public. Like Wilde, Jones chose to reproduce on stage the brilliant surfaces of an opulent consumer society, constructing a precise visual language out of the products of West End couturiers, jewelers, and – in Jones's case – restaurateurs. His society folk attend Henley, dine at the Café Royal or (recently opened) Savoy, and buy their diamonds at Hunt and Roskell's. They fall, moreover, into an easier form of genteel speech than do Wilde's dandies or exquisites. Yet Jones, ultimately, was not of the worlds he made – nor did he seek to be. If Wilde's critiques of Mayfair life amount to dispatches from the drawing-room front, Jones's are invariably qualified by the flinty skepticism of a rural outsider. The *Theatre* likened him to W. T. Stead, a prude describing "fast life" from hearsay (1 November 1897, 249). Clayton Hamilton, still close enough, in the 1920s, to have observed the gaps of class, taste, and sensibility that separated Jones from his Criterion public, put a more sympathetic construction upon the phenomenon: "Mr. Jones enjoyed the great advantage of holding up a mirror before the very people who were seated in the stalls, and showing them how they appeared to a representative English mind that was not natively aristocratic in its outlook" (Jones, *Representative Plays*, II, p. xvii).

In 1894 Jones's "representative English mind" put him on a collision course with his producer and leading man. The occasion was the opening in October of that year of *The Case of Rebellious Susan*, a revenge comedy of reciprocal infidelities. Jones, together with Mary Moore and Madame Eroom, a Maddox Street dressmaker "coming fast into repute for her style and taste" (*Illustrated Sporting and Dramatic News*, 27 October 1894, 265), had placed upon the Criterion stage a flawlessly clothed but unpleasantly smug collection of society figures. At the work's center stood Wyndham himself as Sir Richard Kato, a divorce court lawyer surrounded by the unhappy marriages of his family and acquaintances. Chief among these was that of the play's heroine, Lady Susan Harabin, whose vow to even the score with an unfaithful husband formed the mainspring of Jones's plot. In dressing his action for Wyndham's audiences, however, Jones did not play fashion groups off one another, as Wilde had done in his Haymarket comedies, nor did he, after the manner of *Lady Windermere's Fan*, clothe opposing types in disturbingly similar gowns. His method was rather to preside over what the *Queen* described as an "agon" of fancy dress, allowing the production's women to compete openly for sartorial applause (13 October 1894, 640). Madame Eroom, who had outfitted two previous Criterion plays, had primary responsibility for the work. To the surprise of Florence she built wardrobes not only for Mary Moore (Lady Susan) and Fanny Coleman (Lady Darby), but for Nina Boucicault in the low comedy role of Elaine Shrimpton, an aesthetic young woman, who by mid-play exchanges her sea-green gowns for the tweed suits of a proto-suffragette. Both Boucicault's "artistic" and New Woman costumes were used to reinforce social and sexual stereotypes, cutting off "non-fashion" and "anti-fashion" as serious alternatives to the dress codes of Lady Susan and her world. Taking as his fashion text a barbed comment by Worth about women dressing not only "for the pleasure of making themselves smart, [but]...for the still greater joy of snuffing out the others" (de Marly, *Worth*, p. 134), Jones arranged the play's comings and goings to accommodate the appearance and reappearance of his leading ladies in increasingly spectacular outfits. The process culminated in an Act III squaring off of Mary Moore and Gertrude Kingston. Kingston, as the merry widow Inez, made her penultimate entrance in a ruby velvet skirt and vermilion silk blouse described in the *Daily Telegraph* as "enough to make male eyes ache and water" (4 October 1894, 3). After a brief absence she returned with "an entire sable placed over each shoulder" (*Queen*, 13 October 1894, 640). Moore countered with a gown of "black watered silk with sequined bodice, and soft billowy sleeves of white chiffon and lace," by consensus the visual climax of the piece. Indeed, Moore was so taken with the garment she had it copied for private use – only to learn something of the efficacy of on-stage advertising. Upon wearing it to a society function at Brighton's Metropole Hotel, she found herself confronted by three admirers in identical outfits (Moore, p. 243). On Moore's final entrance the dress was complemented by a theatre cloak of black satin. One of two additions to Moore's wardrobe supplied by Jay's of Regent Street, it became, according to the *Illustrated Sporting and Dramatic News*, "the talk of society; or anyway, the feminine portion thereof" (27 October 1894, 265).[31] The irony was that as Lady Susan shifted into more ostentatiously consumed forms of luxury, she was drawn inexorably back to the wretched world and unfaithful husband she had rebelled against at the outset. That the two actions were meant to be read as one is made plain in the play's Act III reconciliation. James Harabin, who had earlier proposed compensation for his infidelities in the form of "a diamond ring and bracelet" from Hunt and Roskell's Bond Street showroom, concludes the work by completing his wife as society object, solving, in effect, his domestic problems by accessorizing: "How well you look, Sue! I'll take you down Bond Street tomorrow morning and buy you – the whole street!" (p. 161).[32]

The uneasiness felt by Wyndham's audiences may be traced in the drama columns of the popular and fashion press. Spectators, we are told, were unsure whether they had witnessed a celebration of or attack upon society objects and values. To be sure, the play's social and sartorial closure seemed to hint at comic reintegration. Yet many were disturbed by the sense of tragedy, or at least pathos, that seemed to wash over the work. In a special souvenir supplement, *St. Paul's* magazine spoke of Lady Susan as a woman "beating against the bars of her domestic prison," reclaimed by a brutish husband to the applause of those who admired her stage wardrobe (26 January 1895, n.p.). Archer found the Bond Street proposal "unforgivable," suggesting that on like principles a lady's jewel case might become "a sort of bead-roll of her husband's conquests – a Leporello register engrossed in gold and diamonds" (*Theatrical World 1894*, p. 271). The *Sketch* was equally appalled, dismissing Harabin's contrition as the "frail assurance... [of] a tiger that has tasted man-flesh" (10 October 1894, 568). For many, the depth of the play's despair depended upon whether Susan had, in the parlance of the period, sinned in more than thought. And here is where Jones's project ran afoul of Wyndham's hard-won carriage trade. In the play's initial draft, Jones had left no doubt that Lady Susan had not only committed adultery, but lied about it when returning to her husband. Wyndham objected on a number of grounds. Lecturing Jones on the impropriety of extracting humor from the subject of "a woman's impurity," he wondered what lesson viewers might draw from such experiments. From what quarter, he asked, did Jones expect to attract audiences "since it is evident... that married men will not take their wives, and mothers will not bring their daughters" (Doris Arthur Jones, p. 165). During rehearsal, Wyndham removed lines that made plain Lady Susan's guilt, substituting on his own initiative a more ambiguous version. In so doing, he insisted, he acted not as a moralist, but a practical man of the theatre who knew what audiences would take and how they would take it. Jones responded by dedicating the published play to Mrs. Grundy. Restoring the offending passage, he lashed out against "self-righteousness" and "our belief in our own moral superiority," providing in a dedicatory epistle "a thoroughly shocking moral" for those who insisted upon such things: "if you must have a moral in my comedy, suppose it to be this – that as women cannot retaliate openly, they may retaliate secretly – and *lie*!" (p. 107). He concluded with a postscript in which costume, metaphorically treated, was used to underscore what he had tried to do with text and dress on Wyndham's stage: "My comedy isn't a comedy at all. It's a tragedy dressed up as a comedy" (p. 107).

That Wyndham's objections were, as he claimed, more pragmatic than moral is suggested by his collaboration with Jones on *The Liars*. The play, which opened the Criterion's 1897 season, bears a superficial resemblance to *The Case of Rebellious Susan*. Like the earlier piece, it revolves about the intrigues of a society wife, finally restored, through the efforts of a gentleman *raisonneur*, to social respectability and an unprepossessing husband. Mary Moore appeared as Lady Jessica Nepean, with Wyndham playing opposite her as the worldly-wise Sir Christopher Deering. Yet while Jones, once more, struck the pose of a disapproving outsider, he did not this time let his play's recalcitrant wife consummate her affair. It was a concession that seems to have freed Wyndham to connive in a squint-eyed view of smart life that outdid *Rebellious Susan* in the sheer scope of its cynicism. Not only did lying – as the play's title made clear – provide a controlling metaphor for the behavior of Jones's Mayfair folk, but the inclusion in their world of the semi-public events that marked London's social calendar left no escape for what the *Lady* termed the "well-dressed people" who "filled to overflowing…the prettiest theatre in town" (14 October 1897, 531). While *The Case of Rebellious Susan* never moved beyond the family drawing rooms of Kato or the Harabins, Lady Jessica's initial flirtation takes place in a planked and carpeted tent at Henley Regatta. The site – one of Davidoff's privileged "cages" set firmly within public view – drove home obvious parallels between the play's reproduction of society rites and its own place in the social round. It was, moreover, a device reinforced by Wyndham's selection of Maple and Company, an interior decorator then prominent in society circles, to build his Henley set as well as to refurbish the Criterion stalls for the play's October debut. As Wyndham's program credited Maple for work on both sides of the proscenium, patrons of the recently redecorated auditorium – "gay as a box of sugar plums" *The Times* informed its readers (10 October 1897, 6) – were aware of settling into seats reupholstered by the same hands responsible for the comfort of their on-stage doubles. The move had the effect of erasing what barriers remained between the society worlds of stage and stalls, creating a new intimacy that brought with it an increased vulnerability.

The most telling use to which such vulnerability was put appears in Wyndham's decision to have *The Liars* dressed by Lucile, West End London's most notorious couturière. Through the previous decade, as Mrs. James Wallace, Lucile had worked out of her Davies Street residence, making gowns primarily for friends and family members. Yet the alternatives she offered to Parisian formalism soon attracted the attention of London's avant-garde. When, in the early nineties, an aging Worth began to focus his energies upon nice subtleties of cut and color, Lucile responded with calculated impudence. To Worth's line for 1891, consisting of bias-cut gowns and seamless dresses in cream faille, otter brown (spring), iron gray, pale heliotrope (summer), and a subdued shade of yellow called "Cleopatra," she opposed an exuberant collection of "personality gowns," provocative creations in light fabric meant to harmonize with the characteristics of her clients. Lavishly trimmed, and worked in a bold palette of scarlet, jade, viridian, and tyrian purple, such outfits anticipated by two decades Bakst's designs for the Ballets Russes (Etherington-Smith, p. 42). Introduced at Court by the intrepid Mrs. Willy James, they formed the outer limit of what was permissible to wear in good society. By 1895, the year of Worth's death, Lucile had taken commercial premises in Old Burlington Street. Here she compounded her reputation for the risqué by providing a much talked of "Rose Room" for the marketing of scanty undergarments. Shown to an exclusive clientele (by appointment only), Lucile's transparent nighties, lace knickers, and chiffon petticoats were intended to replace "the ugly nun's veiling or linen-cum-Swiss embroidery which was all that the really virtuous woman of those days permitted herself." In her autobiography, Lucile notes both the initial shock and eventual acquiescence of her society patrons: "Those cunning little lace motifs let in just over the heart, those saucy velvet bows on the shoulder might surely be the weapons of the woman who was 'not quite nice'? They all wanted to wear them, but they were not certain of their ground. They had to fly in the face of the conventional idea as to how a good woman went to bed at night – and it took a little coaxing for them to do it." Among those successfully "coaxed" was Adeline, Duchess of Bedford, who bought, Lucile tells us, "different sets to match every one of her dresses, and even ordered satin corsets in the same colors" (Duff Gordon, pp. 41–43).[33]

In the summer of 1897 Lucile, with little stage experience, was commissioned to design *The Liars*, a task that included personal responsibility for the gowns of Mary Moore, Irene Vanbrugh, and Cynthia Brooke. She had been brought to Wyndham's attention by Moore who had advised her on Marion Terry's wardrobe for *The Physician* the previous spring. Moore had been impressed by Lucile's dramatic instinct as well as her willingness to subordinate her craft to larger concerns of text and production. She was, Moore tells us, "the first costumier to ask us to let her read the play, so that she might the better understand how to garb the different characters" (Moore, p. 242). For Wyndham and Jones, the collaboration had other advantages. Lucile's earlier stage work had been informed by the same flamboyant eroticism that had characterized her off-stage garments. Indeed, her costumes for a charity tour of *Diplomacy*, organized by Lord Rosslyn, had noticeably shocked audiences in both London and Edinburgh. In *The Liars* such smart wickedness would be used to argue through the language of clothes a moral bankruptcy Wyndham was loath to let Jones put into words. Lucile did not disappoint. Not only did she dress all five of the play's women in revealing combinations of lace, net, and chiffon, but, capitalizing upon her reputation for chic impropriety, stripped bodices of their linings, a remarkable move that enabled playgoers to see clear through her costumes to their corset covers (Vanbrugh, p. 50). Irene Vanbrugh, as Lady Rosamund Tatton, refused to wear an especially clinging gown of buttercup yellow, until Lucile convinced her that her own fine figure might itself be a marketable asset (Duff Gordon, p. 45) (plate 4). Moore's Act I outfit, worn while Lady Jessica carried on her potentially adulterous flirtation, consisted of little more than an appliqué of lace and sequins, resting upon an undergarment of flesh-colored chiffon. The device was clearly meant to look "naughty" to the stalls and gallery, an impression reinforced by Lady Jessica's entrance line, spoken through "*a very merry peal of laughter* ... Oh, no, no, no, no, no! Please keep away from my dress!" (p. 169). The critic for *Modern Society* noted the manner in which light playing upon the sequins of Moore's overgown seemed to pick out

4. *The Liars*, Act I. "Miss Irene Vanbrugh's dress in shades of yellow" (*Sketch*, 13 October 1897).

what he slyly called "a tracery of deeper pink" (16 October 1897, 1558–1559) (plate 5).

The impact of such costumes was twofold. Individually, they appeared to accuse their wearers of a variety of sins, from frivolity to outright lust. Clement Scott explicitly linked Lady Jessica's "smart dresses and pretty hats" to her "vain, empty-headed" coquetry (*Daily Telegraph*, 7 October 1897, 9–10). The handiwork of Lucile had, in addition, a cumulative effect that clearly upset fashion writers. While dressmakers like Savage and Purdue and Madame Eroom had, previously, designed entire productions, Lucile's style was so unique that displayed *en masse* her costumes called attention to themselves in unsettling ways. Virginia, who in 1897 had transferred her "Diary of a Daughter of Eve" from *Black and White* to the *Sketch*, questioned the wisdom of allowing "one dressmaker [to] make all the gowns." "Each scene," she maintained, "should show diversity of style, and, as your true artist always has an individuality, several true artists should be employed" (13 October 1897, 513–514). The correspondent for the *Lady* concurred, faulting the play's costumes for being "rather alike in style and effect" (14 October 1897, 531). Unity of concept, expected of musical comedy and historical romance, had, it would seem, disturbing implications for plays of modern life. The more co-ordinated a production looked the less it resembled the milieu it was meant to replicate. Miss Aria in the *Queen* condemned the effect as "theatrical." What she had in mind was the impossibility of a drawing room filled with the work of one designer (16 October 1897, 738). Such displays were, however, a conspicuous part of the play's meaning. In offering what announced itself as a histrionic mock-up of smart society, *The Liars* reduced Lucile's individually conceived "personality gowns" to troubling uniforms, intended to catch the attention and consciences of the Criterion's more affluent spectators. Their success in so doing is recorded, once again, in the fashion press, which resigned itself to the work as a telling, if misogynistic, attack upon the sensibilities of its public. The critic for the *Lady's Pictorial* sums up much of the play's contemporary reception in reading Jones's text and Wyndham's production as an "object lesson in social morality":

I should be sorry ... to have to accept without question or qualification some of Mr. Jones's pictures of smart society; yet I am inclined to think that he has only indulged in a perfectly legitimate and moderate amount of caricature in showing us these trivial, vain, and conscienceless women, ripping up

5. *The Liars*, Act I. "Miss Mary Moore's dress of pink and silver tissue" (*Sketch*, 13 October 1897).

reputations like rags, and flinging brazen lies about like largesse in the hope
that it will be accepted by male fools as sterling coin. (16 October 1897, 520)

Beyond this society comedy could not go. To push any further would
have meant breaching the boundaries of the genre itself, moving into
the no man's land that divided the form from the darker world of the
"sex problem" play. Significantly, Jones's next work for Wyndham
was the grim scapegoat drama of *Mrs. Dane's Defence* (Wyndham's
1900). Lucile, for her part, carried her Criterion experience back to
the world of retail dressmaking. If Jones and Wyndham, like Wilde
and his producers, worked on stages that had been turned into
couturier's shops, she transformed her new showroom in Hanover
Square into a theatre. Building a stage, hanging curtains, and
installing crude limelight devices in makeshift wings, she presented
London, at the century's close, with its first formal fashion show. It
was a move that generated, in turn, its own iconography of modiste,
mannequin, and (male) voyeur-consumer – a reverberant triangle
that would, in time, find its way back to commercial and repertory
stages.

CHAPTER 2

Dressing Mrs. Pat

The selling of women's bodies as well as gowns is implicit in much society comedy. Wilde's women, the playwright tells us, "wear" their waists and chins as surely as their skirts and bodices, while Lucile's advice to Irene Vanbrugh about the marketability of her own "fine figure" betrays the extent to which dressmakers connived in a mutually profitable traffic. Indeed, the commercial drama's identification of haute couture with female sexuality was complete enough to deflect the course of a revitalized national theatre, and reshape the phenomenon Harley Granville Barker would later call "the coming of Ibsen." Ibsen's heroines, most simply put, did not dress to West End standards. Responding to Charles Charrington and Janet Achurch's trailblazing production of *A Doll's House* at the Novelty Theatre in June 1889, critics noted costume effects from Mrs. Linde's Act I traveling coat to the large, black shawl Nora threw about her shoulders as she made her final exit.[1] Yet there was no escaping the fact that the play's world of clerks, housewives, nursemaids, and bank managers left little scope for the type of spectacular display West End consumers had come to demand of domestic drama. For every enthusiast, like American actress Elizabeth Robins, who cheered Achurch's decision to breach tradition by making her initial entrance in a shabby gown meant to signal Nora's precarious finances and depleted dress allowance (Robins, *Ibsen*, p. 10), groups of playgoers shook their heads over a drama of modern life without "pretty ladies ... in smart frocks, half a dozen at least, and as many more as the playwright could provide for and the management afford." "Not lowest of the barriers between Ibsen and the 'recognized' London theatre," Granville Barker reminds us, "was the distressing fact that there is hardly a fashionably dressed woman to be found in his plays. Hedda Gabler to be sure; but heaven help us, even she *walks* home after a party!" ("Coming of Ibsen,"

p. 166). Beyond such immediate disappointments lay a deeper disturbance. Asking why Nora's exit from her doll's house prison should
have caused an uproar in 1889, in an England that had already seen
the establishment of Newnham and Girton Colleges as well as the
passing of a Married Women's Property Act, Granville Barker
replied by citing the particulars of what Clement Scott had termed
Ibsen's "suburbanity." It was one thing for "distinguished ladies,
irreproachably married" to have to curtsey to the likes of George
Eliot, quite another to ask them to countenance similar antics in
provincial parlors: "This Nora...with her little household, her
work-basket and her Christmas shopping, her children and her bank-
manager husband – caricature though he might be, Norwejans [*sic*]
all of them in their outlandish ways! – this was still far too like
Balham to be pleasant. And was the flag of domestic revolt to be set
flying there?" (p. 161). In brief, Ibsen's decision to "dress down" not
only deprived society viewers of fashion markets, it substituted for the
comforts of a well-dressed drawing room the disquieting specter of a
radicalized bourgeoisie.

For playwrights who wished to exploit Ibsen's topicality without
alienating West End clients, a solution appeared in the partial
exception Granville Barker had made for *Hedda Gabler*. Staged for the
first time in Munich in January 1891, the most outwardly modish of
Ibsen's works brought audiences at least to the fringes of smart
society. With its great house, handsome sitting room, and genteel
hostess who talked snobbishly of "our circle," the piece became the
acceptable face of Ibsen for spectators weaned on a diet of Dumas,
Scribe, Augier, and Sardou. No matter that Hedda's surroundings
were part of a calculated assault upon the values and prejudices of
just such viewers, the play's surfaces were in their own right enough
to make claims upon the sensibilities of its public. Indeed, the work's
potential to be played as "parlor comedy" was demonstrated in the
year of its debut by French comedienne Marthe Brandès, who
dismayed Parisian Ibsenites by presenting Hedda as "a Madame
Bovary who gets her frocks on the Rue de la Paix" (Marker, p. 163)
– a pointed reference to the precinct in which Worth had maintained
premises since 1858. In London, where *Hedda* first appeared in
Elizabeth Robins's 1891 Vaudeville staging, the work's elegance won
it ready acceptance in fashionable circles. The *Lady's Pictorial*, which
had twice dismissed Achurch's *Doll's House* as "not to the taste
of English playgoers" (15 June 1889, 873; 22 June 1889, 907),

announced that Robins's *mise-en-scène* had reconciled it to a text it had previously condemned in print. Likening Robins's production to recent works by Henry Arthur Jones and Haddon Chambers, its critic spoke feelingly of "a scathing satire upon *Marriage à la Mode*" thundered forth in well-to-do drawing rooms (25 April 1891, 677).[2] Hedda's wardrobe, that of "a woman of position," was singled out for particular comment. *Black and White* accompanied a mixed review by critic Justin McCarthy with engravings of Hedda in three separate gowns (25 April 1891, 382), while provincial papers like the *Leicester Daily Post* supplied readers with full fashion-plate analyses. Robins first appeared, we are told, "in a sweeping tea-gown of serpent green, with a draped front of orange coloured silk." Her second dress, in sapphire blue velvet, was constructed "with a good deal of white vandyked lace about the throat and wrists," while the "wrapper" of white silk, worn as she burned Løvborg's manuscript, featured an impressive "train lined with primroses" (27 April 1891, 6). Robins's Act IV ensemble, a daring combination of a sleeveless black evening gown and a black feather boa, which "became the rage of fashionable women throughout the city" (Cima, 153) – Hedda, we recall, is in mourning for Tesman's Aunt Rina – enabled Robins to stage Hedda's suicide as a sumptuous study in contrasting textures. A final view of the play's inner room, revealed when Tesman pulled back the draperies, disclosed, according to William Archer's production notes, Hedda arranged on a sofa with "head thrown back, face upward ... white-metal ... pistol in [her] right hand, fallen somewhere on [her] black dress" – a tableau that assured viewers Ibsen's heroine had indeed "done it ... beautifully" (Postlewait, p. 74).[3]

The point was not that Robins or her collaborators had capitulated to West End tastes. Although McCarthy, writing this time for the *Gentleman's Magazine*, complained of a production "calculated to appeal to the sympathies of London audiences" (June 1891, 638), most critics praised the integrity of the venture. In fact, the subtlety of Robins's performance helped to brand her an "intellectual" actress ill-suited for commercial roles.[4] It was rather that the play itself participated in a tradition of up-market opulence absent in Ibsen's previous work. Set alongside *A Doll's House*, or *Ghosts*, with which J. T. Grein had launched his Independent Theatre the previous month, Robins's *Hedda* had the effect of offering West End viewers a choice of Ibsens, or at least alternative modes of "unpleasant" playmaking. If Shaw built into his first dramas the

moral relativism and discussion sequences he had come to value in
the former pieces, the most considerable of his rivals, Arthur Wing
Pinero, chose, after the pattern of *Hedda*, to join the bright surfaces of
society comedy to the darker aims of a problem playwright. What
resulted was the phenomenon Shaw called "Pineroticism," a
compulsive whirl of furs, fans, and female flesh, from which Shaw
himself instinctively recoiled. To Pinero and his imitators, Shaw
would later complain, "it seemed... that most of Ibsen's heroines
were naughty ladies. And they tried to produce Ibsen plays by
making their heroines naughty. But they took great care to make
them pretty and expensively dressed" (*Puritans*, p. 18). Yet if Shaw
condemned Pinero for peddling what amounted to an Ibsen without
brains, Pinero might have countered by accusing Shaw of championing an Ibsen without glands. The chic morbidity Pinero had tapped,
however selectively, was an essential part of *Hedda*'s effect. The
direction in which he wished to take it is suggested in a pair of
cartoons that celebrated the success of *The Second Mrs. Tanqueray*
some two years after *Hedda*'s London debut. On 10 June 1893, the
Illustrated Sporting and Dramatic News depicted a nattily dressed Pinero
touting the wares of a gentrified new drama to a shabby, ill-clothed
Ibsen. His taunt: "I think we have something now which will suit
you!" (522). The association of progressive theatre with sartorial
exclusivity was pursued in a *Punch* caricature published the same day.
Under the rubric "Proceeding by Leaps and Bounds" readers
encountered Mrs. Patrick Campbell, the play's leading lady, jumping
a literal "Hurdle of Convention." She is clad in a full-length evening
gown with shoulder frills, leg-of-mutton sleeves, and sequin-spangled
net. Pinero stands to one side, mopping his brow (10 June 1893, 273).
Between them, the images help to locate Pinero's place in the drama
and fashion worlds of the 1890s, suggesting how his compromises with
avant-garde theatre – his attempts to both dazzle and unnerve his
viewers – would be mediated by the wardrobes and physicality of one
of the era's most remarkable women. They also anticipate Shaw's
response two decades later when, in *Pygmalion*, he worked to demolish
the premises and values of "a wicked Pinerotic theatre" by redressing
that movement's most redoubtable icon as a Mayfair duchess and
Covent Garden flower-girl.

With the première of *The Second Mrs. Tanqueray* on 27 May 1893 two
reputations were made. The event effectively established Pinero,

hitherto known as a farceur and author of sentimental comedies, as a writer of "serious" drama. It also created an overnight success of Mrs. Patrick Campbell, the 28-year-old actress who had taken its title role. The meteoric rise of Mrs. Pat, as she would be known, and the reaction of Pinero's first audiences have been ably documented in recent studies by Margot Peters and John Dawick. The section that follows is indebted to both. Its subject, however, is not biography or theatre anecdote, but the peculiar and often volatile chemistry between actor and author, and the attendant problem of how individual performances get folded into the overall meaning of a work. In part, the triangular relationship between Pinero, Mrs. Pat, and her dressmakers was dictated by the kind of texts that brought them together. Both *The Second Mrs. Tanqueray* and *The Notorious Mrs. Ebbsmith*, which followed in 1895, were read by their contemporaries as "best circle" tragedies – curious amalgams of drawing-room melodrama, well-made play, and Ibsen adjusted for Mayfair markets. Robins's 1891 *Hedda* had shown the way. *The Second Mrs. Tanqueray* was Pinero's attempt to push that most pliant of works from the shadows to the center of smart society. If Hedda had walked home from parties, Paula Tanqueray would arrive by carriage. Where Hedda talked of dancing herself out the previous season, Paula's translation from courtesan to bored wife would be marked by reminiscences of Mediterranean cruises, diamond tiaras, and a frustrated desire to host dinner parties for "the nicest set imaginable ... the sort of men and women that can't be imitated" (p. 89).[5] Indeed, from the beginning Pinero had intended his play for just such a set. When John Hare rejected it for his Garrick Theatre, worried about the effect even accommodated Ibsen might have on carriage-trade patrons, the playwright turned to George Alexander, whose championing of Wilde the previous season had transformed the St. James's into a glittering fixture in London's social round. At no point, we should note, did Pinero consider the little theatres or stage societies that had played Ibsen (and, after 1892, Shaw) to small groups of select viewers. Indeed, when Archer proposed production by Grein's Independent Theatre, Pinero snapped that he would sooner see his manuscript burned. Such venues, he maintained, merely preached to the converted. The drama as an essentially popular art had to reach a larger, more commercial public. Pinero also knew that the "look" he needed to argue his case was beyond the resources of even the most willing small companies. Alexander's production meant, among other things, that the world of "*wealth and refinement*" Pinero had set forth in his stage directions would be realized with convincing polish and solidity. In the event, Aubrey Tanqueray's Act I bachelor dinner took place in Walter Hahn's closely observed replica of Albany chambers Pinero had himself reconnoitered months earlier. "*Richly and tastefully decorated ... elegantly and luxuriously furnished,*" the set with its practicable fireplace, oak table, Venetian glass, and fine china helped to establish the "little parish of St. James's" Aubrey's second marriage would lead him to forsake. The following acts were likewise played in a painstakingly recreated social environment, here "Highercoombe," Aubrey's great house in the Surrey hills, modelled upon an estate near Haslemere in which Pinero himself had once lived (Dawick, p. 79). From the bright breakfast room of Act II, we are brought, in Acts III and IV, to the inevitable parlor with its verandah, mirrors, and pairs of French windows. It is here that Paula, after dinner, and in her best evening frock, would determine to take her own life.

Performance at the St. James's also assured that the play's gowns would be built by Mesdames Savage and Purdue, who by late 1892 were functioning as Alexander's in-house couturières. Fresh from their triumphant dressing of *Lady Windermere's Fan* the previous winter, they responded by using the wardrobes of Pinero's four principal women to mark the boundaries of his stage world. At its perimeter they placed Mabel Orreyed, like Paula, a courtesan who marries out of the trade. Unlike Paula, however, Lady Orreyed is incapable of shedding her pre-nuptial manners. "Paint her portrait," we are told by Cayley Drummle, the play's *raisonneur*, "it would symbolize a creature perfectly patrician; lance a vein of her superbly-modelled arm, you would get the poorest *vin ordinaire*" (p. 80). For Edith Chester, who created the role, Savage and Purdue produced a dinner gown of crimson silk, trimmed with scarlet passementerie and red-tipped ostrich feathers. The *Sketch* found its gaucherie "photographic of the class to which Lady Orreyed belongs" – by which it meant the class from which she had come (6 December 1893, 296). Virginia in *Black and White* pronounced the garment "appropriately garish," declining, as had the *Sketch* and *Queen*, to illustrate it in her column (10 June 1893, 712). In sharp contrast, Mrs. Cortelyon, a society dame with impeccable credentials, was dressed as befitted the only figure in the play capable of introducing Paula's step-daughter to fashionable circles. Amy Roselle, in the part, made her initial entrance in a gown of electric-blue broché with a full knee-height flounce, an innovation so recent Florence congratulated herself on having introduced it to her readers only three months earlier. Step-daughter Ellean, a convent-bred innocent, played by perennial ingenue Maude Millet, appeared in a succession of outfits described by the *Sketch* as "extremely simple, and for that reason ... all the more becoming to her sweet girlish beauty." Her third act skirt of vieux rose crepon was particularly praised for "being devoid of any trimming, save two insertion bands of cream lace" (7 June 1893, 330). It was, however, the ensembles of Paula herself that offered Savage and Purdue their greatest challenge – how to document a woman's passage from *demi-mondaine* to the legal chattel of a West End gentleman, while keeping her in saleable gowns. Their solution was to steer a middle course between flamboyance and respectability. In Act I the former predominated. Paula, paying a late-night call to Aubrey's Albany chambers, arrived in a *décolleté* dress of flame-colored satin with epaulettes of rose velvet and lemon ostrich plumes. It was, in fact, the gown of *Punch*'s "hurdle" cartoon, mitigated by the same ultra-smart flounces Florence had noted in Mrs. Cortelyon's first costume. Act II readjusted the balance. Paula, now rusticated at "Highercoombe," wore a simple walking-dress of fawn-colored cloth. Such decorum, however, was shattered when, during the scene, Paula shifted into an elegantly cut double-breasted coat and brown straw hat, the latter festooned with ornaments of cream guipure. Next to the puritanical Ellean both items looked unsuitably fast. Indeed, a cartoon by Alfred Bryan showed Ellean responding with horror to her stepmother's bonnet ("Oh Pa – look at her hat!" *Illustrated Sporting and Dramatic News*, 10 June 1893, 522). Paula's wardrobe was completed in the play's final acts, in which Pinero put both Paula and Lady Orreyed into "*sumptuous dinner gowns.*" Yet with Lady Orreyed, rather than Ellean, as her foil, Paula's ensemble of gray bengaline, gray beads, and white lace was a model of deportment. Even the jewels and crystals "cleverly curved" on her bodice to accentuate her bosom (*Sketch*, 7 June 1893, 330) seemed a rebuke to Lady Orreyed's open vulgarity. Shimmering in the light of the up-to-date straw shades Alexander had ordered for the occasion, they appeared to hover between respectability and provocation. It was, all in all, an impressive performance, showing how Savage and Purdue had managed, since *Lady Windermere's Fan*, to fit marketable products to the texts of their authors.

How such costumes would be animated in performance was another matter. Pinero was aware that in *The Second Mrs. Tanqueray* he had created a work neither melodramatic nor modern. Gone were the soliloquies, asides, formal attitudes, and tableaux that had served him well through the previous decade. In a watershed letter to Alexander, his leading man as well as his producer, Pinero even declined the orchestral support that had (literally) defined melodrama since the days of Holcroft and Pixérécourt. Such devices, Alexander was told, belonged more properly to what Pinero now dubbed "the 'Blood-on-the-Breadknife' order of play" (Wearing, p. 139). Pinero's heroine would, likewise, demand a more sophisticated response than that claimed by her melodramatic forebears. Indeed, Paula Tanqueray is best seen as the playwright's attempt to hold in tandem the opposing sexualities of melodrama's good and bad women. Part victim, part villainess, both *demi-mondaine* and "Hedda Gabler Shrew," she is finally destroyed by her belief in the values of a respectable world that will not have her. The complexities of the role, however, arose from its overlay of disparate types rather than the psycho-sociologizing Anglo-Ibsenites had come to expect of *their* New Drama. And here, Pinero was helped by his reliance upon the form as well as the style of the French society play. Scribe's lockstep march from exposition to denouement, signposted with significant properties and prepared coincidences, became for Pinero a means of commenting upon the closed systems of society itself. In *The Modern Stage and Other Worlds*, Austin Quigley has shown how *The Second Mrs. Tanqueray* exploited the inherent limitations of the well-made play to bring audiences to "an uneasy awareness" of that form's "spatial, generic, and moral horizons" (p. 90). Paula's suicide, into which she is "plotted" by dramatic conventions built squarely upon social prejudices, was designed, Quigley claims, to make playgoers question the aesthetic structures Pinero had inherited as well as the values such structures traditionally embodied. Quigley's reading goes far to explain much of the genuine discomfort that surrounded the play's first reception, and for the fact that critics ranging from the enthusiastic Archer to the openly hostile Clement Scott were prepared to see the work as a potent attack upon the mores of their public. It also underscores what Quigley calls Pinero's "successful thematization" of the well-made play's inevitable conflict between character and plot. If Paula is played exuberantly enough to convince us of her integrity – if she seems more than a palimpsest of theatrical poses – the play can be made to yield a chilling image of flesh and blood caught in the cogs of social mechanism.

It must have occurred to Pinero in the course of composition that *The Second Mrs. Tanqueray* required a kind of acting he had not seen on West End stages. Some restiveness, at any rate, appears in the search for an appropriate Paula that occupied Pinero and Alexander through the winter of 1893. Pinero, especially, was concerned that the heroine of what he would later call his first "play for grown up people" not carry excess baggage from previous roles. Olga Nethersole and Marion Terry were early possibilities. The former had played Janet Preece in Pinero's *Profligate* (Garrick 1889), the latter, Wilde's "clever" Mrs. Erlynne. Both were passed over. Nethersole, Pinero argued, had grown too old for the part and Terry too fat (Wearing, pp. 138, 143). More to the point, the recent appearance of each as a West End fallen woman could make Paula seem conventionally *déclassé.*[6] Janet Achurch was a less obvious contender, as was Elizabeth Robins. As representatives of London's new crop of Ibsen actors, each might have lent to the piece a sense of committed modernity. Achurch, however, had developed a distractedly mannered style since her *Doll's House* debut. She was also rumored to be suffering from dipsomania and morphine addiction. Robins, who at one point was actually signed for the role, was Alexander's choice. Pinero found her too robust and American-looking – an important objection as we shall see. An intelligent and subtle actress who, by 1893, had brought not only *Hedda* but *The Master Builder* (Vaudeville 1893) and *Rosmersholm* (Opera Comique 1893) to London playgoers, Robins had been praised for her ability to send "thought across the foot-lights" (Campbell, p. 65). Yet what some saw as a subordination of the physical to the intellectual – her Hedda, at Archer's urging as it turned out, suppressed all references to that character's pregnancy – put her at a disadvantage as far as Pinero was concerned.[7] In the end designer Graham Robertson and Florence Alexander were sent to scout London's principal theatres in search of new talent. Robertson, in an often cited passage in his memoirs, recalls their discovery that March of an unknown actress with an impressive ability to play against type. They had gone to the Adelphi to consider Evelyn Millard in *The Black Domino*, a purpose-built melodrama by George Sims:

Miss Millard was very beautiful, very gentle, very sweet, about as like Paula Tanqueray as a white mouse is like a wild cat; another evening was evidently to be spent in vain – when the scene changed and the wicked woman of the play came on. She did not look wicked – a startling innovation. She was almost painfully thin, with great eyes and slow haunting utterance; she was not exactly beautiful, but intensely interesting and arresting. She played weakly, walking listlessly through the part, but in one scene she had to leave the stage laughing; the laugh was wonderful, low and sweet, yet utterly mocking and heartless. (Graham Robertson, p. 248)

The unlikely villainess was listed in the playbill as Mrs. Patrick Campbell. Her resistance to the conventions of domestic melodrama convinced Robertson of her serviceability: "If she would only move, speak, look, above all laugh like that, the part [of Paula Tanqueray] would play itself." Once, however, she had been brought to Alexander's St. James's, Mrs. Pat proved as uncontainable as she had been at the Adelphi under the Gattis. She quarreled with Florence Alexander about hairstyles, and refused to wear the theatre's obligatory wrap while waiting for entrance cues. It had upon her, she complained, "a candle-snuffer effect" (Campbell, pp. 69–70). She was particularly irritated by Alexander himself, whose stiff formality seemed to her comically pompous. She would later compare playing Paula to his Aubrey with having to act opposite a walking-stick. For the moment, his lectures on theatrical deportment – "Don't forget you are not playing at the Adelphi now, but at the St. James's" – produced in her only "a wild desire to laugh and play the fool" (Campbell, p. 67).

Pinero, to his credit, saw possibilities in such friction. A martinet who exercised absolute control over his works in performance, the playwright had publicly maintained that "rehearsal is not – or should not be – a time for experiment." Yet in spite of his insistence that "all that we call 'business' is in the printed matter which I carry into the theatre" (Fyfe, p. 259), he found himself deferring to a new and relatively inexperienced actress whose instinct for sabotaging stage attitudes seemed a signal advantage. To Paula's ferocity Mrs. Pat was able to add an inbred, almost nonchalant, refinement, gaining her points by working against Pinero's dialogue and proverbially explicit stage directions. When Paula confronts Ardale, her ex-lover, towards the play's close, Pinero had required her to storm across the stage, sweeping from a piano a collection of photographs and bric-à-brac. Mrs. Pat refused: "Oh, I could not make her rough and ugly with her hands, however angry she is" (Campbell, p. 69). Ben Webster, Pinero's Ardale, recalled more spirit in her rebellion: "she stormed on cue; she reached the grand piano; she picked up a very small ornament: 'Here,' she said, in tones of black ice, 'I knock something over,' and dropped it delicately onto the carpet" (Margaret Webster, p. 160). Whichever the case, Pinero gave way, and the critic for the *Era* found himself praising the episode for its inventive restraint (Dawick, 82). Similar underplaying helped Mrs. Pat defuse the melodrama of Paula's earlier plea that she be given a second chance with step-daughter Ellean:

> I could get neither shape nor form into my sobbing ... the empty noises, the moans and snuffles I made were all false and silly. After much striving I thought of "breaking up" the sounds by a natural blowing of my nose. (Campbell, p. 71)

Kate Terry Gielgud, one of the few women to have left us with an account of the play's first night, thought the effect "quite the best of its kind" (p. 11). A more studied contribution was Mrs. Pat's musicianship. In Act III Pinero had called for Paula to "*sit ... at the piano and strum ... a valse.*" An accomplished pianist with a Leipzig scholarship to her credit, Mrs. Pat scorned strumming. When, at rehearsal, Alexander insisted that something be improvised, she replied with a polished recital of a Bach piece for the left hand alone. From this moment, she tells us, Alexander and Pinero began to treat her as one of the company. Such talent, they felt, might invest their heroine "with not a little glamour."[8] In the end it enabled Mrs. Pat to complete for Paula the genteel past Pinero had failed to suggest in his text – a matter of no little importance in a play about social barriers and eligibility. The *Punch* reviewer who asked of Paula "what was her bringing up? What ought by right to have been her position in life?" found in Mrs. Pat's playing his only clue to the character's early history (10 June 1893, 273).

Physically, Mrs. Pat helped to evoke Paula in more disturbing ways. In a recent essay, art historian Bridget Elliott has suggested that Aubrey Beardsley's rendering of Mrs. Pat as Mrs. Tanqueray used the somatotype of the New Woman to subvert the meaning of Pinero's play. Beardsley's portrait, which first appeared in the *Yellow Book* for April 1894, shows a distressingly slender Mrs. Pat in Savage and Purdue's second act gown, complete with full cravat of fine lace, and "graduated frills" falling over "tightly fitted wrists." The

6. Aubrey Beardsley, "Portrait of Mrs. Patrick Campbell" (*The Yellow Book*, April 1894).

likeness even incorporates a variant of the decorated hat that so shocked step-daughter Ellean (plate 6). Calling attention to the intemperate reaction of Beardsley's critics, Elliott claims that the "extreme thinness" of the portrait forced upon viewers "an unpleasantly advanced interpretation" of Paula "as a struggling but socially victimized New Woman" ("New and Not so 'New Women,'" 50). The point is well taken. Yet if we begin, not with the conventions of New Woman iconography – something Pinero *would* use two years later in *The Notorious Mrs. Ebbsmith* – but with Mrs. Pat herself, we arrive at some very different conclusions about how both play and picture seem to have struck their contemporaries.[9] We might start by noting that to Pinero's role, and to the outfits of Savage and Purdue, Mrs. Pat brought a sensibility itself described as Beardsleyesque, Baudelairean, and "fin-de-sickly" (Peters, p. 171). In part, this was an accident of physique. She was, by the standards of the day, "ridiculously thin" (Campbell, p. 40). So much so, that through the nineties she was cast (like Dickens's Smike) in "starved business." At the decade's outset she appeared as Astrea, the lean villainess of Sims's *Trumpet Call* (Adelphi 1891); nine years later she created for Frank Harris the rake-like Hilda Daventry (*Mr. and Mrs. Daventry*, Royalty 1900). In practice the effect was often exaggerated by ill-health and a tendency to work to exhaustion. As Clarice Berton, the Adelphi role in which she was discovered, she appeared "physically feeble, white and fragile." She had only recently recovered from typhoid, and her hair was just beginning to grow back. (We recall Robertson's description of her as "almost painfully thin.") At the St. James's, preparing Paula, she was often close to collapse; by her own account Pinero was reduced to spoon-feeding her beef extract backstage to get her through one rehearsal. It was, however, an appearance that Mrs. Pat cultivated. "I look my best," she would confess in her autobiography, "when I am very ill ... the bones of my face are good and my features are well placed" (Campbell, p. 291). The effect, a peculiar blend of Pre-Raphaelite sexuality and *memento mori*, appears to best advantage in an 1895 photograph of Mrs. Pat as the dead Fedora (Campbell, p. 100).

Pinero, too, saw advantages in the look. His play, after all, dealt with a sensual woman haunted by her past and frightened by a future that necessarily contained her own breaking up. Presented, in Bert States's nicely turned phrase, as a "raconteur of her own decay" (p. 188), Paula reaches her first crisis in Act III when forced to confront her ruined image in a mirror held by Cayley Drummle. The scene closes as she gazes in the glass once again, this time on her own initiative. Paula's suicide in Act IV is, similarly, linked to a passage in

which she transforms, for her husband's sake, the lines and hollows of
her face into a grim vision of an epicure "gone off":

> You'll see me then, at last, with other people's eyes: you'll see me just as your
> daughter does now, as all wholesome folks see women like me. And I shall
> have no weapon to fight with – not one serviceable bit of prettiness left to
> defend myself with! A worn out creature – broken up, very likely some time
> before I ought to be – my hair bright, my eyes dull, my body too thin or too
> stout, my cheeks raddled and ruddled – a ghost, a wreck, a caricature, a
> candle that gutters, call such an end what you like! (p. 129)

In performance the passage was delivered in what Mrs. Pat called her
"Channel steamer" voice, a tombside manner meant to convey both
nausea and despair. Pinero, she later told John Gielgud, had coached
her in the technique especially for the role (Gielgud, p. 67). The
overall impression was that of a death's-head in the drawing room, as
actress and playwright used Mrs. Pat's anorexic eroticism to reveal in
a flash both skin and skull beneath. This sense of fatality incarnate –
the critic for the *Theatre* felt himself in the presence of rotting shrouds
and burst sepulchers (1 July 1893, 142) – seems the most likely source
of Beardsley's morbidity, which apprehends rather than subverts the
meaning of Pinero's play.[10] It is also the impulse behind Edward
Reed's ghoulish cartoon, "Played Out; or, The 252nd Mrs.
Tanqueray" (*Punch*, 5 May 1894, 208), which, under the guise of
presenting Mrs. Pat as overworked actor, metamorphoses Beardsley's
image into that of a skeleton lover whose bones, Elliott observes, seem
"about to break through the skin" (plate 7). Reed's costume, we
might note, turns silk into cerecloth, transforming even the guipure
ornament in Paula's Act II hat into what Elliott calls "a grotesque"
(50). The process implied in both portrait and parody – Paula
Tanqueray as predatory victim – is made explicit in Philip Burne-
Jones's painting *The Vampire*, in which Mrs. Pat's attenuated body,
now *en déshabillé*, appears straddling a male cadaver. A lurid study in
green, black, and crimson, the figure asserts its membership in Bram
Dijkstra's company of polyandrous blood-drinkers, grave ladies of
the *fin de siècle* whose anemic constitutions drove them to prey upon
male vitality (pp. 333–351). When displayed at the opening of the
New Gallery in 1897 the picture was accompanied by Kipling's now
familiar lines identifying its subject as "a rag, a bone and a hank of
hair" (Peters, pp. 142–143, 486; Dent, p. 225).[11] Throughout, Mrs.
Pat was conscious of the contributions she was making, both
substantive and accidental, to Pinero's art. Years later she would

7. Edward T. Reed, "Played Out; or, The 252nd Mrs. Tanqueray" (*Punch*,
5 May 1894).

boast to Shaw that "the Portuguese Jew knew there would have been
no 'Mrs. Tanqueray' if he had interfered with the amateur" (Dent,
p. 327). For his part, Pinero seemed to concur. Relinquishing
something of the absolute control he believed to be a dramatist's

prerogative, he allowed his new leading lady to transform in performance both his work and that of his costumiers.

Through the extended run of *The Second Mrs. Tanqueray* the image of the bony lady in couture house gowns continued to haunt the imaginations of West End playgoers. So potent, in fact, was its effect that Mrs. Pat soon found herself cast in a sequence of roles cut much to the same cloth. At the St. James's, Alexander followed Pinero's piece with Henry Arthur Jones's *The Masqueraders*, in which Mrs. Pat, in an ill-suited blonde wig, played Dulcie Larondie, a barmaid turned society wife. This was, in turn, succeeded by Beerbohm Tree's Haymarket staging of Haddon Chambers's *John a' Dreams*, a drawing-room drama in which a reformed prostitute was reclaimed by an opium-eating poet. In the part of Kate Cloud, Mrs. Pat, dressed entirely in sables and silks, was applauded for the "morbid touch" with which she endowed her musings upon an unpleasant past (*Saturday Review*, 10 November 1894, 507).[12] Pinero, however, had other plans. The previous summer he had begun work on a new project that, unlike *The Second Mrs. Tanqueray*, was from the beginning designed to capitalize upon Mrs. Pat's unique corporeality. Commissioned by actor-manager John Hare the play, soon to be called *The Notorious Mrs. Ebbsmith*, opened at the Garrick Theatre on 13 March 1895. Its central role, that of a feminist platform-speaker, was, Mrs. Pat declared, a greater part than Paula Tanqueray. She harbored, nevertheless, some doubts about the general drift of Pinero's action: "The role of Agnes Ebbsmith and the first three acts of the play filled me with ecstasy. There was a touch of nobility that fired and inspired me, but the last act broke my heart." What stoked Mrs. Pat's imagination was Pinero's decision to place her upon the stage as "a new and daring type, the woman agitator, the pessimist, with original, independent ideas – in revolt against sham morals" (Campbell, pp. 98–99). A blood-and-thunder orator with radical views about the institution of marriage, Agnes Ebbsmith is, at the play's outset, living openly with Lucas Cleeve, a married MP. Their plan, announced in Act I from a decayed lodging-house on the Grand Canal, is to trumpet to the world a program of "free union," presenting themselves as living examples of "man and woman ... in the bondage of neither law nor ritual! Linked simply by mutual trust!" (p. 51).[13] What broke Mrs. Pat's heart was the manner in which Pinero's plot seemed to connive in the dismantling of his heroine. When in Act II Agnes learns, to her horror, that her hold upon Lucas is primarily sexual she exchanges her plain brown dress for a low-cut one of shimmering black gauze. The ensuing episode in which she is transformed into a conventionally beautiful woman, was as Archer recognized, an attempt on Lucas's part to "have her put on the gown and prejudices of his caste" (*Theatrical World 1895*, p. 88). A further humiliation awaited Agnes at the close of Act III. In a mood of game defiance she hurls a Bible into a wood-burning stove. Moments later she plucks it out and, in a gesture dismissed by Shaw as gross theatrical claptrap, clutches it to her breast as the curtain descends. The play's conclusion, which particularly dismayed Mrs. Pat, dispatches the former free-thinker (her hand in a bandage) to a Yorkshire parsonage for an extended period of rest and recuperation. "I knew that such an Agnes in life could not have drifted into the Bible-reading inertia of the woman she became in the last act." It was, she protested, a regrettable "rounding off... to make the audience feel comfortable" (Campbell, pp. 98–99). Had Pinero, as Mrs. Pat went on to suggest, "miss[ed] an opportunity?" Or was it the playwright's turn to create from the materiality of Mrs. Pat's body and stage wardrobe a more troubling work than she herself had at first realized?

Before looking at Mrs. Pat in the role of Agnes Ebbsmith, it might be useful to consider the New Woman as she had previously appeared in the West End drama of the nineties. The phrase, to begin with, is best understood as a catch-all for a variety of distinct but overlapping types, each of which had migrated to the stage from the fiction and popular iconography of the period. The liberated bachelor girl, unmanageable wife, frustrated spinster, and street-corner demagogue were not so much life studies as embodiments of male fears and fantasies spun about the prospect of female emancipation. What they had in common was their status as grotesques, the laughter directed at them ranging from indulgent to savage depending upon their degree of militancy. Gaunt, drawn, or angular in appearance, such figures also shared a common body type meant to suggest "unnatural" sexuality. In 1894, the season before Mrs. Ebbsmith made her debut, London audiences had applauded two works that freely celebrated such stereotypes. Sydney Grundy's *The New Woman*, which opened at the Comedy in September of that year, offered playgoers a quartet of mannish females who espoused advanced causes by anathematizing their sex. Agnes Sylvester, the leader of the troupe, condemns her husband to meals of cold mutton in order to write on "The Ethics of Marriage." When, in Act I, we find her batting her eyes at her male collaborator, Grundy's agenda becomes clear. His New Woman is a fraud, a neurotic humbug designed to collapse in mid-play. Draped throughout in chiffons, silks, and feathers – the work of Ellen Terry's dressmaker, Mrs. Nettleship of Wigmore Street – she becomes a fashionable diversion for spectators who wait smugly for biology to triumph.[14] One month after the première of Grundy's play, Jones's *The Case of Rebellious Susan* opened at the Criterion. Elaine Shrimpton, its New Woman, was also conceived as a figure of fun. Her decision, however, to step into the political arena subjected her to rougher handling. Raw and assertive from her first appearance in a gown of aesthetic cut, she is by Act III maneuvered into what the *Sketch* recognized as the uniform of her tribe: "tweed coat and skirt, double breasted waistcoat and wide-brimmed felt hat" (10 October 1894, 613). Her ideas are similarly placed. The message she carries of "an immense future for Women" is cut short on two occasions by Sir Richard Kato, the play's *raisonneur*.[15] In the second instance, in a passage that would gain its own notoriety, Elaine is scolded for harboring "distorted and defeated passions." When she departs "in a glow of martyrdom" – to howls of laughter in Wyndham's production – Sir Richard wonders "How it is that women never will understand the woman question?" (pp. 153–154).

To such displays *The Notorious Mrs. Ebbsmith* offered both a rebuke and corrective. It is not so much that Pinero wished to champion the New Woman – a figure he had himself lampooned in pieces like *The Weaker Sex* (1889) and *The Amazons* (1893) – but that by 1895 he had come to see in her a broader range of stage effects than those possible in farce or low comedy. Agnes Ebbsmith is, ultimately, no more fortunate than her theatrical predecessors. Indeed, the surfacing of what she calls her repressed womanhood links her directly to her namesake in Grundy's comedy. Pinero's adjustment lay in transposing her to a minor key – asking us to be distressed rather than amused at her progress. In practice such disturbance was created by the playwright's juggling of familiar types. His protagonist is, on closer inspection, an unsettling amalgam of New Woman attributes, meant to be articulated by the mannerisms and (above all) the physicality of Mrs. Patrick Campbell. In Acts I and II the actress becomes an armature on which to hang the shabby spinster of popular myth. "*Her dress,*" we are told, "*is plain to the verge of coarseness; her face, which has little colour, is at first glance almost wholly unattractive"* (p. 14). *The Times* recognized in her "a dowdy New Woman, in a plain brown dress with carelessly tied up hair," a figure both forbidding and unkempt (14 March 1895, 10). The *Era* would later speak of Mrs. Pat's unhealthy physique as peculiarly apt for the role (2 March 1901, 12). Although she and Lucas have been lovers, she proposes before the act is out a union "devoid of passion." Lucas, in turn, accuses her of "perpetual slovenliness" – which he emends to "shabbiness" – and of going through life with pursed lips. Through this neurotic puritan, however, Pinero lets us glimpse a more threatening type, "a gaunt, white-faced" political agitator, who dreams of "standing, humbly-clad, looking down upon a dense swaying crowd – a scarlet flag for [her] background" (p. 158). This is the "notorious" Mrs. Ebbsmith of the play's title, a stump demagogue with shrill voice and sunken cheeks. Her leanness is that of deprivation, her ferocity bred of solidarity with the people. Her presence in the work is most vividly evoked by her nemesis, the wicked Duke of St. Olpherts, who in Act II recalls an encounter five years earlier with "the lean witch" of Ironmongers' Hall. *Punch* illustrator E. J. Wheeler depicted the figure with clenched fist and flashing eyes, addressing a meeting of an anti-marriage league (Hankin, *Mr. Punch's Dramatic Sequels*, p. 223). Pinero's heroine oscillates between the two, creating an impression of typological instability. A photograph by Alfred Ellis, used by the *Sketch* for its 3 April 1895 cover, shows the passion of the rabble rouser seeming to burn through the reticence of the prude (plate 8).

In the play's second half the question of what to do with the New Woman becomes largely a matter of how to clothe her. The low-cut, bare-armed evening gown Lucas orders from "Madame Bardini" is met by Mrs. Ebbsmith with calculated disdain: "When would you have me hang this on my bones?" (p. 61) (The force of this seemingly casual image would not have been lost upon viewers in 1895.) Once, however, she suspects that the relationship with Lucas may be sensual on her part as well, the garment becomes an erotic weapon. Fearful of Lucas returning to his wife, she makes a sensational end-of-act entrance "*handsomely gowned, her throat and arms bare, the fashion of her hair roughly altered*" (p. 109). The effect, once again, builds upon Mrs. Pat's disruptive angularity, now read as the tight-laced provocation of the decade's "fast" woman. Cartoonist Alfred Bryan of the *Illustrated Sporting and Dramatic News* underscored the point,

8. Mrs. Patrick Campbell as Agnes Ebbsmith in Act I of *The Notorious Mrs. Ebbsmith*.

presenting a transmogrified Mrs. Ebbsmith lighting a cigarette while mouthing slang phrases associated with the type: "How's this for ALL RIGHT!" (30 March 1895, 129). The boldness of the move seemed to arouse many of the play's (male) first-nighters. In an accompanying text that publication's Captious Critic congratulated Mrs. Ebbsmith for abandoning "dowdy gowns fastened at the neck for a low cut costume which show[ed] more of her charms." The *Punch* reviewer nudged and winked about her coming out *of* – rather than out *in* – an evening dress (30 March 1895, 148). Even Shaw, who kept a clinical distance, described the garment as "cut rather lower" than he expected (*Saturday Review*, 16 March 1895, 347). The point, however, was not the costume's chic impropriety, but its violation of its subject. When Mrs. Ebbsmith puts on what was cheered in its own right as a "smart frock," her head droops and her voice becomes hard and dull – Mrs. Pat's "Channel steamer" tones again. Her ambiguous triumph shatters the composite New Woman of Acts I and II. It also offers a telling gloss on the Cinderella myth, fashionable on West End stages since the première of Tom Robertson's *School* in 1869. Here our workaday drudge dons her fairy gown and feels shame (plate 9). When, like Paula Tanqueray, she surveys herself in a mirror, she falls into a dead faint (p. 99).

The play's achievement to this point may be gauged by the reactions of its society critics. Although *The Notorious Mrs. Ebbsmith* had opened at an awkward time of year, with fashionable London preparing to leave for points south, the prospect of Mrs. Pat in a new wardrobe at the Garrick had caused many to postpone their departures. Both the *Sketch* and the *Lady's Pictorial* provide impressive roll-calls of those who attended, appending detailed catalogues of their hats, gowns, jewels, and accessories. Even the final destination of Hare's most affluent patrons, a midnight reception hosted by Lady Brassey, was noted by one enterprising reporter (*Lady's Pictorial*, 28 March 1895, 394). For such spectators, Mrs. Pat's initial ensembles were an obvious disappointment, especially after the expectations raised by her appearances as Paula Tanqueray, Dulcie Larondie, and Kate Cloud. "They do not take much description," began Florence's column of 20 March, "these gowns, in which Mrs. Patrick Campbell enacts the part of the heroine of the new Garrick piece." Her first outfits, "a trailing robe of...dark-brown woollen fabric, held in at the waist," and a clinging gray skirt "of equally severe simplicity," were, Florence noted with some asperity, "as different as

9. Mrs. Patrick Campbell as Agnes Ebbsmith in Acts II and III of *The Notorious Mrs. Ebbsmith.*

... can be from the outstanding fullness in which we are rejoicing nowadays" (*Sketch*, 20 March 1895, 433). The *Queen* and the *Lady's Pictorial* were likewise chagrined. The latter, in an editorial called "Beauty v. Brains," read in Mrs. Pat's Act I entrance a cautionary tale, instructing "the modern restless woman" against making herself willfully unattractive (23 March 1895, 382). Such reactions were predictable enough. What is surprising – indeed, unprecedented, in the fashion journalism of the day – is the response of such critics to the play's pivotal "transformation" gown. While paying lip service to its generic brilliance, its "rustle of silk, glare of arms and throat," fashion writers were unable to free the garment from its dramatic context, pronouncing it, in the same breath, both "gorgeous" and "unbecoming" (*Sketch*, 20 March 1895, 390). The gown was, in the process, rendered unmarketable. Not that its note of sexual advertisement had transgressed society standards, but that the sinister meaning it had acquired on stage had made consumers understandably purse shy. In spite of its admitted modishness, no columnist sought to identify, let alone recommend, its maker – other than as Pinero's "Madame Bardini." Nor, while it was reproduced in photographs and engravings of the play in performance, was the gown admitted to the costume illustrations accompanying dress reviews. In sharp contrast, the outfits of Ellis Jeffreys and Eleanor Calhoun, in relatively minor roles, were repeatedly sketched by fashion artists. For the ensembles of both, Hare had gone to Messrs. Jay of Regent Street, a firm whose origins as a smart mourning house had made it peculiarly apt for the two dresses worn by Jeffreys as the widow Gertrude Thorpe. Calhoun, as Sybil Cleeve, the play's deserted wife, was likewise praised for the veiled outfit of black passementerie in which she made her single appearance. Indeed, the trio of gowns with their distinctively tied Jay's bows became, by default, the play's fashion text. Both the *Queen* (30 March 1895, 549) and the *Lady's Pictorial* (23 March 1895, 393) ran full-page fashion plates, and the *Sketch* (20 March 1895, 433) a series of three separate blocks, from which Mrs. Ebbsmith's climactic evening gown was conspicuously absent. In creating a smart dress, contaminated by thematic content, Pinero had gone beyond the paradoxical "fashion statements" of Wilde's society comedies. In erasing his leading lady's *pièce de resistance* from the fashion tableaux of artists like Paulette and Pilotelle, the playwright had moved it, unambiguously, from the realm of haute couture to that of drama.

Oddly enough, the Bible-burning that so annoyed Shaw and Archer seems not to have been a problem for Pinero, Mrs. Pat, or the majority of their patrons.[16] Indeed, the sight of a charred Testament clutched to Mrs. Pat's nearly exposed bosom allowed spectators to thrill to the same kind of fleshly religiosity that had made toga drama so popular in the period – although there it was the masculine chest of Wilson Barrett that stirred so much excitement (Granville Barker, "Coming of Ibsen," p. 162). The pietism of the play's conclusion was another matter, and one upon which playwright and actor found themselves in sharp disagreement. Pinero had constructed an ending to comfort and reassure his audience. After three acts of emotional distress, the Bible-hugging Magdalen of the play's close was a peace offering – an endorsement, at his heroine's expense, of his spectators' codes and mores. Mrs. Pat's objection was not to the conversion itself, but to its scope. Where Pinero saw reaffirmation, she found only diminishment. Her response was a passionate but oddly deracinated performance that alerted the play's more attentive viewers to the possibility of alternative readings. Edmund Gosse talked of a "whirlwind of battling instincts" that ultimately "swamped the play" (Campbell, p. 101). Shaw, with malicious delight, chronicled the effect as a contest between author and actor clearly decided in the latter's favor:

Mrs. Patrick Campbell... pulls [Pinero] through by playing him clean off the stage. She creates all sorts of illusions, and gives one all sorts of searching sensations. It is impossible not to feel that those haunting eyes are brooding on a momentous past, and the parted lips anticipating a thrilling imminent future, whilst some enigmatic present must no less surely be working underneath all that subtle play of limb and stealthy intensity of tone. Clearly there must be a great tragedy somewhere in the immediate neighbourhood; and most of my colleagues will no doubt tell us that this imaginary masterpiece is Mr. Pinero's *Notorious Mrs. Ebbsmith*. But Mr. Pinero has hardly anything to do with it. When the curtain comes down, you are compelled to admit that, after all, Mrs. Patrick Campbell is a wonderful woman. (*Saturday Review*, 16 March 1895, 346)

It was not merely that Mrs. Pat was, in Shaw's terminology, a "creative" rather than an "interpretative" artist – Shaw's description of Irving's Shylock playing Shakespeare "off the stage" is remarkably similar (*Saturday Review*, 26 September 1896, 340) – but that in *The Notorious Mrs. Ebbsmith* her body had become a site of resistance, inviting viewers to "rewrite" Pinero's play. Mrs. Pat was specific about the conclusion she had in mind:

A fourth act – I wanted – with Agnes preaching the doctrine of selfless, unexacting love; stern and unyielding only when baseness, lying, and fear invades its purity – her conversion, a sudden revelation of the Love of God; not a mere creeping back into the shell of a narrow morality – how I should have loved to speak that harangue in Hyde Park if only it had been written. (Campbell, p. 99)

The point was that she played as if such an harangue *had* been written, animating her character with an energy alien to Pinero's copy. Her example, moreover, incited others to similar irreverence. St. John Hankin devoted one of *Mr. Punch's Dramatic Sequels* to "The Unfortunate Mr. Ebbsmith," a satiric sketch in which he argued the case for Mrs. Ebbsmith's deceased husband. Another *Punch* critic spoke of marrying Agnes to the play's north-country parson (30 March 1895, 148), while Shaw proposed returning her to political life as "the Radical Duchess of St. Olpherts" (*Saturday Review*, 25 May 1895, 693). For the moment, however, Mrs. Pat had set her own limits upon how she would be used for Pinerotic purposes. Whether or not she had intended to reshape Pinero's conclusion, her refusal to be gathered into his text on any but her own terms amounted to the same thing. Indeed, the very ability to act against the grain that had helped Mrs. Pat "make" Paula Tanqueray, effectively worked to "unmake" Agnes Ebbsmith. In her autobiography Mrs. Pat attempted a reconciliation. Noting that in 1895 "the suffragette, with her hammer in her muff, had not yet arisen on the horizon," she wondered whether Pinero might not have been right in gauging the tastes and sensibilities of his public (Campbell, p. 100). This was, however, twenty-seven years after the fact. The immediate outcome of their second collaboration was less tentative. Although Pinero and Mrs. Pat maintained a cordial relationship for the next four decades, in spite of the financial success that attended their joint ventures of the nineties, the two did not work together again.[17]

For Bernard Shaw, the picture of Mrs. Pat dressed to Pinero's specifications came to epitomize all that he loathed about West End drama. Not only did it superimpose a cheap eroticism upon an already meretricious theatre, it pretended, in the process, to be intellectual entertainment. The appearance of Mrs. Pat as both Paula Tanqueray and Agnes Ebbsmith also served to remind Shaw

that a "perilously bewitching" actress, who might be impressed into
his own program of problem playmaking, was, for the moment, in the
camp of his rivals. Through the early nineties, Shaw had tantalized
himself with the prospect of Mrs. Pat as Kitty Warren, Julia Craven
(*The Philanderer*), and the Strange Lady in *The Man of Destiny*. Later,
he would model directly upon her the figures of Cleopatra, Eliza
Doolittle, Mrs. Juno (*Overruled*), Hesione Hushabye, Orinthia (*The
Apple Cart*), and the Serpent in *Back to Methuselah*. As drama critic for
the *Saturday Review*, Shaw wrote at length on Mrs. Pat's performances
in plays by an orthodox opposition that included Shakespeare as well
as Pinero and Sardou. Attempting to lure her from what he saw as a
decadent repertoire, he tactfully worked to separate Mrs. Pat's acting
from the dramatic texts in which she appeared. If her Mrs. Ebbsmith
"play[ed] Pinero off the stage," her Fedora "threw Sardou out of the
window" (1 June 1895, 726). As Juliet, she succeeded, as she had
with Pinero's heroines, "simply [by being] a wonderful person"
(28 September 1895, 410). At the same time, however, Shaw opened a
second front, directed at Mrs. Pat's wardrobes, which were made to
bear the brunt of his exasperation with her as a stage voluptuary.
Modishly gowned for the role of Rita Allmers (*Little Eyolf*), Mrs. Pat
was contrasted, to her disadvantage, with Janet Achurch, whom she
had replaced in the part. "Her dresses," Shaw noted caustically,
"were beyond reproach: she carried a mortgage on the 'gold and
green forests' on her back" (12 December 1896, 623). Clad in period
garb for John Davidson's romantic pot-boiler *For the Crown*, Mrs. Pat
provided Shaw with an opportunity to remind his readers of the
milieu in which they habitually found her: "Mrs. Patrick Campbell's
dresses," he announced, "are not made by Worth: no controversy
can possibly arise over her sleeves: worst of all, she does not appear
in a hat. It is true, on my credit – four acts, and not one hat"
(7 March 1896, 248). The campaign embraced the already cited
attack upon the *décolleté* evening gown worn in *The Notorious Mrs.
Ebbsmith*. Feigning surprise at the reactions of the play's on-stage
viewers, Shaw proceeded to demolish the very assumptions upon
which such costume "effects" had been built:

I should, by the way, like to know the truth about the great stage effect at
the end of the second act, where Mrs Patrick Campbell enters with her plain
and very becoming dress changed for a horrifying confection apparently
made of Japanese bronze wall-paper with a bold pattern of stamped gold.
Lest the maker should take an action against me and obtain ruinous

damages, I hasten to say that the garment was well made, the skirt and train perfectly hung, and the bodice, or rather waistband, fitting flawlessly. But as I know nothing of the fashion in evening dresses, it was cut rather lower in the pectoral region than I expected; and it was, to my taste, appallingly ugly. So I fully believed that the effect intended was a terrible rebuke to the man's complaint that Mrs. Ebbsmith's previous dress was only fit for "a dowdy demagogue." Conceive my feelings when everyone on the stage went into ecstasies of admiration. (16 March 1895, 347)

A like complaint was lodged against the costumes Mrs. Pat wore in Forbes Robertson's 1895 Lyceum revival of *Romeo and Juliet*. Calling attention to the production's marriage of antiquarianism and modern marketing, Shaw noted the "toning down" that substituted for the bold colors of Shakespeare's Verona the muted shades of Marshall and Snelgrove. The device, he observed, enabled "the stalls [to] contemplate the 14th century and yet feel at home there." His fiercest attack, once again, was directed at the gowns created for Mrs. Pat, this time by a well-known Mayfair modiste: "'Mrs. Patrick Campbell's dresses,' says the programme 'have been carried out by Mrs. Mason of New Burlington Street'. I can only say that I wish they had been carried out and buried. They belong to Mrs. Mason, and are her triumph, instead of to Mrs. Campbell." Likening Mrs. Pat, unfavorably, to Gertrude Kingston ("an artist in dressing fashionably") and Ellen Terry ("an artist in dressing originally"), Shaw argued that "a lady who is dressed by somebody else, according to somebody else's ideas, like any dressmaker-made woman of fashion, is artistically quite out of the question." Mrs. Pat's only recourse, he advised, was to claim that her Juliet ensembles were intended to suggest "the tutelage of a girl of fourteen who is not yet allowed to choose her own dresses" (28 September 1895, 409).

Shaw's concern, however, was less that Mrs. Pat "dress" herself, than that she abandon the garments of fashionable Mayfair for outfits of his own devising. Indeed, the one Shavian role Mrs. Pat did, in the end, create, began with the playwright's wish, expressed in an 1897 letter to Ellen Terry, to clothe her as "an east end donna in an apron and three orange and red ostrich feathers" (*Collected Letters*, I, p. 803). Much has already been written about the origins of *Pygmalion*, from such casual first thoughts, to Shaw's reading of an initial draft to Mrs. Pat some fifteen years later. The play's tempestuous rehearsals under Beerbohm Tree at His Majesty's Theatre have themselves attained the status of green room legend, while the playwright's infatuation with Mrs. Pat has been exhaustively analyzed by biographers, editors, and literary critics.[18] Yet whatever tangle of psychological and professional motives can be teased out of Shaw's personal correspondence, the author was himself precise about how he expected his "romance in five acts" to receive and reform its leading lady. The two themes that weave paradoxically through Shaw's letters of 1912–1913 are Mrs. Pat's affinity for the role of Eliza Doolittle and "the enormous joke" of casting her so completely against type (Dent, p. 42). "I am," Shaw insisted in a particularly telling image, "a first class ladies tailor." Eliza Doolittle, he assured Mrs. Pat, would "fit" her as snugly as Cicely Waynflete had "fit" Ellen Terry a decade earlier (Dent, p. 21).[19] At the same time, Shaw boasted that in recycling the West End's "Queen of Snobs" as "a dusty petticoated ... girl" he would "astonish the young lions of the St. James's stalls" (Dent, p. 106).[20] It may be, as Arnold Silver has suggested, that in composing *Pygmalion* as an equivocal "love gift" for a "prototypical siren" Shaw was driven by childhood fears of aggressive female sexuality (pp. 223–250). To be sure, his flirtation with Mrs. Pat has a sexual edge absent from similar encounters with Ellen Terry, Janet Achurch, and Lena Ashwell. Yet in a larger sense, the demons Shaw was exorcizing were as generic as they were personal, and we should, perhaps, take him at his word when he insists that Mrs. Pat's "overpowering *odor di femmina*" was endangering not merely his individual well-being, but "the very health of ... the English theatre" (Silver, p. 229). The culprit, once again, was "Pineroticism," its cult of elegant morbidity, and the persistent popularity of the actress who had remained its most formidable emblem. The "bombardments" Shaw had begun in his *Saturday Review* columns of the mid-nineties were renewed, at the century's close, in a militant Preface added to the published text of *Three Plays for Puritans* (1900). Here, after decrying, yet again, Mrs. Tanqueray and her "fashionable dressmaker," Shaw called upon a new Cromwell to rise up and smash the icons of a foolish, degenerate stage. In *Pygmalion* the playwright would provide himself with the opportunity to (literally) redress such grievances, deconstructing in full view of her adoring public the actress he had most closely identified with "sham Ibsen" and drawing-room naughtiness.

In an anti-Cinderella play that claimed language as its principal subject, Shaw's first line of attack was obvious enough. Mrs. Pat's voice, a thrilling contralto with rich bottom notes and pinched articulation, was as idiosyncratic as her body. In his *Saturday Review* columns, Shaw, "a mere critic with a very superficial knowledge of phonetics," had praised what he termed the actress's "instinctive" enunciation, while damning the affected vowels – especially a clipped English "a" – through which she mimicked lady-like behavior (8 February 1896, 149). The speech patterns of Eliza Doolittle were, as Mrs. Pat recognized, consciously built upon such peculiarities. In later correspondence, the actress would remind Shaw of how he climbed onto the stage after her debut as the femme fatale in Robert Hichens's *Bella Donna* (St. James's 1911), and accused her of "speaking too carefully" (Dent, p. 326). Her rejoinder, a challenge to write for her a "cockney role" that might permit her to show her versatility, allowed Shaw to invent a street argot close enough to Mrs. Pat's stage cadences to suggest uncomfortable similarities between social pretension and open vulgarity. To acquire the Cockney dialect needed for Shaw's opening scenes, Mrs. Pat drilled as assiduously as the play's Eliza learning the accents of Mrs. Pat's Mayfair. At one point, it was rumored, she was actually tutored by an authentic flower-seller. In the end, the actress's quick ear enabled her, like Eliza, to beat her "creator" at his own game. Anthony Asquith, directing the play's 1938 film version, incorporated into Shaw's text at least one variant Mrs. Pat had introduced in performance (Peters, p. 366). As the malfunctioning automaton of Act III Mrs. Pat, as Shaw anticipated, parodied herself. Even the play's great "sensation," the "not bloody likely!" with which Eliza swept out of Mrs. Higgins's elegant "At Home," depended for its full effect upon being projected with the performer's celebrated precision, "slow but always sure over the aspirates" (*Queen*, 18 April 1914, 740). The stunned silence with which the line was greeted, followed by laughter so tumultuous it threatened to wreck the production, was a response not only to Eliza's yielding to what *Vanity Fair* called her "cockney instincts" (30 April 1914, 26), but to Mrs. Pat, creator of Paula Tanqueray, Agnes Ebbsmith, and Kate Cloud, breaching the decorum of a stage drawing room in a particularly outrageous manner. The complexity of the effect – part linguistic, part phenomenological – helps to explain the lopsided emphasis placed upon it by contemporary critics and satirists. Although the Lord Chamberlain's Office had found the adjective harmless enough, both popular and society publications titillated readers by hinting broadly at the "unprintable" word Mrs. Pat uttered nightly on His Majesty's stage.[21] For *Sketch* readers, *Pygmalion* became "Bernard Shaw's Naughty Word Play" (22 April 1914, 74), while on the boards of the plebeian Palace, "Mrs. Pat's voice was very cleverly mimicked" by review artist Nelson Keys, who, gowned as Eliza, pronounced fellow actor Arthur Playfair a "vermilion rotter" (*Sketch*, 15 May 1914, 170–171). Mrs. Pat, ambivalent about her new notoriety, saw the phrase as Shaw's attempt to knock the Pre-Raphaelitism out of her. It was, she claimed, part of a larger program bent upon "breaking up" her voice, carriage, and figure (Campbell, p. 268; Dent, p. 326).

Visually Mrs. Pat was vulnerable to such attacks. When *Pygmalion* opened in April 1914, she was in her fiftieth year and already a grandmother. Her anxieties about playing an 18-year-old "guttersnipe" pepper her correspondence with the playwright, from Shaw's first gibes about her "acting a girl" (Dent, p. 42), to her own declaration a quarter of a century later, that she had been "twenty five years too old for the part" (Dent, p. 326). At rehearsal, Shaw exacerbated matters by shouting from the stalls that she looked "forty years too old for Eliza" (Peters, p. 337), and sketching in the margin of his rehearsal book a likeness both fatigued and middle-aged (*Pygmalion*, rehearsal notes, 2 April 1914). Mrs. Pat, who in 1906 had complained that the "days of dewlaps have arrived," drew in her own script her Edwardian profile, hatching over its double chin to restore her 1890s features (*Pygmalion*, acting copy, Act III, p. 14). On stage, the problem of Mrs. Pat's age was compounded by the weight she had gained since her Pinero debuts. Not yet the "obese" object cruelly guyed by Cecil Beaton ("Twice as large as any man on the stage"), she had nevertheless acquired a matronly girth obvious to the pit and stalls. In Alexander's 1913 revival of *The Second Mrs. Tanqueray*, her stoutness had been cloaked by generously cut garments, and a less animated playing style.[22] Yet Shaw's purposes demanded a warts-and-all Mrs. Pat, dressed to accommodate his anti-romantic vision. The flower-girl's ensemble of "apron" and "ostrich feathers," from which *Pygmalion* had originally sprung, was an attempt, in the nineties, to overlay Mrs. Pat's "erotic sentimentality" with squat drudgery and a coarse flamboyance. By 1912, however, when Shaw had completed his play, London flower-sellers had abandoned ostrich-plumed hats for more practical ones of dark straw. The previous season, actor Charles Brookfield had noted the exchange, by flower-girls outside the Haymarket, of "marvellous picture-hats laden with ostrich feathers" for "sailor-hats – severely unadorned – which are unbecoming and out of character" (*Random Reminiscences*, p. 196). The *Evening News* similarly observed that "the up-to-date flower girl invariably wears a black sailor cap... and for high days and holidays a black velvet coat much beaded." "The purple plush hat with its three brightly coloured, contrasting feathers, all waving at outrageous angles," it added, "is surely... behind the times" (Tree, Clipping Book 1914, p. 275). Shaw, loath to lose his effect, retained Eliza's "coarse apron" as part of her Covent Garden uniform (plate 10), but shifted her "hat with three ostrich feathers" to the following act, where, worn with a second "nearly clean" apron, it became a best calling toilette, accompanying Eliza on her "state" visit to Wimpole Street.[23] Indeed, a cancelled 1912 passage, which adds to the outfit a "yellow" ostrich feather, may have been meant to recall the yellow ostrich plumes worn by Mrs. Pat on her earlier journey, also "in state" and unannounced, to Aubrey Tanqueray's Albany chambers (*Pygmalion*, printer's copy, Act II, p. 3). In *Pygmalion*, however, such "finery" was meant to be patronized. Not only was Eliza's hat a demonstration of working-class vanity to which stalls viewers could comfortably condescend, it was, in the bargain, lousy – a detail that offended the authentic flower-seller Tree had engaged to help promote his production (Huggett, p. 145).[24] In the end, Eliza's anachronistic hat, pretentious, gauche, and pest-ridden, would become the play's most enduring symbol.[25] Its final appearance, at the close of Act II, strutted about by Mrs. Pat, while wearing a kimono that showed her legs to disadvantage, rendered its wearer openly ridiculous.[26] When, at the close of the episode, Mrs. Pearce announced the delivery of Eliza's new wardrobe, viewers were teased with the prospect of sartorial relief. It was, needless to say, an expectation Shaw did his best to upend.

The bet to transform Eliza into a duchess makes her, as Mrs. Higgins is quick to point out, a creature of her dressmaker's art as well as Higgins's phonetic skill. Indeed, Higgins's claims in Act I for the great leveling powers of language, had visual parallels in a variety of *ad hoc* social experiments. On 23 March 1910, while Shaw was casting his play into draft form, the *Sketch* featured the story of American socialite Alma Powell, who, in an effort to demonstrate her "pet theory" that "a Paris gown will make a Society woman," floated her own cook as an Irish heiress. Under the rubric "Fine Feathers *Do* Make Fine Birds," and a photograph of the two women

10. Mrs. Patrick Campbell as Eliza Doolittle in Act I of *Pygmalion* (*Sketch Supplement*, 22 April 1914).

elegantly gowned, gossip columnist Cosmo Hamilton described the translation of one Nora Corrigan, giving an account of how "during the few evenings of her debut in Society the cook's hand was sought by a well-known Hungarian Count" (354). Such transformations, Shaw was at pains to point out, were common enough. Rather than present them as "Cinderella" miracles, he sought in *Pygmalion* to distinguish between "faked up" ladies and the more difficult task of creating an emancipated woman. The play's Alma Powell, in this sense, is not Higgins, but the more conventional Colonel Pickering, who proposes the bet, pays its expenses, and, we are told, buys Eliza's clothes. Even his traditional chivalry, which Eliza credits with striking her ladyhood into being, is sharply contrasted with Higgins's insistence upon treating both sexes with equal disdain, and his claim, after her threat to earn her own living, that he has made her not "a lady" but "a woman."[27] Pickering's success comes with Eliza's society debut, her complete mastery of what he calls the "social routine," signaled by her acceptance at a garden party, an embassy reception, and the same opera house outside of which she had once sold flowers. This, however, is precisely what Shaw elects not to show. Although he would later add a ball episode to the film version of the play, and this would, in turn, be incorporated into his authorized text, Shaw initially withheld from his public what theatrical convention had led it to expect, the social accreditation of a rags-to-couture-house heroine. Disingenuously blaming Tree for excluding the kind of spectacle Tree had in fact wished to include, Shaw presented instead an isolated Eliza, disabused, after her triumph, by Higgins's indifference to her own part in the venture. The sumptuous ballgown and chiffon wrap created for Mrs. Pat by Madame Handley Seymour, a Bond Street dressmaker who had received her first court commissions the previous year, was in its own right handsome enough. Yet Shaw went out of his way to insure that neither the dress nor the values it embodied would be shown to best advantage. Fashion columnists later complained that Eliza's wrap was discarded so rapidly they had no time for fair perusal, while the gown beneath, a delicate construction "of palest pink satin" with "a deeply pointed and flowered tunic," was compromised by its display in a sequence of increasingly demeaning postures (*Lady's Pictorial*, 25 April 1914, 664). Eliza, immediately after her Act IV entrance, is made to sit up-stage in a dark corner, glaring at Higgins and Pickering for a full twenty minutes. By the scene's close, after fetching Higgins's slippers

and flinging them in his face, she is directed to crawl about on all
fours searching for a ring Higgins had given her in happier days.
Throughout, we are told, the weeping Eliza "look[s] ugly as the
devil." Under the circumstances, it is hardly surprising that, in spite
of its structural virtues and sales potential, the outfit that might have
served as the play's visual climax was fleetingly noted by the fashion
press.

The purpose of such sabotage was to heighten Shaw's distinction
between a lady's drive for social acceptance, and his own counter-
myth of independent womanhood. Yet if Shaw sought to bring Mrs.
Pat into the orbit of disquisitory playmaking, Mrs. Pat, determined
to remain both "lady" and "woman," fought back with the two
gowns Madame Handley Seymour had built for her Act III and Act V
appearances. We cannot say at this remove how much Mrs. Pat had
to do with the actual cut of these garments. We do know that she had
personally sketched and then rejected "the sort of dresses...men
would have chosen" (Dent, p. 158), and that Madame Handley
Seymour, her dressmaker of choice, boasted of her ability to fit
costumes to the actress's unique personality and style. In a later
interview, the couturière talked of putting Mrs. Pat into outfits
designed to transcend mere modishness (Peters, p. 463). For *Pygmalion*
this meant coming to terms with the colors and motifs of pre-war
Futurism. Through 1913–1914, London had been much occupied
with the paintings of Severini and "plastic ensembles" of Boccioni,
both exhibited at the Doré Galleries. It had also cheered readings
and lectures by poet and group spokesman Filippo Marinetti. During
the first month of *Pygmalion*'s run, the *Sketch* would devote its front
cover to Marinetti's "exploded" self-portrait, and turn staff artist
W. Heath Robinson loose upon the movement's rhetoric and iconography. In "Fireside Futurism," Robinson depicted a society lady
and her maid debating the propriety of "leaving one's eye on the
mantelpiece." The maid's defense, "it is not my eye, but merely the
dynamic conception of its lyrical form," shows how thoroughly the
movement's aims and imagery had soaked into the small talk of smart
society. Debate over the so-called "Futurist fashions" which appeared with much fanfare in the summer of 1913 presented Madame
Handley Seymour with a ready vocabulary. Loose fitting and brightly
colored, the outfits had been both praised for their avant-garde
boldness, and denounced for a dynamism that threatened to
overwhelm the post-Directoire silhouette. Taking advantage of the

controversy, Madame Handley Seymour constructed two outfits designed to catch Eliza at crucial points in a traditional Cinderella progress. For Act III, set in Mrs. Higgins's Chelsea drawing room, in which the half-finished flower-girl mixes Mayfair enunciation with Lisson Grove diction, she created an "ideal visiting dress" of corn-colored satin with an elegantly cut bolero corsage (*Lady's Pictorial*, 25 April 1914, 664). The problem, as far as fashion critics were concerned, was what the *Daily Graphic* called its "Futurist" palette, which seemed to betray a "flower girl's lavish taste" (Tree, Clipping Book 1914, p. 259). The gown's pattern of electric green foliage and scarlet roses on a background of yellow taffeta convinced the *Westminster Gazette* that Eliza, in spite of the outfit's formal subtleties, had "no more lost her affection for the gaudy hues [of Act II] than she had grasped [true] refinement of speech" (14 April 1914, 9) (plate 11). The self-assured Eliza of Act V, in sharp contrast, was praised for having acquired a more "cultivated taste for low tones and neutral tints" (14 April 1914, 9). For her second appearance at Mrs. Higgins's, Madame Handley Seymour contributed a dress of a "wonderfully rich matelassé silk … in the palest shade of grey" with a wide hem in "puttee-coloured cloth" and a sash of "sombre" tulle. Its one concession to Futurist "flash" was the contrasting lining – "black silk patterned with circles of pink, purple, and green" – of an accompanying sleeveless coat (see frontispiece). In its restrained application of one of the season's most exuberant fads, the garment won the applause of both fashion critics and society first-nighters. The implication was that Mrs. Pat had achieved, by the evening's end, sartorial credibility. Cutting clear across the grain of Shaw's text, the sequence helped to establish Eliza as clothes-conscious as well as free-thinking. An ironic observer might almost have called it "playing Shaw off the stage."

The ensuing debate over the meaning of Shaw's heroine would occupy author and actress for the next quarter-century. Shaw, who had once boasted to Mrs. Pat that his *Saturday Review* columns had "rolled Pinero in the dust beneath [her] feet," was no doubt discomfited to find publications like *Vanity Fair* marking the "Pinero stride" of Eliza's final moments, or noting how, in spite of his attempted sabotage, the flower-girl of Acts I and II "faded before one's memories of Paula Tanqueray and Mrs. Ebbsmith" (30 April 1914, 26). Seeing his script destabilized by what he had formerly patronized as Mrs. Pat's "Tanqueradiance," Shaw countered with a

11. *Pygmalion*. Mrs. Patrick Campbell (center) in Madame Handley Seymour's Act
III visiting ensemble.

co-ordinated campaign designed to regain the aesthetic initiative. Critic Arnold Silver has argued with some ingenuity that the Preface and lengthy Postscript added to *Pygmalion* in 1916, as well as revisions Shaw made to the text itself in the 1930s and 1940s, were attempts to diminish both Mrs. Pat's contribution and the stature of her Eliza (pp. 253–279). We might add to his list a note sent to Mrs. Pat after a successful remounting of the play in 1919, in which Shaw attacked both her Act III and Act V gowns, denouncing them, respectively, as "horrible" and "dramatically nonsensical" (Dent, p. 211). Yet the conflict was not simply, as Shaw sought to suggest, between a progressive playwright and a "dressmaker-made woman of fashion." Mrs. Pat, in reconciling emancipation with couture house culture, was, in fact, emulating the "dress code" of Edwardian feminists, who, as we shall see, embraced modishness as a necessary weapon with which to fight caricatures of the hammer-wielding suffragette.

Her attempt to steer Eliza away from such stereotypes was, accordingly, cheered by suffrage sympathizers like Edith Lyttelton, whose own play, *Warp and Woof*, a biting attack upon fashion-trade abuse, had been produced by the actress a decade earlier. In the end Shaw found himself, as had Pinero after *The Notorious Mrs. Ebbsmith*, outmaneuvered by a performer he had sought to reform. Indeed, Pinero's comment to fellow playwright H. F. Maltby, that "If [Mrs. Patrick Campbell] is absolutely fitted in a part, she can wear it – but she can't wear anyone else's" (Peters, p. 388), anticipates Shaw's 1938 challenge to Mrs. Pat to "write a true book entitled WHY, THOUGH I WAS A WONDERFUL ACTRESS, NO MANAGER OR AUTHOR WOULD EVER ENGAGE ME TWICE IF HE COULD POSSIBLY HELP IT" (Dent, p. 328). As a response to what both playwrights read as a celebrity's *gran rifuso* it was unfair and ungrateful. So was Shaw's decision to withhold further roles, even those he publicly boasted were inspired by her qualities. Citing, but dramatically transposing, images associated with Mrs. Pat's earlier triumphs, Shaw ungraciously acknowledged his own indebtedness: "I exploited you, made money out of you ... Why, oh why do you get nothing out of me ... You are the Vamp and I the victim; yet it is I who suck your blood and fatten on it whilst you lose everything!" (Silver, p. 263). Mrs. Pat, in return, accused Shaw of "want of respect," insisting that after the success of *Pygmalion* she "deserved another chance" (Dent, p. 304). She also recalled what, in retrospect, seemed a turning-point in her career. During one particularly ill-tempered rehearsal, she had decided to stand her ground, insisting, before the assembled *Pygmalion* cast, that "If Mr. Shaw doesn't leave this theatre I will." She watched as Shaw silently gathered up his papers and departed. How different matters might have been, she would later ask, if, playing a conventional woman's part, she had instead "burst into a flood of tears" (Dent, p. 327).

CHAPTER 3

The ghost in the looking-glass

Camden Theatre in less than fashionable Camden Town witnessed its own Cinderella-like transformation as "rank and fashion" converged upon it on the evening of 6 June 1904 (*Echo*, 7 June 1904, 4). "Just ten minutes drive from Piccadilly," the faint-at-heart were reassured by advertisements encouraging their attendance at the première of Edith Lyttelton's full-length play, *Warp and Woof*. Why, the *Sketch* asked, should Society transport itself to the opening of what was reported to be "a drama ... showing [the] 'smart' world at what a sacrifice some of its pleasures ... are produced" (4 May 1904, 83). Because, we are told, the play's author, the "clever wife of the Colonial Secretary," was herself in Society, and because the piece was produced by Lyttelton's close friend, Mrs. Patrick Campbell, whose picture-post-card likeness joined those of society beauties in shop-window displays. The combination of Society and "theatrical personages" was, observed the *Illustrated London News*, "the making of a huge 'draw'" (30 July 1904, 72) and the press predicted that *Warp and Woof*, in spite of its venue, would be "one of the social as well as one of the dramatic events of the Season" (*Sketch*, 4 May 1904, 83). Sufficiently rallied, Society did descend upon the theatre, its insistence upon its own presence causing the *Times* reviewer to complain that "it was characteristic of the occasion that we found it more difficult... to procure a programme than a list of the distinguished persons present" (7 June 1904, 10). Indeed, the play's first-nighters helped to produce a spectacle of their own, creating a celebrity crush at the Cobden Memorial outside the theatre in Camden High Street. To the *Pall Mall Gazette*

it seemed that a Cobden centenary celebration was afoot. Round about his statue was a crowd that must, one way and another, have numbered between 4,000 and 5,000. But nobody regarded the statue: what the crowd had come forth to see were the distinguished persons who flocked to witness the production of a play by the wife of the Colonial Secretary. The crowd was not always sure of its man. Some celebrities passed unremarked. A gentleman who is not a public character, who has never even been elevated to picture post-card rank, was cheered as if he were a saviour of the Empire, whereat he was greatly puzzled. He could not think of any notable for whom he could possibly be mistaken, and his friends could not help him. It was a great day for Camden Town. (7 June 1904, 3)[1]

Smug in its exclusivity, Society used the opportunity for self-worship and class condescension. Moving among the *hoi polloi*, whose ignorance of membership betrayed its position as outsider while its presence as onlooker bestowed status, a privileged elite affirmed its position at the same time that its boundaries were secured – literally, in this case, as law and order in the form of mounted police were "called to keep the curious crowd from the door." Such a gathering of supernumeraries had occurred, Mrs. Pat surmised, as a result of a desire "to see all the 'fine ladies and gentlemen'," for, she explained, "it had leaked out that the play was by the wife of a distinguished Member of Parliament, and that all the smart world would be present" (Campbell, p. 248). The *Evening Standard*, receiving the theatre's press release, noted both Lyttelton's object of "draw[ing] attention to the over-working of shop-girls in large dressmaking establishments" and Mrs. Pat's request "to mention that all seats for [opening night] ... have been sold to Society people" (6 June 1904, 4).

Just who was performing for whom was a vexed matter through the period as actors, themselves seeking social inclusion, reproduced on stage a society world eager for emulation. Mrs. Pat, who "could act her best on the news that a lord or lady was out front" (Peters, p. 248), served as audience for such admirers, even while she performed for them. Society, in turn, enjoyed rubbing shoulders with its surrogates, seeing them as fellow players whose professional activities were echoed in their own private theatricals, pageants, and *tableaux vivants*. The first meeting of Mrs. Pat and Edith Lyttelton (then Balfour) in the grounds of Wilton House in 1890 was informed by just such intermingling. The socialite, at the urging of her hostess, Lady Pembroke, had "disguised" herself, with thick rouge and a red cloak, as a member of Ben Greet's Shakespeare company. Mrs. Pat, an actress with the troupe, had arrived with Greet's players to perform in touring productions of *As You Like It* and *A Midsummer Night's Dream*. The friendship that developed between the two women had

practical advantages for both. For the society-struck Mrs. Pat it
meant a ready entrance to smart circles – Lyttelton was a member of
the exclusive "Souls"[2] – that would culminate in Lyttelton's presentation of Mrs. Pat's only daughter at Court. For Lyttelton it
assured a professional venue for her stage writing, and the services of
one of the era's most glamorous celebrities, to both produce and
appear in her plays. In 1906 Mrs. Pat staged and acted in *The
Macleans of Bairness* (Criterion), Lyttelton's history of Bonnie Prince
Charlie, and three years later produced her "miracle play" *St.
Ursula's Pilgrimage*, a rehandling of the legend of St. Ursula and the
11,000 virgins. The latter, presented at the Royal Court, was notable
for including in its cast a number of society beauties, including the
golden-haired Cynthia Charteris Asquith as St. Ursula and Lady
Diana Manners in the emblematic, if uncharacteristic, role of "a
thousand virgins." Their presence on stage was greeted by "young
men [who] roared applause ... and sent them bouquets and baskets"
(Peters, p. 299). Mrs. Pat, in her memoirs, no doubt reflecting upon
her experiences with both Pinero and Shaw, talked of the unique
rewards of staging a friend's work, especially when "the authoress
was a woman of much more than ordinary intelligence" (Campbell,
pp. 202–203).

Warp and Woof, the first and most considerable of Mrs. Pat's
Lyttelton productions, took the form of a three-act dramatic "tract"
or "sermon," designed to demonstrate to society audiences the sweat
and blood that went into the manufacture of fancy dress gowns. The
argument was not in itself original. In broad form it can be traced
back to the publication in 1843 of Thomas Hood's "Song of the
Shirt" (*Punch*, December, 260). A humanitarian poem that had its
own origins in the journalistic exposés that followed R. D. Grainger's
parliamentary report for the Children's Employment Commission
(1843), Hood's ballad popularized the plight of the sweated
seamstress. Its impact was startling. Turning its light upon the
habitually unseen, it provided what social historian Christina
Walkley has termed "a common ground of awareness" (p. 133), a
ready-made stock of images that could be appropriated with equal
facility by artists, writers, philanthropists, and social reformers. A
sentimentalized portrait of domesticated womanhood, the poem's
lone seamstress plies her needle "in poverty, hunger and dirt,"
the wages of such work "A bed of straw, / A crust of bread –
and rags." Its appeal was directed to "men, with sisters dear! / O

men, with mothers and wives!" to act the manly part, to perform the chivalrous rescue of deserving women whose destitution was marked by "unwomanly rags." It was, all in all, a powerful image that would loom large as an emblem of social exploitation. Its literary analogues were prodigious, from the Blue Book reports of government commissions to the fiction of writers like Gaskell, Dickens, and Kingsley, from the investigative journalism of Henry Mayhew to Charles Booth's empirical studies of poverty, from Gertrude Tuckwell's and Clementina Black's detailed examinations of women's labor[3] to illustrations of female exploitation in the work of Karl Marx and Friedrich Engels. Such writings were complemented, as art historian T. J. Edelstein has shown, by a proliferation of visual realizations, "shirtmakers, milliners, dressmakers – often accompanied by lines from 'The Song of the Shirt' – stitch[ing] away in pictures on the walls of the Royal Academy, British Institute, and Society of Artists" (184–185). Richard Redgrave's painting of *The Sempstress* was one of the first and most influential (plate 12).[4] Shown first at the 1844 summer exhibition of the Royal Academy, its image of a solitary needlewoman gazing heavenward illustrated Hood's "Song" at the same time that its meaning was illuminated and extended by appending to it lines from the poem's final appeal to manly valor. Something of an "ur-image," Redgrave's painting generated a precise visual vocabulary – the outward gaze of the lone figure, the lateness of the hour, the single candle, the dying plant, the cup of tea and bit of bread, the garret room – that informed most subsequent handlings of the motif. It was not, however, the intention of Redgrave or his followers to put on canvas the squalor and misery of Hood's seamstress. In their renderings, "unwomanly rags" are translated into neat gowns, their wearers into images of attractive if vulnerable womanhood.

Alongside such portraits of anonymous shirtmakers there developed an alternative iconography focusing upon either workroom tableaux or the contrast between the dressed lady and her makers. In both types we witness a shift from romantic appeals to the chivalric male to a condemnation of production and consumption as practiced by women. For when the ballgown replaces the shirt as the object under construction, women join the portrait as victimizers as well as victims. In an engraving typical of the genre, "Madame Dobière's workroom," used to illustrate Camilla Toulmin's 1845 short story "The Orphan Milliners" (279), womanly women ply their craft in

12. Richard Redgrave, *The Sempstress* (1846). Reproduced by courtesy of the Forbes Magazine Collection, New York.

diverse attitudes of prettified suffering amidst such immediately recognizable signs as burning candles, a dark skylight, and a clock marking the late hour. New to the image, however, is the figure of the overseer, a "hard, passionless, yet scolding woman," who does not minister to her languishing sisters but, as the caption borrowed from Hood's poem insists, drives them to "work – work – work."[5] Not attempting an economic or social analysis, the formula presents "unnatural" women as the enemy, their perversion of "caring" femininity the immediate cause of dressmakers' suffering. The other contributing cause of the seamstress's hard lot was seen to be the consuming vanity of well-bred ladies. *Punch*, for example, was not averse to using the laboring dressmaker's demonstrable want as a stick with which to beat her indolent sisters. Placed in visual proximity, conventionally sentimentalized images of the exploited seamstress served to condemn juxtaposed portraits of her customers. The archetypal image here is "The Haunted Lady, or 'The Ghost' in the Looking-Glass" (*Punch*, 4 July 1863, 5), in which a woman dressed in the height of fashion gazes into a mirror to see not her own reflection but that of her half-starved and fainting dressmaker (plate 13). The real culprit in the cartoon, however, is not the lady herself but a third figure, the gown's presenter "Madame la Modiste," a task-driving employer whose angular jaw and jutting nose are imagistic shorthand for the mannish spinster. The lady, to the end, remains a lady; her fault, unlike "Madame's," lies not in her look (which is after all fashionably feminine) but in how she obtained that look. Hence the caption, in which "Madame la Modiste" addresses her anonymous client: "We would not have disappointed your ladyship, at any sacrifice, and the robe is finished *à merveille*." Well-dressed women are not being asked to moderate their dress, here a reassuring sign of class and gender, so much as their method of consumption in circumstances in which their leisure is placed in a complex relationship with other women's toil. So in Redgrave's *Fashion's Slaves* (1847), a later companion-piece to *The Sempstress*, we see a languid young woman, sentimental novel in hand, reclining on an ottoman as she rebukes a dressmaker's assistant for being late with an order. The latter's "refined face and meek bearing," Walkley observes, "tell us that she has seen better days" (p. 17). Certainly hers is a classic Victorian countenance of lovely passivity, her meekness a telling rebuke to the other's arrogance which sits uneasily upon her womanly form. The message is clear – to be unreasonable

THE HAUNTED LADY, OR "THE GHOST" IN THE LOOKING-GLASS.

Madame La Modiste. "WE WOULD NOT HAVE DISAPPOINTED YOUR LADYSHIP, AT ANY SACRIFICE, AND THE ROBE IS FINISHED *A MERVEILLE*."

13. "The Haunted Lady, or 'The Ghost' in the Looking-Glass" (*Punch*, 4 July 1863).

in one's demands for a gown shows an assertiveness that threatens the womanliness the gown itself is meant to evoke. Passivity is celebrated in such image-making, the seamstress's sweet refinement designed to be read as a lesson by ladies threatening to stray from that model.

That women's unseemly aggression in consumption was taken as a real cause of the unhappy condition of needlewomen is apparent in the charters of organizations such as the Association for the Aid and Benefit of Dressmakers and Milliners. Established in March 1843 "chiefly through the exertions of a committee of ladies," it set out to ameliorate the appalling conditions exposed in Grainger's report of that year. Listed third among its five stated objects, which included reducing the work day to twelve hours, improving ventilation in the workshop, furnishing financial assistance to deserving recipients in temporary distress, and providing medical assistance where required, was the desire "to aid in obviating the evils connected with the present system, by inducing ladies to allow sufficient time for the execution of orders" (Thompson, *Unknown Mayhew*, p. 435). And it was certainly the case that the finger of blame was often pointed at women's failure to order in advance. Mayhew, writing for the *Morning Chronicle*, provides a striking instance in his account of the workings of an unnamed "first-rate milliners' establishment at the West-End":

The first hand comes in with the dress, and throws it down on the first table she comes to. The young ladies look up to see what is the matter. At last one ventures to ask, "Who is it for?" "Oh," the first hand answers, "it's for Lady or Mrs. So-and-so, and she wants it tomorrow morning." "Tomorrow morning," cry half-a-dozen voices, "how is it possible, when we have so many other dresses to do? Why, she has kept us up three nights this week already." "Well, it's of no use," replies the first hand, "she must have it; so we must all sit up tonight again." (Thompson, *Unknown Mayhew*, p. 431)

As late as 1910, when mourning wear for King Edward's funeral produced a glut of orders and subsequent overwork at dressmakers' establishments, the newspapers were still sounding the same refrain:

One wishes some punishment, or at least some incentive to considerateness, could reach the wearers of the dresses. National mourning, of course, furnishes an excuse for haste more valid than most, but it remains the fact that hardly any kind of consumer purchases with less regard to the workers' convenience than the purchaser of Court dresses. (Arncliffe-Sennett, vol. x, p. 44)

But if women's inconsiderate purchasing of gowns, prompted by the demands of the Season, was deemed culpable, the consumption of images of suffering and exploitation was not. In fact, paintings of both the solitary seamstress and her oppressors, intended for a middle- and upper-class clientele, were displayed at Royal Academy openings that were themselves part of the social calendar. Works detailing exploitative conditions served a didactic function, reading a lesson on appropriate womanliness (as that was manifested by poor seamstresses) to moneyed wives and daughters. Emulate her manner – if not her circumstances – such works insisted. In broad popular appeal, however, the sole needlewoman triumphed. Capitalizing upon sentiment as the chief carrier of meaning, renderings of her alone evoked a pleasurable sense of sympathy and pity as much for the sensation of the emotion itself as for the seamstress (Edelstein, 189). The effect of their sentimentality, and implicit faith in manly rescue, soothed any concern such paintings might have stirred, viewer inertia flowing from the salvation promised within their conventional narratives. So much for Hood's lament in the "Song of the Shirt"'s final stanza, "Would that its tone could reach the rich!"

Yet "reaching the rich" was precisely what Lyttelton had in mind. In *Warp and Woof* she began by exploiting the fact that well before 1904 the theatre had moved up-market, and as an occasion for spectacular display and cultural merchandising had joined regattas, races, and Royal Academy openings in the round of semi-public events that made up the London Season. In this respect the play parted company with earlier efforts to bring to the stage the plight of the sweated seamstress. Taking Redgrave's 1844 painting as a model, mid-century melodramas, such as Mark Lemon's *The Sempstress* (City of London 1844) and Tom Taylor's *The Bottle* (Haymarket 1847), had spun pathetic narratives about the lives of hypothetical piece-workers. Yet in elaborating their circumstances, and adding a host of subsidiary figures designed to raise tears in the pit and gallery, such works diluted the integrity of their copy. Indeed, the occasional tableau, "realizing" on stage the particulars of Redgrave's painting, only invited critics to observe the manner in which popular playwrights fell short of their goal. "The embodied representation of Mr. Redgrave's picture," observed the *Athenaeum* in its review of *The Sempstress*, "would have been more impressive without speech-

making: nor does the presence of an imbecile old father and a
desperate husband add to the wretchedness." Such distractions, it
was concluded, rendered the misery of Lemon's needlewoman
"accidental and isolated" rather than "the result of a system, or state
of things, and shared by hundreds of thousands" (8 June 1844,
533–534). Lyttelton, too, was less concerned with "accidental"
suffering than with exposing trade abuse. Building upon the Blue
Book dramas and problem plays of the 1890s, including Shaw's *Plays
Unpleasant*, she accordingly turned her gaze from the iconography of
Redgrave's *Sempstress* to that of multi-peopled representations like
"Madame Dobière's workroom," "The Haunted Lady," and
Fashion's Slaves. On stage, before society spectators, the juxtaposition
of wretchedness with vanity or unwomanly "push" took on new
resonances, detailing not only the particulars of an oppressive
business, but the nature of a trade that prided itself on its "making"
of women. The raw ambition of *Punch*'s "Madame La Modiste" as
well as the indolence of Redgrave's consumer both served Lyttelton's
purpose, but took their place as parts of a larger design that focused
not upon good or bad individuals, but upon what *The Times*
identified as the "economics and ethics" of a culture determined to
explain women sartorially (7 June 1904, 10). Indeed, such resolves
were so firmly held that a number of critics commented upon the
play's "distinctly feminine theme" (*Pall Mall Gazette*, 7 June 1904,
3), one that having "to do with dress" was particularly suited to
treatment by a woman (*Lady's Pictorial*, 9 July 1904, 48).

Linked by the figure of Theodosia Hemming, a fitter at Madame
Stefanie's dressmaking emporium, the plot of *Warp and Woof* follows
the process of gown construction from fitting to delivery, Lyttelton's
set shifting, in turn, from a West End showroom, to a workshop,
to the society parlor in which Madame Stefanie's products are finally
worn. Objecting to such dispersal of action, the *Pall Mall Gazette*
blamed the play's "diffusiveness" upon Lyttelton's gender: "As is
the wont of lady-playwrights, she fritters away her time in entertaining strangers, when she should be diligently developing her
theme." "A dramatist," the paper insisted, "would have had no
other act" but the second, which passes in the workroom; the first
and third are "superfluous and tiresome. We do not want to see the
dresses ordered ... We do not want to see them delivered and worn"
(7 June 1904, 3). What was wanted, in other words, was a
confirmation of the play's visual sources. By confining action to its

Act II workroom, Lyttelton's drama would take its place as one more
tale of pathetic workers abused by a driving proprietress and grasping
clients. Society, safely out of sight, might continue to elude scrutiny.
Yet, in *Warp and Woof*, Society is made to meet its makers. Lyttelton's
seamstress, in a final act, actually moves into the drawing room to
denounce in a passionate speech the society figures she has made to
her cost. In such a context, the finery she has fashioned stands newly
constituted as an emblem of female oppression. Here is "the ghost in
the looking-glass" with a vengeance, for in Lyttelton's drama that
passive icon of female suffering sheds her timidity and, in the
imposing figure of Mrs. Patrick Campbell, steps through the
"mirror" to demand a reckoning. It is an effect made possible by the
fact that society playgoers were as much a part of, as apart from, the
action taking place in the "drawing room" that extended from stage
to stalls. Critics who were not themselves in Society were invited to
read the play's lesson in the responses of both "on-" and "off-stage"
consumers. The socialist *Clarion*, noting that "the audience consisted
in a large measure of those very Society dames," concluded that
"there can be little doubt... that many of the titled and well-known
people present left the building with eyes opened to the sufferings and
temptations of their sisters" (10 June 1904, 3).

The play's first confrontation between society-consumer and
dressmaker-producer occurs in Act I, at Madame Stefanie's West
End showroom, an environment whose exclusivity is evoked by thick
carpets, large mirrors, and "plate glass" windows. It serves as an
acceptable meeting-place for representatives of labor and capital
normally separated by the physical distance between Mayfair and
Camberwell, where, we are told, Theodosia lives with her consumptive sister. During the Season increased demand resulted in
closer proximity as seamstresses worked through the night, a
circumstance used to theatrical effect by Lyttelton, who appropriates
the "showroom" set to display, at curtain rise, the sleeping bodies of
exhausted dressmakers. It is not "blooming fancy gowns" we see but
the women who have "been at them all night," sewing until "about
five ... [when] all gluey with sleep ... we was told to lie down where
we could" (pp. 7–8).[6] The tableau is meant to shape our response to
the collection of ladies who subsequently come to the showroom to
buy. Among these is Lady Jenny Barkstone, a *"fashionable smart
woman, not quite young, but struggling to be so,"* whose arrival is heralded
by a telegram announcing her need for a fancy dress costume that

same evening. Having already been turned away by her own dressmaker and Worth's London branch, she triumphs here by means of male intercession. For Percy Wilson, a self-proclaimed "maker of women," interferes on her behalf. It is he who places the late order and then appeals to Madame Stefanie's ambition and greed to see it through:

My dear soul, you must – it's a chance for you. Lady Jenny is one of the smartest and best dressed women in London. If you do this for her she'll rave about you, and it'll mean hundreds of orders – come, you know you can. (p. 24)

The upwardly climbing Madame Stefanie, her Cockney accent concealed beneath a "frenchified" veneer, capitulates. The point is worth stressing, because in the inherited tradition of the shirt-making seamstress the man is conspicuous by his absence. Indeed, in the prospect of his return resides the promise of chivalric rescue. In group portraits of dress construction we are, likewise, made privy to the mysteries of a "woman's world" of which men, it is suggested, have little knowledge and play no part. It is a notion Lyttelton is at pains to correct, taking as her cue events like the press exposure of a Mr. (as well as a Mrs.) Isaacson behind the exploitative court dressmaker "Madame Elsie."[7] In the hierarchy of the play's dressmaking trade, Madame Stefanie, "an aggressive personality" ready to sweat and bully her workers, is overtopped by Percy Wilson, a "hanger-on of fashionable women" who, in spite of Madame's objections, declares himself free of her establishment.[8] A journalist of sorts, Wilson explains his deitic place in the dressmaking firmament: "I'm not a dressmaker – but all the same I can make a dress – ha! ha! – by what I write" (p. 70). It was, in fact, his direct intervention that secured Theodosia her current place. Throughout the piece she is referred to as his "protégée" by which he means "property." As the play unfolds, however, Wilson's gaze is itself brought under examination, his pleasure in Theodosia's subservience and suffering revealed to be aggressively prurient: "I'm not going to let you lose your youth and your lovely figure from overwork, though I must say I've never seen you look so pretty" (p. 43). "How clever you are with your needle. I love to see you kneeling like that" (p. 73).

Mrs. Pat's agreement to herself play Theodosia was here turned to good account (plate 14). Preceding *Pygmalion* by some ten years, *Warp and Woof*, in spite of Shaw's claims to the contrary, offered the

14. Mrs. Patrick Campbell as Theodosia Hemming in *Warp and Woof*.

actress what was in effect her first "low life" part. Yet the manner in which Lyttelton put her colleague on stage – and into unlikely garments – could not have been more different. Like Shaw, Lyttelton, abetted by Mrs. Pat, played against viewers' expectations. In 1904 the actress was still, in the eyes of her admirers, the modishly dressed temptress of Jones, Haddon Chambers, and, above all, Pinero, whose plays were revived regularly through the decade that separated *Warp and Woof* from *The Second Mrs. Tanqueray*. Mrs. Pat in a play of modern life, especially one that announced as its provenance the procurement of society gowns, meant for most a vision in tulle, furs, and feathers, gliding gracefully through a succession of West

End parlors. Yet by casting Mrs. Pat as seamstress rather than consumer, Lyttelton created an effect not unlike that in Wilde's *A Woman of No Importance*, in which a striking figure in anonymous black stood out handsomely against the finery of the conventionally well-dressed – indeed, we might recall that in Wilde's earliest drafts Mrs. Arbuthnot had herself been a seamstress. In *Warp and Woof*, however, the emphasis falls not upon the virtues of "anti-fashion," but upon an impressively austere Mrs. Pat, who articulates what the *Lady's Pictorial* called "a woman's sympathy with her sisters" (9 July 1904, 48). A contemporary drawing by A. L. Becker suggests how effectively Lyttelton went about her business. Engraved as a three-quarter-page plate to mark the play's successful transfer to the Vaudeville in late June, it depicts a towering Mrs. Pat, clad entirely in dressmaker's black, hand on heart in a grandly tragic stance. Her tape measure, draped about her shoulders, is worn with the authority of holy vestments.[9] A kind of allegorized Every-seamstress, as her name insists, Theodosia Hemming has come to read a devastating *j'accuse* to her buyers in the boxes and stalls. That such clients were among Mrs. Pat's most devoted followers only underscored the point. Anticipating a smartly dressed heroine, in gowns they themselves had come to copy, they were instead confronted by the grim image of her (and their) makers. What remained of the morbid vampirism Pinero had evoked in the nineties was transferred, as we shall see, to the gowns themselves, as Lyttelton insisted upon the manner in which such garments effectively "bled" their workers.

The myth of chivalric rescue, to which Hood's "Song of the Shirt" and Redgrave's *Sempstress* had appealed, is likewise subverted. Wilson's offer to back Theodosia in a dress-shop of her own as long as "I can get you along with it" (p. 121) reveals beneath such fables the crass reality of sexual blackmail. In Theodosia's temptation and final refusal, Lyttelton gives theatrical shape to the connection between economic deprivation and prostitution, one spelled out in depressing repetitiveness in Mayhew's *Morning Chronicle* letters on needlewomen. Chronic underpayment, particularly in circumstances in which dependants figured, compelled sexual activity that paid better. In Lyttelton's view, one shared by sister playwrights like Inez Bensusan and Gertrude Vaughan,[10] blame fell squarely on the shoulders of men who used their institutionalized power over money to beggar women as a means of ensuring their sexual availability. Within this context, Christabel Pankhurst's 1913 slogan, "Votes for Women and

Chastity for Men," was both cumulative and inevitable. Such portraits deny out of hand the possibility that men will freely choose to exercise their influence to ensure adequate pay and working conditions for women. So, in *Warp and Woof*, when Lord Lickwood, *"eldest son of a Duke, tall, strong, stupid,"* musters a diffident query to make conversation: "Do they have proper seats for the girls, I wonder? I read something about it in the papers the other day – makes them ill standing, or something – some fuss or other," Wilson shrugs it off as "such a lot of sentimental nonsense talked" (p. 40). If, however, as the drama critic for the *Lady* noted, "Mrs. Lyttelton is not gracious in her treatment of masculine characters" (23 June 1904, 1058), Madame Stefanie and her society customers fare no better. Advocating gender rather than class loyalties, the playwright urges a form of consumer radicalism that has little patience with women who connive in the oppression of their sisters. Lady Jenny is condemned as much for her indifference to Wilson's sexual interest in Theodosia as for her collusion with him in the procurement of a sweated gown. Such conscious collaboration is yoked with the willed ignorance of Poppy Price, a *"vivacious young pushing wife of a rich stockbroker,"* who feels she has done her part to lighten the dressmaker's load when she bestows upon Madame Stefanie's seamstresses flowers from her country home.[11] A ruse to avoid paying her bill, it is evidence of the parsimony of wealthy clients, regularly cited as contributing to seamstresses' deprivation. Certain proprietors claimed to "have four and five thousand pounds of debts in their books, for which two and three years' credit has been given to persons apparently able to pay, and who have yet been unable to raise one or two hundred pounds to meet a bill that was coming due... [As a result] they often have not ready money enough to pay their quarter's rent or even the day-workers at week's end" (Walkley, p. 25). Madame Stefanie's response is direct and to the point: "Damn the flowers. Why don't she pay her bills?" (p. 53). Poppy Price becomes both an easy butt for Lyttelton's humor, and an object-lesson to ladies to know themselves, although her position as a parvenu may have blurred the message. Insisting loudly upon her own kindness and generosity ("I love flowers so much myself I like you all to have a share – some people are so selfish") she agrees to accept delivery late into the evening as "that will give you more time, and you can go on working at the gown till ten o'clock. There! Not many ladies would do that – would they? But I hate to be inconsiderate" (p. 51).

In the play's second act, by means of a workroom recreated in the theatre, complete with sewing machines from Jones[12] and an authentic corps of "thirty to forty work-girls," Lyttelton brings home to her audiences the actual conditions of dress manufacture. In so doing she joined a widening circle convinced that social reform could be facilitated by confronting the public with "real" evidence of social ills "so that an effect may be produced which will not be transitory and will lead to the serious consideration of remedies which shall be permanent, and which shall embrace not only individuals, but the whole" (Black, *Sweated Industry*, p. 10). Such was the impetus behind the *Daily News* Anti-Sweating Exhibition of 1906, which was deliberately held in London's fashionable West End, and displayed, in twenty-three separate stalls, workers engaged in manual production. The Exhibition was, however, faulted for equivocating, the affluence of the Queen's Hall, with its plush carpets and neat stalls, transforming proletariat drudgery into a middle-class spectator sport (*Clarion*, "Cannibal Exhibition," 18 May 1906, 5). The editor of the *Daily News* expressed his regret that for many the display proved but "a painful interlude between a visit to the shops in the morning and a visit to the theatre in the evening" (Beckett, p. 72). Such limitations, however, might be overcome in the theatre proper, where the visual lessons of anti-sweating tableaux could be coupled with a dramatic narrative whose argument was unmistakable. In *Warp and Woof* viewers were accordingly made to hear as well as see images of industrial oppression. Silent suffering, the result of economic bullying rather than inherent womanliness, is given voice in the play's Act III drawing room in which on- and off-stage consumers are made to bear witness to the women they contrive not to see: "We're always upstairs in the workrooms. There we are always stitching – cold often, when you're warm round your fires – hot, stifling hot, when you're in your cool rooms – stitching when you're all fast asleep" (p. 113). When, in the same scene, Theodosia builds a gown literally on the body of its wearer, she translates its meaning into flesh and blood, inviting us to read society dress as itself cannibalistic:

Everyday for three weeks we've been at work from seven in the morning till eleven, twelve, and sometimes one at night. We never went to bed at all last night or the night before ... drive, drive, drive, with only a few minutes to cram the food down our throats. Perhaps you don't know it's against the law to work more than twelve hours – but it is – and so it ought to be. We could do the work if you gave us time. But here's her ladyship angry because we're behind with the gown. When did she order it? Only this morning... Oh, don't any of you fancy your gowns are made of silk and satin only – our life and strength goes into them too. (p. 114)

Similar imagery was evoked in the fashion pages of the *Queen* just weeks before the play's opening. Society columnist Mrs. Evan Nepean, documenting a gown that was "a perfect maze of manipulation," wondered if readers ever "think of all the eyesight that has been been sewn into it. One does not like to think of that, does one?" (7 May 1904, 775). Lyttelton theatricalizes such circumstances to insure that "one" does.

The open mockery of legislative remedies helped to remove a final buffer between Lyttelton's stage and stalls. In Madame Stefanie's Act II sweatshop, gowns are constructed beneath a posted notice of the Factory Act. Since 1901, hours of employment had officially been limited to a maximum of twelve a day and eight on Saturday, with a minimum of one and a half hours allotted each day (except Saturday) for meals. Overtime was confined to a maximum of two hours a day over a total of three days in a given week to a maximum of thirty days in a calendar year. Yet in spite of Theodosia's complaints, Madame Stefanie allows only "ten minutes for dinner to-day – there's fifty minutes saved. Tea served in the workroom, there's thirty minutes more, and the work must go on to-night – till every gown is sent off" (p. 54). She could do so with impunity because the law did little to protect workers who reported infractions to factory inspectors. As one of Lyttelton's male characters pointedly asks "Did the last visit of the inspectors do any good? Or the one before? The girls whom the inspector speaks to are dismissed, you know that. Take my advice and keep clear of it all" (p. 57). Yet in choosing herself not to "keep clear," in appealing to the lawmakers as well as the consumers in her audience, Lyttelton created a powerful piece of stage propaganda. Not only was income from a benefit performance in aid of the Industrial Law Indemnity Fund used to relieve the immediate misery of "women and girls wrongfully dismissed from their employment" (*Clarion*, 15 July 1904, 3),[13] but the play became an important tool of the Women's Trade Union League, which used it in its efforts to organize dressmakers and millinery workers. Laborite Mary Macarthur, for one, was quick to see its value as "a peg to hang propaganda articles on and a means of enlisting interest for the struggling Dressmakers' Union" (Mary Hamilton, p. 48). Her organization's preliminary meeting, held less than two weeks after the play's opening night, cited Lyttelton's *mise-en-scène* in justifying its program to improve working conditions, regulate employer-employee relations, provide free legal aid, and assure that existing legislation was scrupulously enforced (*Clarion*, 17 June 1904, 2).[14]

Yet the play's significance was not limited to monitoring, or even remedying, worker abuse. Its novelty rests equally with its sartorial re-valuation of women's fancy dress, which, as a result of occasion-specific use, licensed display that carried an aggressive, extra-erotic charge. Or as Adern Holt, fashion columnist for the *Queen*, put it, "there are few occasions when a woman has a better opportunity of showing her charms to advantage than at a Fancy Ball" (*Fancy Dresses Described*, p. xiii), a claim echoed in *Warp and Woof* by a customer's request to have "her fancy dress cut low and left rather short. 'I wish to show my ankles – one so seldom has the opportunity'" (*Era*, 2 July 1904, 12). In the course of Lyttelton's play, we witness the translation through dress of three representative society women, the manufacture and fitting of their ballgowns transforming them respectively into a "Water Nymph," a "Medusa," and a "Spanish Dancer," figures associated in the male-fixed iconography of the period with an unleashed or predatory sexuality (Dijkstra, pp. 244, 258, 310). At society balls, such eroticism would be regulated, less potentially subversive than effectively tamed, the general types as well as the specifics of the costumes familiar matters to Lyttelton's viewers. Indeed, Lyttelton's own circle was particularly enamored with fancy-dress gatherings, characterized by lavish preparation and ostentatious expenditure for ensembles meant to be worn only once.[15] The play's costumes, built for the occasion by court dressmaker "Madame Viola" – a Mr. Otto Viola according to *Trade Directories*[16] – were variations upon common motifs. Viola's designs for the production have not survived. Yet we may reconstruct them in their essentials by turning to Adern Holt's *Fancy Dresses Described*, a series of illustrated order books published through the period by Debenham and Freebody. Holt's "Spanish Dancer," not surprisingly, wears "a satin skirt... with black lace flounces, beaded bands of velvet or gold, low bodice of the same; senorita jacket of velvet trimmed with ball fringe, made with long sleeves; high comb; lace mantilla fastened over it with red and yellow roses" (p. 242). For a "Water Nymph," a variant of the Siren or Lorelei, Holt recommends

a dress of frosted gauze or silvered tulle over green, looped up with seaweed, coral, shells, crystal, and aquatic flowers, for the salt-water nymphs; water-lilies and grasses for those who rule over lakes and rivers ... A veil of tulle to match the dress falls over the hair, which should be covered with frosting powder and be allowed to float on the shoulders. A cuirass bodice of silver gauze, the tunic silver gauze, is a good rendering of the character. The bodice, whether a cuirass or made a la Vierge, should be trimmed with a fringe of the shells, etc., a dragonfly on one side of the hair. The silver tulle that is used should as nearly as possible resemble water, an effect best produced by waved stripes. Diamonds, coral, and aquamarine with silver are the most appropriate ornaments, and silver fringe should be introduced wherever it can be placed. (p. 279)

A "Medusa" costume – the outfit ordered by Percy for the flirtatious Lady Jenny – consists, we are told, of a green dress "trimmed with lizards, scorpions, and dragons," complemented by a crown of "snaky" ornaments (p. 169). In the play's earliest draft Percy refers to "a sudden vision of shimmer and glitter – a sort of embodiment of all the snakes from Eve's downwards" (LCP, Act III, p. 3).

In *Warp and Woof*, however, such costumes are used not as provocative disguise, but correctives to challenge licensed eroticism. At the first appearance of the "Water Nymph," for instance, Lyttelton removes the nocturnal, private social setting, which rendered sexual display acceptable, exposing the figure instead to the unexpected gaze of male eyes in the unkind light of early morning. "Shy" in her get-up, which savors of "professional" calculation, the play's "well-bred" siren objects, "I'm only trying it on. It looks absurd in the daylight" (p. 37). So too in the case of the "Spanish Dancer," who makes her first appearance only half dressed: "like a Spanish dancer as far as her waist ... [but with] an ordinary evening skirt, and ... a thin chiffon wrap over the whole" (p. 97), her potential to arouse undercut by Lyttelton's exposure of the obviously constructed nature of such display. In Percy's presentation of the "Medusa," the imposition upon women of such dress becomes unmistakable:

Look here, Madame Stefanie, I'll save you all the trouble of thinking. I've got a little idea for her. (*Turning to Lady Jenny*.) I think you ought to be all glittering – a serpent – or a mermaid. Or – yes ... Medusa. You know you can look so wicked, and I do love wicked eyes. Everyone does. I can see you with wriggling snakes in your hair, all shining, and your eyes darting. (p. 34)

It is left to female dressmakers to translate the woman's figure (which she confesses isn't her "best point") into fashionable form, "correcting any little mistakes the Almighty has made" (p. 28). Urging the transformative function of clothing – Theodosia at one point notes "the way [that] a hat makes you into a different person" (p. 22) – Madame Stefanie observes that although Lady Jenny is "badly made," she can "make madame look quite different. Lengthen here – pad there – pull the waist down" (p. 34). So blatant in fact is the suggestion that women are their clothes that Madame Stefanie observes of one customer: "Oh Lord, if you could have seen her in that dress, and then she wants it made shorter and lower. There won't be enough of her left to hold the clothes on with." Nor should we lose sight of the fact that if women are made by their dress, men, as the case of the "Medusa" makes plain, may be said to "define" such dresses. Not surprisingly, under the circumstances, clothing is also seen to determine women's desirability. As Wilson observes of Theodosia, "properly dressed she'd be a beauty" (p. 27) although the reverse is apparently not the case. The "good figure" of a mannequin cannot "save" a badly designed dress. Thus we see society women reduced to clothing, and beauty situated in dress that the play has already exposed as a product of sweated female labor. Lyttelton's message is double-edged. Taking her audience on a sartorial odyssey, she pushes into view women in the making, her revelations of the process of dress manufacture prompting a revisionist look at a product which can be said to wear women as much as it is worn by them. That women should be seen in terms of their clothes is, in *Warp and Woof*, not a pretty sight. It was a point not lost upon fashion columnists who, in spite of Lyttelton's social standing, the reputation of "Madame Viola," and the fashionable audiences whose patronage contributed to the play's success, maintained a tactical silence regarding the work's society wardrobes. The closest we come to comment is the *Era*'s generalized, and in context surely perverse, insistence that "a great attraction of the performance, is the exhibition of some of the prettiest costumes imaginable. Several of them might be described as perfect symphonies in colour" (2 July 1904, 12), the reviewer's callousness in the face of Lyttelton's presentation making her case as effectively as any other. The rest, even with their practiced journalese, could not wrestle the gowns free of their context, a little knowledge effectively translating such garments into what Gertrude Tuckwell identified as "burning shirts of Nessus."[17]

What Lyttelton did for the sweated seamstress, Elizabeth Baker and Cicely Hamilton attempted to do for the more problematic figure of the shop assistant. In the 1850s, shortly after the appearance of Hood's "Song of the Shirt," Victorian feminists had begun to argue the case for female employment in shops. To that end, publications like the *English Woman's Journal* urged readers to exercise their influence by expressing a preference to be waited upon by women.[18] The cause prospered due largely to changes in marketing and distribution that led to the welcoming of "shop girls" as a cheap source of labor. From 1890 to 1914 the employment of women sales assistants, at half the salaries of their male counterparts, was attractive enough to result in a threefold increase of women who worked on shop floors or behind counters. Trusting to their work to lend them an aura of middle-class respectability, female shop assistants, themselves poorly paid, looked down upon their working-class sisters. They were, in turn, often "despised by industrial workers" as obsequious "counter-jumpers,"[19] while their upper- and middle-class customers regarded them as little more than domestic help. The paradox of their position appears in the reports of philanthropists and social reformers who found it difficult to agitate on behalf of a group whose appearance so argued against it. As social historian Wilfred Whitaker has noted:

The traditions of the shop-assistants' work meant the maintenance of an appearance of prosperity and well-being. In all but the poorest neighbour-hoods, the shop-assistant was apparently well-dressed and evinced a simulated interest in the needs and whims of the customer. It was difficult to conceive that such a person was in as much, or more, need of pity and protection as the dirty, badly clothed person whose picture you might see representative of the typical factory worker or coal miner. (p. 174)

Ironically, shop assistants' clothing precluded aid at the same time that it represented a major drain upon the budgets of workers expected "to make a very neat and prosperous appearance... dress[ing] as well as their customers on half the wages of a cook" (Holcombe, p. 113). To put their case more effectively the National

Union of Shop Assistants was formed,[20] an organization which, despite its disproportionately small size, did much to publicize the actual plight of shop workers. Legislation introduced in response to its agitation offered some relief, although many bills were passed in such compromised form as to render them virtually useless. Of more immediate importance were the reports of Margaret Bondfield, who drew upon her own experience as a shop worker to aid the Women's Industrial Council in exposing conditions of retail employment. Bondfield's specific targets included long workdays which effectively "deprived shop workers of liberty and of social intercourse with people outside their own workplace," and, above all, the notorious "living-in" system which required employees to board on shop premises, the inflated cost of such lodgings deducted directly from their salaries (*A Life's Work*, p. 62). In theory designed to protect the morals of a largely female work force, the custom, in practice, meant bad food, crowded sleeping rooms, and lists of rules, violations of which resulted in fines often disproportionate to the offense.[21] In 1898 the *Daily Chronicle* popularized Bondfield's work in a series of articles entitled "Life in the Shop." These were, in turn, followed by a profusion of reports, tracts, and fictionalized exposes,[22] including S. Gertrude Ford's 1911 ballad "The Song of the Shop Slave." Declaring its kinship with Hood's "Song of the Shirt," Ford's "lyric of living-in," published in *Common Cause*, the organ of the National Union of Women's Suffrage Societies, spoke feelingly in the first person of "my life; what other life have I? ... A life in death" (6 April 1911, 857–858).

On the popular stage such case histories were eclipsed by a succession of musical comedies that celebrated the shop assistant as part of a larger tribute to the glories of British trade. The vogue for what would become one of Edwardian England's most persistent sub-genres had begun in 1894 with J. T. Tanner's Gaiety production of H. J. W. Dam and Ivan Caryll's *The Shop Girl*. Composed, we are told, in response to the public's taste for the "local and real," the piece set the first of its two acts in "the Mantle Department of the Royal Stores," where the winsome Bessie Brent finds employment with shop proprietor Septimus Hooley (*Sketch*, 28 November 1894, 216).[23] Breaking with a tradition of fantastical garb long associated with Gaiety burlesque, lyricist Harry Dam had specified that in Act I the play's women would be seen in "contemporary dress." By this he meant, the *Sketch* elaborated, "such costume as they might wear in

the street." Yet if the verisimilitude of the play's first act, "inflict[ed]
... a strain upon the imagination of its patrons," its second was
designed to assure viewers that their "evening would not be spent in
vain" (22 April 1896, 571). Bessie Brent, it turns out, is heiress to an
estate of £4 million. Her initial appearance, independent and behind
the counter, became, accordingly, the prelude to a "rescue" action
that would, by the evening's end, put her into society dress and find
her an appropriate husband. Creating a pattern that would prove
both popular and lucrative, the play shifted mid-evening from an
opening department-store set to a sumptuous site of carnival activity,
here a Fairy Bazaar in South Kensington. Changing her dress to
participate in an impromptu performance of "a Modern Society
Drama" – *Rebellious Susan* is mentioned as a possibility – Bessie is
sought by suitors both wealthy and titled, and is, at the final curtain,
presented with "the finest obtainable house in Mayfair" (pp. 42, 49).
The transformation of shop girl to society object was repeated in a
series of musicals that retraced much the same ground. In 1906
Leedham Bantock's *The Girl Behind the Counter* (Wyndham's) introduced the well-to-do Winnie Willoughby, who masquerades as a
shop assistant at the Maison Duval in order to escape a disagreeable
match. By Act II, Winnie is engaged to the man of her choice, the
action having been moved to an Ice Carnival at the Barons Court
Exhibition, and Winnie herself into a gown "in the Greek style, with
floating sleeves and a jewelled girdle of pearls and diamonds" (*Play
Pictorial*, 47:8, 52). In *Our Miss Gibbs*, written by a syndicate called
"Cryptos" and staged by George Edwardes at the Gaiety in 1909,
Mary Gibbs, a shop assistant at Garrods [*sic*] Department Stores,
finds herself whisked off to a life of fashionable ease after being
"garbed *en Pierrot*" for a harlequin "Moondance" at the Court of
Honour at London's Franco-British Exhibition. In each case
reviewers found themselves echoing the critic for the *Theatre*, who,
commenting upon Tanner's 1894 prototype, noted of both the genre
itself and its shop-girl heroines "that occasionally one is tempted to
forget 'she' is anything more than a lay-figure, intended for the exhibition of magnificent costumes" adding that "in this respect...'she'
merely fulfils the law of her being" (Mander and Mitchenson, p. 17).

Elizabeth Baker's *Miss Tassey*, a one-act tragedy produced by the
Play Actors at the Royal Court in March 1910, responds to both the
desperation of Ford's "Song of the Shop Slave" and the cynical
escapism of the shop-girl musical. An active member of the Women

Writers' Suffrage League, Baker had won high praise the previous year with *Chains*, a full-length drama that drew upon her own experience as an office typist to examine the privations of petty clerkdom. The piece would eventually earn her "a position of honour among what was, before the War, the 'young' Naturalistic Group" (Clark, p. 306). The need for a similarly sympathetic handling of shop employees was underscored three seasons earlier during the run of Henry Arthur Jones's bootmaker drama, *The Heroic Stubbs* (Terry's 1906). Objecting to sentiments voiced by one of that play's sales assistants – "What's the use of being virtuous in a shop?" – women workers responded so violently that the management was obliged to host a "Shop-Girl Matinee" at which "lady representatives of the assistants" were asked to intercede with their rank and file (*Sketch*, 14 February 1906, 144; 28 February 1906, 219). In *Miss Tassey* Baker rendered her own verdict, aligning herself with the anonymous contributor to *Common Cause*, who had insisted that "only women can understand how their fellow-women suffer, and can bring plainly before the country the hardships of a shop girl's lot" (19 May 1910, 89). Set in a dormitory at Messrs. Trimmers drapery establishment, the play takes as its subject both the immediate ills of "living in" and the larger issues raised by dress – especially fancy dress – as a means of defining and controlling women. Its central action is the ritual gowning of shop assistant Rose Clifton, "*a pretty girl with a quantity of fair, fluffy hair, and a habit of giggling*" (p. 10). Anticipating an evening out with a young swell, Rose slips out of her "*black shop dress*," reducing herself to a "*petticoat and bodice*." The remainder of the play consists of her reconstruction as a fancy-dress pierrette. One by one, she is put into a pair of "*scarlet slippers*" (p. 12), "*scarlet gloves and white hat with scarlet pompoms*" (pp. 16–17), and "*a scarlet and white pierrette's frock, very short and fluffy*" (p. 16). The outfit is completed when, we are told, she "*shak[es] out a pair of scarlet and white stripe stockings with scarlet bows at top*" (p. 17). Throughout, the image of her "young man" gazes down from a photograph over her bed. Miss Postlewaite, a more experienced colleague, jests about the propriety of "dressing up in front of a young man," punctuating the scene with sly comments about Rose's *décolletage* and petticoats. When Rose is laced so tightly that she begins to pant, Miss Postlewaite notes the like manner in which she will be squeezed by her lover. The scarlet bows at the top of her stockings elicit similar remarks about how much she intends to show. It is, all in all, a clever reworking of the shop-girl's progress as presented in musical comedy, the transition from utilitarian black to dazzling fancy dress, posted with enough markers to remind viewers of the new markets in which Rose is preparing to trade.

Baker, however, is not content merely to suggest links between erotic effect and commercial calculation. Summoning up the gritty particulars of shop-girl literature as bodied forth in *Common Cause* and Bondfield's labor tracts, she places Rose's fancy-dress metamorphosis in the bleak world of "living in." The play's single set, identified only as "Bedroom Number 52," is a grim cubicle containing "*three beds only, of the ordinary hospital cot pattern,*" "*three wash-stands in a row,*" "*a gas bracket with a frosted globe,*" and, on the floor, a "*brown oilcloth*" (p. 9). A ubiquitous "*card of rules hangs on the wall,*" reminding Rose both of the "permit" she lacks, and the perils of "sleeping out" without one. The critic for the *Stage* noted how, from the outset, viewers were made brutally aware of "the living-in system at a drapery establishment with all its malignant conditions and abuses still permitted by a Christian community" (29 May 1913, 23). Here, in an environment so oppressive that marriage, to virtually anyone, was viewed as a route of escape, Rose's "harlequinade" takes on a desperate quality.[24] The savvy Miss Postlewaite, who urges Rose to "trade" while she still has the goods, helps to argue the case. Afraid that her own shelf life is drawing to a close, she speaks with "*affected jocularity,*" turning suddenly "*sharp*" when Rose "*thoughtlessly*" asks her age. The point is driven home in Baker's presentation, upstage behind a discreet bed screen, of the suicide of a middle-aged co-worker. This is the Miss Tassey of the play's title, a 45-year-old spinster who has apparently "missed her chance" at matrimony. Having lost her job as a result of her age and infirmity, the latter a direct consequence of her conditions of employment, and facing a future without friends, family, or sufficient income, she finds in a drug overdose a second means of escape. That the *Times* critic, on the occasion of the work's 1913 revival, could persist in calling Miss Tassey the play's "other girl" (23 May 1913, 10) acknowledges the parallel, while it perpetuates the values under attack. Indeed, the very yoking of "shop" and "girl" with its implicit connivance in a system that cashiers workers too old to sell themselves behind a counter, is Baker's ultimate target. By juxtaposing the two incidents, *Miss Tassey* also challenges what Mariana Valverde has identified as attempts throughout the period to link female "love of finery" to an overflowing, and often vicious, sexuality (pp. 169–188). In Baker's hands, negotiating the mysteries of fancy dress becomes rather a strategy for survival, the accusation of "vice" redirected against a society that forces women into the service of male sexuality, at the same time that it reduces their lives to "everyday flirtations and silly little concerns" (*The Times*, 23 May 1913, 10). After the discovery of Miss Tassey's body, the play ends with Rose, her metamorphosis complete, looking "*incongruous in her scarlet finery.*" As she is led out, in a state of near collapse, a final stage direction tells us, she "*fingers ... her dress like one distraught*" (p. 29).

Many of the issues raised in *Miss Tassey* are anticipated in Cicely Hamilton's four-act drapers' comedy *Diana of Dobson's*, produced by Lena Ashwell at the Kingsway Theatre in the winter and spring of 1908. Like Lyttelton and Baker, Hamilton was an active supporter of the suffrage movement. A member of the Actresses' Franchise League, and a founding member of the Women Writers' Suffrage League, her *Pageant of Great Women*, produced by Edith Craig at the Scala Theatre in 1909, became the organization's most spectacular get-penny. *How the Vote was Won* (Royalty 1909), a one-act satire written in collaboration with Christopher St. John (Christabel Marshall), used the devices of Aristophanic farce to present a world in which women obtain the vote by collectively withholding their labor. Its humiliating reduction of anti-suffrage arguments rendered it, too, an essential weapon for the cause. Yet Hamilton's sympathies, in her own words, were more broadly feminist than they were suffragist. Her own involvement in both the Pankhursts' Women's Social and Political Union, and, after 1907, Charlotte Despard's Women's Freedom League, is put into context in an often cited passage from her autobiography, *Life Errant*:

I never attempted to disguise the fact that I wasn't wildly interested in votes for anyone, and ... if I worked for women's enfranchisement (and I did work quite hard) it wasn't because I hoped great things from counting female noses at general elections, but because the agitation for women's enfranchisement must inevitably shake and weaken the tradition of the "normal woman." The "normal woman" with her "destiny" of marriage and motherhood and housekeeping, no interest outside her home – especially no interest in the man's preserve of politics! My personal revolt was feminist rather than suffragist; what I rebelled at chiefly was the dependence implied in the idea of "destined" marriage, "destined" motherhood – the identification of success with marriage, of failure with spinsterhood, the artificial concentration of the hopes of girlhood on sexual attraction and maternity. (p. 65)

It was a position Hamilton most emphatically argued in *Marriage as a Trade*, a 1909 polemic Elaine Showalter has described as being "on the brink of a feminist criticism" (p. 225). Using commercial models to explore women's "professional" interest in marriage and fashion, the work demonstrates the manner in which woman is "the product of the conditions imposed upon her by her staple industry" (Hamilton, *Marriage as a Trade*, p. 17). Personal adornment, under such circumstances, is less a matter of vanity or "romance" than business calculation. Women, under patriarchy, simply acquire the skills needed to pursue the careers to which they have been apprenticed.

Such beliefs both underpin and inform *Diana of Dobson's*, described by its author as "a romantic comedy" in which a sweated shop assistant "on the strength of a small legacy, makes a Cinderella-like appearance in the world that does not toil or spin" (*Life Errant*, p. 61). The play's first act occurs on familiar terrain. In "*a bare room of the dormitory type*" at Dobson's Drapery Emporium, we find ourselves, once again, in the presence of "*a single gas jet ... turned very low,*" a simple washstand, and "*five small beds ranged against the walls – everything plain and comfortless to the last degree*" (p. 7). Margaret Bondfield, then an organizer for the National Federation of Women Workers, was enlisted to insure the accuracy of Hamilton's stage picture. "Happy to be taken into consultation," she pronounced it "the real thing, with boxes under the bed, clothes hanging up on the hooks, the general dinginess, and a reproduction of the actual furniture" (*A Life's Work*, p. 73).[25] Hamilton, who confessed in an interview with the *Pall Mall Gazette* (8 February 1908, 2) her intention of arousing public indignation at "the want of consideration with which some [workers] are treated by their employers," introduces to the scene five shop assistants and their overseer, Miss Pringle. In addition to her heroine, the rebellious Diana Massingberd, we meet both the 20-year-old Kitty Brant ("pale and tired"), whose recent engagement means release from a world of "grind and squalor and tyranny and overwork," and the "faded" Miss Smithers, "well over thirty" and reconciled to being, like Miss Tassey, "one of the left ones." Yet the much praised action of the scene, such as it is, consists neither of fines nor scolding from the po-faced Miss Pringle, but the evening toilette of Hamilton's workers (plate 15). The London correspondent for the *New York Herald* watched with some incredulity as "five tired out girls [came]

15. The Act 1 undressing scene in *Diana of Dobson's*.

straggling up to their mean and dingy room to tumble into five mean
and narrow cot beds":

There is nothing left to the imagination. They all disrobe in full view of the
audience, take off their regulation black waists and skirts and toss them on
the tin trunks, or the floor, or anywhere...Off come the false curls and
switches, that are held in the mouth, shook out and brushed, in a way with
which all women are familiar. Shoes and stockings, gaudy petticoats and
other articles of feminine apparel are gradually shed and strewn about...
[until] flannel nighties [are] donned ... [and] bare feet protrude beneath the
bedclothes. (15 February 1908; McKinnel)

The potential for prurience was obvious enough. The following
month, music-hall entertainer Miss Valli Valli parodied the scene on
the stage of the Empire, conflating Hamilton's first and fourth acts,
so that her shop assistant undressed, not in the privacy of a women's
dormitory, but on a park bench on the Thames Embankment (*Sketch*,
25 March 1908, 328) (plate 16). Popular playwright Frederick
Melville, likewise, interpolated into what he billed as his "remarkable
bedroom drama," *The Bad Girl of the Family* (Elephant and Castle
1909), an episode in which female shop assistants undressed in view
of a disguised male interloper. Yet the remarkable thing about
Hamilton's "disrobing" was its determined lack of erotic charge.
The *Herald* correspondent concluded by noting that, in spite of its
subject-matter, "somehow" the scene was not "indelicate." And in
this he was echoed by, among others, the critics for the *Stage*
(13 February 1908, 23), the *Illustrated Sporting and Dramatic News*
(7 March 1908, 19), and the *Illustrated London News* (22 February
1908, 266), all of whom commented upon the "mechanical" matter-
of-fact way in which Hamilton's young women disassembled themselves, distributing the parts and parcels of their sales identities into
the appropriate bins and boxes. H. M. Walkley, describing the scene
for the *Pall Mall Gazette*, volunteered that "if any flippant reader
imagines that by booking a seat at the Kingsway Theatre he will get
a view of something rather scandalous and improper – well, all we
shall say is, Let him book his seat! He will deserve his disappointment" (13 February 1908, 4). It was, all in all, a virtuoso
demonstration of the author's contention that "the care, the time
and the thoroughness which many young women devote to their own
adornment" springs neither from vanity nor an overplus of romantic
sentiment, but from a "thoroughly professional" assessment of their
economic opportunities (*Marriage as a Trade*, pp. 90–91).

16. Miss Valli Valli (upper right and lower left) parodies the undressing scene in *Diana of Dobson's* (*Sketch*, 25 March 1908).

The argument is pursued in the play's central episode, which presents a pointed variation upon the shop-girl's traditional on-stage progress. Diana, instead of investing her small legacy for a supplementary income of "nine or ten pounds a year," elects to quit Dobson's to enjoy a month of extravagant freedom. Insisting that, before she dies, she will "know what it is to wear a decently cut frock" and "boots that cost more than seven and eleven pence a pair" her first destination is "Paris – for clothes" (p. 17). In Acts II and III, we find Diana, in Society, parading about a luxury resort in the Swiss Alps first in a smart evening dress of rose-pink silk, then in a kilted walking-skirt in shades of hydrangea blue and mauve. Unlike the press silence that greeted the gowns "Madame Viola" had created for *Warp and Woof* four seasons earlier, there was little reluctance to describe or praise either outfit. In fact, fashion arbiter Mrs. Jack May, declaring that "if it were not for the theatre, life, viewed from the point of clothes, would be intolerably dull," found the play's justification to lie in a simple reading of its "sartorial revelations." In the role of Diana, actress Lena Ashwell, "not one of the most notoriously good dressers," we are told, nevertheless managed to "triumph" in a second-act evening ensemble whose "glorious embroidery of shaded dahlias" was read as "a sure predication" of coming spring fashions (*Bystander*, 26 February 1908, 466). The "essentially charming little morning gown" of Act III also aroused "considerable interest," prompting *The Sunday Times*, in a column headed "Smart Frocks at the Kingsway Theatre" to recommend its "skirt of pale grey and white striped summer tweed, for travelling" (16 February 1908, 12). If, however, such critics hoped to revive the type of "morally blind" costume analysis that had characterized theatrical fashion plates through the previous decade, Hamilton had set them a trap. In Act II, the re-dressed Diana encounters a former employer, drapery boss Sir Jabez Grinley. No longer one of his "unseen" drudges, Diana is now "materialized" by her rose-pink evening gown and a bodice "filled in with cream lace." Indeed, so complete is the identification of "girl" and "garment" that the entrammeled Sir Jabez, while he woos its wearer, surreptitiously "*feels the quality of goods in her sleeve.*" When Diana, in reply, "*withdraws her arm slowly,*" Hamilton's distinction becomes clear. Men may propose to gowns, but it is their flesh-and-blood wearers who will endure the consequences. Diana's achievement in becoming "personally attractive and therefore desirable" not only argues, in

Hamilton's terminology, a "professional" interest in haute couture, but hints at a more comprehensive power to manipulate the products of sweated industry for her own ends. If men have made women what they wear, as Hamilton suggests, there is little, other than her black uniform, to distinguish a sales assistant from her most privileged clients. By defining ladies as fine gowns and modish accessories, an unwitting fashion trade had endowed women with a chameleon potential for self-transformation, one that threatened to loose the very boundaries it had set out to reinforce.

In her final act, Hamilton, characterized by the *Star* as as much a rebel in dramatic technique as her heroine had been in opposing Dobson's drapery practices (13 February 1908; McKinnel), presents "Cinderella" after the stroke of twelve. Diana, having run through her fortune, appears destitute on the Thames Embankment, bundled up in the kind of "unwomanly rags" to which Hood had alluded in his "Song of the Shirt." Having used her earlier acts to respond to the narrative of the shop assistant as it had been plotted in musical comedy, Hamilton here seeks to "problematize" the fable of the rescued seamstress. Diana, in *"a shabby hat and coat, a short skirt, muddy boots and woollen gloves with holes in several of the finger-tips"* meets the Hon. Victor Bretherton, a dashing Captain in the Welsh Guards, who had, like Jabez Grinley, proposed to her society gown in Act III. Dared by Diana, who tells him her story, to find his own market value, Bretherton now appears cold, hungry, and much chastened. Their reconciliation, on a park bench occupied by an old woman *"of the hopelessly unemployed class,"* consists of Victor's realization that his unearned income of £600 a year is sufficient for them both. His second proposal, offering Diana a home, "a fortune," and himself "in the bargain," is accordingly accepted. The rescue will not restore Diana to the "ornamental" position she had occupied in Acts II and III, but will at least free her from "unwomanly rags." Seen in the context of the play as a whole, Hamilton's version of sartorial reclamation is fraught with ironies. Clamped onto a drama that had, as the *Era* reminded its readers, been "produced quite apropos of the agitation against 'living in'" (15 February 1908, 17), such a self-consciously romantic solution raised questions about the work's ultimate meaning. Society publications, like the *Lady's Pictorial*, luxuriating in the sentimentality of Diana's escape, attempted to deny the "hard conditions" of Hamilton's opening act, observing that "if one were to burrow in the underworld of commerce, there might be found nagging forewomen, tyrannical employers, overworked and underpaid assistants, but to suggest that such conditions are general, or even frequent, among the business houses today is unjust" (22 February 1908, 270). The *Clarion*, once again, watching stalls patrons with an eagle eye, focused instead upon "how very pained and shocked ... Miss Ashwell's fashionable audience look[ed]," recording differences between those "jewelled ladies and collared gentlemen" amenable, and those hostile, to being swayed by "a Socialistic piece, written by a Socialist" (21 February 1908, 3).[26] Indeed, Hamilton's decision to make viewers uneasy about both trade practices and the aesthetic conventions that forestalled their remedy provoked an extended debate that helped to insure the play's commercial success. In an ironic comedy that took as its provenance not merely the dress trade but the spectacle and meaning of woman dressed, Hamilton was able to link agitation against trade abuses to broader questions about a woman and her wardrobe. In a comedic close designed to raise more problems than it solved, the play simultaneously built upon and undermined the literature and iconography of both the seamstress and the shop assistant, demonstrating how "the narrowing down of woman's hopes and ambitions to the sole pursuit and sphere of marriage is one of the various disabilities, economic and otherwise, under which she labours" (*Marriage as a Trade*, p. 22). In its attempt to lobby for legislative relief, while insisting upon the need for new myths by which to live, *Diana of Dobson's* must be counted among the period's most comprehensive efforts to grapple with both the public and domestic implications of the Edwardian dress trade. It would remain so until the rise of the modern fashion show and haute couture model helped to extend the terms of debate.

CHAPTER 4

Millinery stages

During the last year of Victoria's reign the couturière Lucile married Sir Cosmo Duff Gordon, a principal backer of her fashion house since 1895. The union, which took place on 24 May 1900, would affect the fortunes of London's West End theatre as well as its dressmaking trade. As Lady Duff Gordon, England's first titled modiste, Lucile was now able to approach society patrons on equal footing.[1] At the same time, her mint-new status encouraged a special relationship with the era's so-called "Dollar Princesses," American heiresses fast marrying into Mayfair's power elite. It was for these markets that Lucile championed the S-bend corset with its mono-bosom silhouette, and, after 1908, following the lead of Parisian counterpart Paul Poiret, a Directoire revival – sheath dresses, cut-away jackets, and outsized hats – whose reinscription of the female form is best summed up by Poiret's boast to have "freed the bust but ... shackled the legs" (Poiret, p. 73).[2] On stage, Lucile exploited both looks in a string of commissions executed for that most opulent of Edwardian pleasure palaces, the refurbished Gaiety. Turning the home of Britain's musical comedy into an adjunct showroom, Lucile completed her construction of turn-of-the-century womanhood by dressing a succession of showgirls for impresario George Edwardes. Indeed, Lucile's role in creating icons of sexuality out of leading ladies like Lily Elsie, Gabrielle Ray, and Gladys Cooper extended beyond the mere gowning of her subjects. For Edward Morton's adaptation of *The Merry Widow*, produced by Edwardes in 1907, Elsie was taken to Lucile's Hanover Square shop for a complete make-over. Here, before her costumes were fitted, she was given a new complexion and *coiffure*, and trained to walk with an elegant Gibson Girl glide. "There was not a movement across the stage," Lucile would later recall, "not a single gesture of her part ... that we did not go through together" (Duff Gordon, p. 109). In performance, Lucile's wardrobes of high-waisted tunics in diaphanous fabrics caught the attention of the young Cecil Beaton, whose memoirs pay tribute to his predecessor's Gaiety reign:

The leading lady's gowns were inevitably made by Lucile and were masterpieces of intricate workmanship ... [She] worked with soft materials, delicately sprinkling them with bead or sequin embroidery, with cobweb lace insertions, true lovers' knots, and garlands of minute roses. Her colour sense was so subtle that the delicacy of detail could scarcely be seen at a distance, though the effect she created was of an indefinable shimmer. Sometimes, however, she introduced rainbow effects into a sash and would incorporate quite vivid mauves and greens, perhaps even a touch of shrimp-pink or orange. Occasionally, if she wanted to be deliberately outrageous, she introduced a bit of black chiffon or black velvet and, just to give the coup de grace, outlined it with diamonds ... In her heyday, Lucile's artistry was unique, her influence enormous. (Beaton, pp. 32–34)

After *The Merry Widow*, with its accompanying craze for slit skirts and black hats with broad brims and bird-of-paradise plumes, Lucile's position as London's first dressmaker of international stature was assured. It was an achievement marked, appropriately enough, by Edwardes's 1909 production of A. M. Willner's *The Dollar Princess*, in which Gaiety showgirls, themselves rumored to be hunting titles, enacted the tale of two "self made Yankee maids" who boast of their ability to buy "Dukes or Counts" on the strength of their dowries and couture-built figures.

If Lucile, through the decade, used the stage to generate sales, her West End showroom indulged in forms of public display denounced by her detractors as openly stagy. As in the nineties, Lucile's most significant innovations were attempts to provide a specifically theatrical context for the selling of women's clothes. Her broadest claim, to have invented the mannequin, or live fashion model, was a blatant piece of self-puffery. Although the early history of the mannequin is obscured by conflicting accounts of rival houses, Gagelin had apparently used *demoiselles de magasin* to display shawls and mantles as early as 1849. Through the sixties, moreover, Madame Worth (Marie Vernet), usually cited as the first professional model, regularly launched her husband's seasonal lines at Longchamps, often in the company of the Princess von Metternich (de Marly, *Worth*, pp. 23–24). Yet, for all this, Lucile's point is well taken. In an age in which many fashion houses still displayed gowns draped over wooden lay figures, or propped up on chairs and stuffed out with tissue paper, Lucile had aligned herself with a group of designers, including Paquin and Poiret, who insisted upon the persuasiveness of fabric in motion. Indeed, Lucile, drawing upon her stage experience, took the concept one step further, harping upon the erotic possibilities of such exhibits. Her mannequins abjured the *malliots* or under-garments of "rigid black satin, reaching from chin to feet" conventionally worn by couture house models, nor were they shod in "unappetizing laced boots" (Duff Gordon, p. 68). Such devices merely perpetuated a Victorian reticence at odds with Lucile's determination to harness the trade aspects of sexual temptation. So much appears in her comments upon the sales assistants selected to model gowns by some of her less flamboyant competitors:

Even the most nervous mamma could safely take her son with her to the dressmaker's when temptation appeared in such unalluring guise, that is to say, if it could be called temptation at all, for as a guarantee of the respectability of the establishment the director could be relied upon to choose only the plainest of girls to show off his creations. (Duff Gordon, p. 68)

Lucile's response was to recruit and train her own corps of "glorious, goddess-like girls" drawn largely from the working-class suburbs of East and South London. Selected for the kind of full-busted, long-limbed figures Lucile would help to make popular,[3] each was drilled in carriage and deportment, before being given a sonorous stage name like Hebe, Gamela, or Dolores. Although the painter "Drian" would later liken Lucile's amazons "mincing about in their turbans and trailing trains" to "impertinent lobsters" (Beaton, p. 34), they were widely admired by the fashion press of the day, which used them to proclaim the arrival of a new English type of glamor. By the decade's close many would be celebrities in their own right, the first supermodels of an emerging couture house industry (plate 17).

In or about 1900 Lucile's drive to theatricalize fashion marketing was made literal with the building of a ramp and curtained recess at one end of her shop. Here, picked out by limelight and accompanied by the playing of soft music, the most accomplished of her mannequins introduced gowns to small groups of invited clients. The resulting mannequin parades, forerunners of the contemporary fashion show, were innovations of which Lucile could justifiably boast. Rival houses advertised similar events, but these, as often as not, were attempts to replicate on a showroom floor the particulars

17. "Paraders of Dream Dresses Before the Four Hundred: Lady Duff-Gordon's Beautiful Mannequins" (*Sketch*, 30 March 1910).

and ambience of society gatherings. Typical was the much discussed "mannequin parade" held at Peter Robinson's Oxford Street store in the spring of 1904, in which "no fewer than thirty mannequins" perambulated about the costume rooms mingling with spectators and one another. "But for the background," the *Sketch* observed, "the scene might have been the lawn at Ascot, or an ultra-fashionable garden-party." Society columnist Sybil, who lavishly praised the event, was reminded of "the Terrace" at Monte Carlo (4 April 1904, 365, 383). Lucile's displays, in sharp contrast, used the paraphernalia of stage representation – ramp, curtains, wings, limelight, and music – to establish a voyeuristic bond between mannequin and spectator. The process was intended to draw a mixed audience of male and female viewers, the former lured to Lucile's premises by the prospect of inspecting flesh as well as fabric. This, in itself, was unusual. As late as 1908 even public displays of women's clothing, like the Earl's Court Dress Exhibition of that year, specifically excluded men from their more intimate tableaux (*Sketch*, 29 January 1908, 75). Lucile, however, encouraged male attendance, using terms like "model" and "gown" to refer simultaneously to her mannequins and their garments. The complex eroticism of her spectacles – working-class women dressed as society ladies promenading silently before audiences of middle- and upper-class men – was further augmented by Lucile's decision to replace the numbers by which gowns had hitherto been identified with suggestive titles like "Passion's Thrall," "Do You Love Me?," and "A Frenzied Song of Amorous Things." Beginning with a series of simple walk-abouts called collectively "Gowns of Emotion," such displays soon took the form of thematic pageants. The most elaborate had texts prepared by Lucile's sister, society novelist Elinor Glyn.[4] The series culminated in 1909, after Lucile's return from North America, with the ambitious *Seven Ages of Woman*, a stage piece in seven acts tracing from birth to death the dress-cycle of a society dame.[5] Playing to an audience that included Queen Marie of Romania, the Queen of Spain, and Princess Patricia of Connaught, Lucile began with "The Schoolgirl," consisting of two dresses, "The Beginning of Knowledge" and "The Awakening of Youth," and progressed, in turn, through "The Debutante," "The Fiancée," "The Bride," "The Wife," "The Hostess," and "The Dowager," the latter, again, represented by two gowns, "Eventide" and "Twilight." The most developed episode, reflecting Lucile's business sense as well as her calculated sensuality, was "The

Hostess," a succession of four scenes and three tableaux designed to appeal to "the married woman who entertained, was entertained and who could indulge in the luxury of a lover." An introductory passage steered spectators of both sexes through a sequence of gowns whose subtext was unmistakable: "The Desire of the Eyes" led to "Persuasive Delight," which was then followed by "A Frenzied Hour," "Salut d'Amour," "Afterwards," and "Contentment" (Etherington-Smith, pp. 89–90).

The full hothouse effect of Lucile's mannequin parades – at least, as they appeared to unsympathetic eyes – is preserved in Marie Corelli's *Bystander* column of 27 July 1904. While neither Lucile nor Elinor Glyn is mentioned by name, Corelli's sub-acid account of a "fashion symposium" held under the joint auspices of "Madame la Modiste" and her would-be novelist sister left few readers in the dark:

Not very long ago there was held a wonderful "symposium" of dress at the establishment of a certain modiste. It was intensely diverting, entertaining and instructive. A stage was erected at one end of a long room, and on that stage, with effective flashes of lime-light played from the "wings" at intervals, and the accompaniment of a Hungarian band, young ladies wearing "creations" in costume, stood, sat, turned, twisted and twirled, and finally walked down the room between rows of spectators to show themselves, and the gowns they carried, off to the best possible advantage. The whole thing was much better than a stage comedy. Nothing could surpass the quaint peacock-like vanity of the girl mannequins who strutted up and down, moving their hips to accentuate the fall and flow of flounces and draperies... There was a "programme" of the performance fearfully and wonderfully worded, the composition, so we were afterwards "with bated breath" informed, of Madame la Modiste's sister, a lady who by virtue of having written two small, rather clever skits on the manners, customs and modes of society, is, in some obliging quarters of the Press called a "novelist." This programme instructed us as to the proper views we were expected to take of the costumes paraded before us.

Among gowns cataloged in Glyn's text we find "Elusive Joy," "Incessant Soft Desire," and the sensationally titled "Red Mouth of a Venomous Flower" – the last, as it turned out, "a harmless-looking girl in a bright scarlet toilette." Corelli's most telling comments, however, were reserved for the show's reception. Surprised at both the number and type of male viewers who had elbowed their way into Lucile's salon for the occasion, she transcribed a range of responses that made clear what, in fact, was being sold:

Curious to relate, there were quite a large number of "gentlemen" at this remarkable exhibition of feminine clothes, many of them well-known and easily recognisable. Certain *flâneurs* of Bond Street, various loafers familiar to the Carlton "lounge," and celebrated Piccadilly-trotters, formed nearly one half of the audience, and stared with easy insolence at the "Red Mouth of a Venomous Flower" or smiled suggestively at "Incessant Soft Desire." They were invited to stare and smile, and they did. But there was something remarkably offensive in their way of doing it. (437–438)

Through such rituals the mannequin effectively replaced the seamstress and shop assistant as the millinery trade's most conspicuous object of male desire. The substitution, moreover, formed part of a concerted sales effort, a point nicely caught in Corelli's phrase about gentlemen viewers being "*invited* to stare and smile." Among Lucile's competitors similar effects were achieved only by Poiret, and here largely through the efforts of the mannequin Andrée, whose gyrations, we are told, resembled those of "an anemone expanding in the sea under the influence of a genial current." Poiret claimed to have seen "more than one duke bite the head of his stick to put himself in countenance, and insert his monocle the better to observe her" (Poiret, p. 146).[6] Corelli's parting suggestion, that such voyeurs might profitably have the "smoothness" kicked out of them by "a few thick boots worn on the feet of rough but honest workmen" hints, none too subtly, at the class and sex antagonisms upon which such showmanship had been built.[7] It also helps to explain why Lucile's type of theatricalized and eroticized mannequin parade would come to offer so resonant an image for those who wished to explore, on commercial as well as repertory stages, both the business and products of Edwardian fashion.

Through the autumn of 1909, the year of Lucile's *Seven Ages of Woman*, producer and playwright Harley Granville Barker was preparing to launch London's second venture in repertory theatre. Two years earlier, Barker had closed the books on the three seasons of innovative drama he had presented in concert with John Vedrenne at the Royal Court Theatre in Sloane Square. Their fabled "Thousand Performances" (actually 946 performances of 32 plays by 17 authors) had helped to establish Shaw as a marketable playwright, presenting eleven of his works in tandem with Gilbert Murray's translations from Euripides and new pieces by John Galsworthy, St. John Hankin, John Masefield, and Elizabeth Robins.

The Voysey Inheritance, Barker's own study of a corrupt solicitor's ironic legacy, enjoyed a healthy run of thirty-four performances during the 1905–1906 season. To the surprise of all, the enterprise made money, although efforts to repeat its success at the Savoy the following year proved financially disastrous. The 1910 venture, backed by American impresario Charles Frohman, was an attempt to bring a similarly "progressive" theatre to London's West End. The venue this time was the fashionable Duke of York's in St. Martin's Lane, the company a troupe experienced in the ways of repertory playing. Indeed, many were veterans of the Royal Court seasons, including Lewis Casson, Dennis Eadie, Edmund Gwenn, Florence Haydon, and Edyth Oliver. Barker's role in the undertaking, while not formalized, included directorial responsibilities for his own scripts as well as those by former Court colleagues (Kennedy, pp. 100–103). His most enduring contribution, however, was made as a playwright. The previous July, with Frohman's season clearly in mind, he had completed the first draft of *The Madras House* (Purdom, p. 94), an aggressively uncommercial drama, anatomizing, in terms drawn from the drapery trade, the manners and mores of contemporary England. Barker's earlier works had dealt at a tangent with various aspects of the Woman Question, including marriage, motherhood, and sexual exploitation. In *The Madras House* the topic was moved center-stage, as Barker used the economic and social implications of the Edwardian fashion world to suggest unsettling relationships between women, clothes, money-making, and what postmodern critics have come to call cultural production and the construction of gender. With a cast of twenty-five and a casual, ramshackle plot that placed before his audiences a world of shop girls, modistes, mannequins, and fashion entrepreneurs, it was an audacious example of what critic Margery Morgan has termed "millinery theatre." If, however, the play's action rambled, its focus remained clear, enabling Barker to turn his four sets – two domestic and two business establishments – into sites for sustained and highly topical debate. Indeed, the talkiness of the piece as well as the issues broached helped to establish its "new drama" look, making unlikely the prospect of revival outside of repertory auspices.

Before opening on 9 March, during the third week of Frohman's season, *The Madras House* underwent two rounds of revision.[8] Yet with few exceptions the play as staged preserved the groundplan of Barker's original draft. Its central action remained economic, the acquisition by American financier Eustace Perrin State of both the high-fashion House of Madras and its poor cousin the retail drapery firm of Roberts and Huxtable. It is, however, misleading to speak of plot in any conventional sense. The actual purchase is bundled into ten lines of quick dialogue at the close of Act III. Indeed, so rapidly and so amiably is the matter concluded that some critics seemed unaware it had taken place at all. The play's interest lay rather in the questions it raised about a variety of commercial and domestic transactions, all revolving about men's attitudes towards women, clothing, and money. Our path through these issues is marked by the progress of Barker's protagonist Philip Madras, although, once again, protagonist seems hardly the right word. Jan McDonald may be nearer the mark in calling him the play's "linkman" (p. 88). Reluctant heir to the House of Madras, and partner in Huxtable's drapery shop, Philip's initial role in the piece is to co-ordinate the sale of both companies. In Act I he announces back-to-back meetings to be held at Huxtable's Camberwell store and the West End showroom of the House of Madras. Acts II and III take us, in turn, to each site, where Barker propounds his central thesis, that by 1909–1910 laissez-faire capitalism, through a collusive fashion trade, had consigned middle-class women to lives that consisted largely of buying and being bought. In Act II, avant-garde playgoers acquainted with the shop-girl dramas of Cicely Hamilton and Elizabeth Baker, found themselves on familiar ground, surveying a tense confrontation between a young sales assistant and her spinster forewoman. Act III, set in the bright rotunda of the Bond Street House of Madras, offered, in contrast, a Lucile-style mannequin parade, punctuated by the fantastical musings of the play's principal men of business. In each case, however, Barker pushes past obvious targets, carrying his attack back to the attitudes that promote and institutions that profit by such behavior. At the same time, he is at pains, in the play's two outer acts, set in contrasting drawing rooms in Phillimore Gardens and suburban South London, to hint at an insidious relationship between domus and market-place, suggesting that, in the end, the consumers of fashion may be its ultimate victims. It is, all in all, a sweeping indictment, set forth with sufficient clarity and period detail to make the play an essential document for social and fashion historians. Yet while Barker notes with some prescience the emergence of modern marketing techniques and dress strategies, his immediate concerns are with social rifts, gender politics, and, above all, the ways in which an increasingly theatricalized fashion world might be brought to the bar of public performance.

The play's method, a subversive tangling of economic, sexual, and domestic motifs, is announced early in Act I. In the Denmark Hill parlor of Henry Huxtable, viewers are offered a dramatic embodiment of the era's much discussed "surplus woman" problem. The six unmarried Huxtable daughters, aged between twenty-six and thirty-nine, are presented as prisoners of their family's upward mobility, and of a society unwilling to let them work, create, or marry beneath their station. The drapery firm of Roberts and Huxtable, whose wealth has created their enforced leisure, also provides, in its "living-in" system, an ironic image for their largely homebound servitude.[9] The gentility to which so much has been sacrificed is likewise cast in millinery terms. Mrs. Huxtable, we are told, "*figures ...for the dignity of the household.*" It is a quality conveyed "*by the rustle of her dress*" and the identical "*Sunday frocks, Sunday hats, [and] best gloves*" worn by her daughters through the act. While no designer is credited for these gowns, Mrs. Huxtable's outfit, reproduced in Langdon Coburn's portrait of Florence Haydon in the role, is appropriately dark, high-necked, and full-skirted (*Graphic*, 19 March 1910, 398). Complemented by a gray mourning cap, it sets a standard of respectability that demonstrates its wearer's exemption from what Thorstein Veblen had called "all vulgarly productive employment" (p. 179). Daughter Julia, who at one point had shown promise in watercolors, had been, we are told, "*dressed in brown velveteen and sent to an art school.*" On family outings to Weymouth she still puts her sisters' noses out of joint by appearing on the parade in summer dresses with bright orange stripes (pp. 2, 96). Emma, the most animated of the brood, adopts a New Woman look, "*run[ning] rather to coats and skirts and common sense*" (p. 3). Both, however, are defeated by their own good breeding: Julia, by the ways of seeing imposed by her art school instructors, Emma by the family's refusal to let her pursue the occupations for which she is dressed. By the time the play opens their acts of sartorial rebellion have dwindled into pathetic outbursts of costume fetishism. An obsession with matinée idol Lewis Waller is particularly telling. When Waller's shirt collar comes back from the laundry in mistake for Mr. Huxtable's it is hidden away by the 34-year-old Julia. Its confiscation by Mrs. Huxtable provokes a teary outburst, with consequent remarks about Julia's "wanton mind" (pp. 23–24). While the incident is, in general terms, damning enough, Barker's use of Waller is astutely topical. In the spring of 1908, the actor's mainly female admirers had been organized into the entertainment industry's first modern fan-club. Taking their cue from Waller's appearance as the cowboy hero of Edwin Royle's *A White Man* (Lyric 1908), they called themselves KOW Girls, alternatively expanding the acronym into "Keen on Waller" and "Keen Order of Wallerites." Sporting KOW buttons, meeting for weekly discussions, and providing "a secret bodyguard" at Waller performances, by 1909 the group formed a potential market for a variety of promotional products. Indeed, by February of that year Waller had posed for the first of a series of "personality puppets," meant to replace what the *Sketch* called "the daubed face and shapeless form" of the traditional rag doll (3 February 1909, 6–7). In bringing the slick packaging of the stage celebrity into contact with the cloistered world of the Huxtable sisters, Barker transforms the shirt-collar episode into a timely fable of class snobbery, sublimated sex, and merchandising opportunities. The relationship between all three will become the subject of Eustace State's Nottingham scheme, set forth in Act III, in which ladies' finery is sold by crews of "Pure Clean-Minded" male athletes, all "bronzed, noble" and over six feet tall (p. 84).

If Huxtable's domestic establishment is seen in commercial terms, his drapery business with its objectification and exploitation of women workers is likened to "an industrial seraglio" (p. 101). Act II, played in a grim suburban office beneath a framed fashion plate of "*twenty faultless ladies engaged in ladylike occupations*" (p. 37), plunges us back into the world of *Diana of Dobson's* and *Miss Tassey*. Here, gathered about a table in "*one of the very ugliest rooms that ever entered into the mind of a builder or decorator*" (p. 36), we find Miss Yates, a shop assistant of ten years standing, Miss Chancellor, spinster overseer of Huxtable's workers, and Mr. Brigstock, Third Man in the Hosiery. What has brought them together is the pregnancy of the unmarried Miss Yates, a condition blamed on the unprepossessing Brigstock. The interrogation that follows, conducted by Philip at Huxtable's request, unfolds as a broad if predictable condemnation of the "living-in" system, with its abuse of both married and unmarried workers. As such, the act was applauded by the labor and suffrage press. *Votes for Women*, the voice of the radical Women's Social and Political Union, urged attendance by "intelligent shop-assistants... who would, if they dared, thoroughly enjoy [its] exposure of the

living-in system" (8 April 1910, 439). Janet Case, writing for the
Common Cause, suggested that "every Suffragist should go and take a
dozen of the unconverted" (7 April 1910, 734), while Margaret
Bondfield, the shop assistant and union organizer whose research on
employment conditions had been incorporated into *Diana of Dobson's*
two years earlier, congratulated Barker for striking "another blow at
the living-in System, and for the exposure of the degrading aspect of
the trade in dress which leaves no room for souls to grow"
(unpublished letter, 25 March 1910). Such points are well taken. Yet
Barker's emphasis through the episode falls less upon trade grievances
than systemic forms of class and gender bias. And here he finds an
especially striking image in the relationship between retail dressmaking and haute couture. Miss Yates's pregnancy, it seems, is
more a result of her "living out" than "living in." Sent by Roberts
and Huxtable to the Madras House for professional training, she has
succumbed to the sensuality of its premises and, more urgently, the
advances of Constantine Madras, Philip's father and the firm's
founding director.[10] "There's something in that...place," she
confesses to Philip, "that does set your mind going about men" (p.
57). During her Bond Street sojourn, Miss Yates's mind is also "set
going" about the invisibility imposed upon drapery workers by a
carriage-trade clientele:

Those ladies that you get coming in there...well, it does just break your
nerve. What with following them about and the things they say you've got
to hear, and the things they'll say...about you half the time...that you've
got not to hear...[while you] keep your voice low and sweet, and let your
arms hang down straight. (p. 57)

In Act II both kinds of subjugation are bodied forth in immediate and
powerful stage symbols, the first, by Miss Yates's obvious pregnancy,
the second by the entry, immediately after the above passage, of
Philip's society wife, Jessica, "*exquisite from her eyelashes to her shoes*"
(p. 57). The juxtaposition is designed to provoke the same kinds of
questions about "ladyhood" and its costs as those raised by
Theodosia Hemming in the last moments of Lyttelton's *Warp and
Woof*. Yet Barker complicates matters by arguing what amounts to a
"best-case scenario" for fashionable life. No gauche caricature, like
Jenny Barkstone or Poppy Price, Jessica reads Shelley, plays
Beethoven, and attends performances of the repertory theatre. Her
arrival, in an elegant visiting dress, brings genuine relief to the bleak

squalor of Huxtable's waiting room.[11] When Barker asks whether this creature "*the result – not of thirty three years – but of three or four generations of cumulative refinement*" is not perhaps "*worth the toil and the helotage of – all the others?*" he does not expect easy answers. Miss Yates, for one, fiercely independent with Philip, is in Jessica's presence reduced "*to her best costume department manner.*" Assuming a professional anonymity, she becomes, with reference to the traditional garb of the West End shop assistant, "*a black-silk being of another species*" (pp. 57–58). To Philip's amazement, she remakes herself on the spot, altering face, posture, tone, and rhetoric: "I'm sure I hope I've not talked too much. I always was a chatterbox, madam" (p. 59). It is, on Jessica's part, a bravura display of wealth and position, meant to complement Miss Yates's sexual exploitation at the hands of her male employer. Barker's next act takes us to the Madras House itself, the ultimate source of both forms of power.

Described in the press as "a kind of millinery symposium," the play's central episode presents the passing of its two dress firms into alien hands. The act is set in the Madras House rotunda, a mock-Moorish salon, in which Barker assembles his moguls of the drapery trade. The playwright, however, is less interested in the details of their deliberations than in catching and commenting upon a propitious moment in consumer history, the passing of the age of luxury dressmaking to that of the franchised clothing chain and purpose-built department store. On one side of the divide stands Constantine Madras, a grand couturier of the old school. Founder of the fashion house that bears his name and *arbitre des élégances* through the seventies and eighties, Constantine has become, for his Edwardian contemporaries, a figure of near-mythic proportions. Since opening his Bond Street showroom, however, Constantine has abandoned both his profession and the society in whose interests he has labored. Withdrawing to a small village on the banks of the Euphrates, where he lives the life of a "Mahommedan gentleman," he has returned to England only to preside over the sale of his business. He will, in the process, lend a critical "stranger's eye" to the scene's deconstruction of Western women, clothing, and sexuality. In all but his rejection of elite society, Constantine evokes the shade of Charles Worth, father of haute couture, who in the 1880s added to his pose of gentleman dressmaker that of bohemian autocrat.[12] Constantine's eccentric but modish ensemble of "*velvet coat, brick-red tie,* [*and*] *shepherd's-plaid trousers*" has its counterpart in the velvet berets, silk scarfs, and fur-lined coats Worth affected through the period, ruling his couture house, until his death in 1895, with a grandeur and solemnity that infuriated his critics. The story of a duchess going down "on her knees" to beg Constantine to make her a ballgown – a tale thrice told in Barker's play – has its origins in Worth's Second Empire reputation. Declining to fit clients at home, Worth compelled even princesses to make the pilgrimage to his offices in the rue de la Paix. To Count Primoli, nephew to the princess Matilda, his *atelier* seemed to "exhale ... some atmosphere of degraded aristocracy, some heady fragrance of elegance, wealth and forbidden fruit" (de Marly, *Worth*, p. 100).[13] Indeed, Worth's *Salon de Lumière*, in which select customers were fitted for evening gowns under simulated ballroom conditions, anticipates Constantine's rotunda, a chamber that "*in the old grand days*" had been "*the happy preserve of very special customers, those on whom the great man himself would keep an eye*" (pp. 72–73). Built by Constantine in 1884, the room's self-conscious orientalism – black marble, fretted archways, striped canopies, and crescent lamps – conjures up both the opulence and aesthetic despotism that has led fashion historian Diana de Marly to describe Worth's professional manner as that of "a sultan in a harem." Even the cushioned divans placed about the chamber's perimeter, and "*sun with spiked rays*" fixed in its ceiling, echo Worth's claim to have "composed" his gowns, while reclining, with "the rays of the setting sun gild[ing] his conceptions" (*Worth*, pp. 105–109).

To Eustace State, Barker's romantic capitalist, such stuff is the matter of legend, and legends, State explains at the outset of the act, are "the spiritual side of facts" (p. 74). Indeed, the play's earliest drafts include an exchange in which State traces his interest in buying the Madras House back to a dog-eared copy of *London Celebrities in Eighty-Eight*, in which he first learned of Constantine's encounter with the kneeling duchess (LCP, p. 68). On entering the rotunda State pays his respects to the site of the incident, later providing the story with his own glittering, fairy-tale conclusion. Such deference to both history and myth distinguishes State from his fellow milliners, who seem, in their collective stolidity, to explain the fate that has overtaken the Madras House since Constantine's retirement. By 1910, we learn, the firm is well on its way to becoming just another shop: its "*special customers are nobody in particular,*" the rotunda merely a place "*where a degenerate management meet to consider the choice of ready-made models from Paris*" (p. 72). To save the House from further humiliation, State preaches a doctrine of messianic consumerism, an audacious yoking of Goethe's concept of an "eternal feminine" with sound principles of bulk distribution. Having amassed previous fortunes in lumber and canned peaches, State has recently acquired the London mantle concern of Burrows and Company. Using the Burrows establishment to smash local competition, he now feels the need to add "poetry" to his venture. State's immediate plan calls for a network of franchises, drawing upon the prestige of Constantine's name to bring to provincial clients the dress opportunities of Mayfair and St. James's. Seeking to align what he calls his "Madras Houses ... New Edition" with "the Great Modern Woman's Movement," he has already begun his own market research:

It's but six months ago that I started to study the Woman Question ... I attended women's meetings in London, in Manchester and in one-horse places as well. Now Political Claims were but the narrowest, drabbest aspect of the matter as I saw it. The Woman's Movement is Woman expressing herself. Let us look at things as they are. What are a woman's chief means ... how often her only means of expressing herself? Anyway ... what is the first thing that she spends her money on? Clothes, gentlemen, clothes. (pp. 84–85)

If, however, State poses as a liberator of bourgeois sensuality, offering to a hypothetical "doctor's wife in the suburbs of Leicester" an equal chance to "Dazzle and Conquer," he assures his business associates that, viewed solely in economic terms, "the Middle Class Women of England ... think of them in bulk ... form one of the greatest Money Spending Machines the world has ever seen" (p. 88). The two aspects of his vision converge in a single passage that manages to suggest both his rewriting of women's history and the fashion trade's quasi-biological interest in the making and mating of its clients:

The Woman's Movement. The Great Modern Woman's Movement. It has come home to me that the man, who has as much to do with Woman as manufacturing the bones of her corsets and yet is not consciously in that Movement is Outside History. (p. 83)

In his exuberant blend of sentimental idealism and hard-headed business sense, State put many of the play's first viewers in mind of department store magnate H. Gordon Selfridge.[14] An American entrepreneur who talked passionately about the romance of commerce, Selfridge had come to London four years earlier to challenge both the organization of that city's drapery trade and the shopping habits of its women. Drawing upon his experience as a junior partner at Marshall Field in Chicago, as well as reports he had filed on the operations of the Parisian Bon Marché, Selfridge worked to introduce to mass markets some of the fruits of carriage-trade fashion. With great fanfare he had opened the store that still bears his name at the west end of Oxford Street on 15 March 1909 – almost a year to the day before the première of Barker's play. Through the process, Selfridge, like State, spoke expansively of the women's movement, focusing his energies upon attracting a middle-class and largely female clientele. To this end his store, with its thirty-odd costume divisions, was conceived as "a social centre not a shop," utilizing plush carpets, soft lights, banks of flowers, and a hidden string orchestra to address consumers as "connoisseurs of their surroundings as well as of what they wished to buy" (Pound, pp. 67, 72). Marketing strategies included the saturation use of newspaper advertising, and in-store exhibits that insisted upon the quality rather than the variety of his goods. Display windows, designed by the Chicago firm of Goldsman and Company, remained lit until midnight, revealing "pictorial fashion tableaux, shown against backcloths painted in the manner of Watteau and Fragonard" (Pound, pp. 66, 70). Throughout, such conspicuous opulence was linked to Selfridge's boast of "LONDON'S LOWEST PRICES – ALWAYS" (*Queen*, 13 March 1909, 15). Indeed, the lure of accessibility was central to his purpose. By such means Selfridge, who was among the first to advertise in the suffrage press, maintained he was "help[ing] to emancipate women" coming along "just at the time when they wanted to step out on their own." In patronizing his store, he claimed, "they ... realized some of their dreams" (Pound, p. 16). To skeptical critics, like the writer for the *Anglo-Continental* who accused him of "employing every art to lure the feminine element into those extravagances which work ruin and misery in the household," Selfridge replied, as would State, by appealing to progress, manifest destiny, and a balance sheet built upon his assumption that "woman is the same the world over when she goes shopping" (Pound, pp. 84–85). It is a tribute to the voracious appetite of venture capitalism that Selfridge, an acquaintance of Barker and enthusiastic first-nighter, recognized and indulged his stage portrait. Shortly after the play opened the *Tatler* photographed both men together on the roof of Selfridge's store. An accompanying caption identified them as "a dramatic genius" and "a business Napoleon" (18 October 1911, 77).

If Selfridge, like Worth, offered an historic reference point for debating the role of fashion in an advertising age, reception of the play was also shaped by the actions, through 1909, of some of Selfridge's more established rivals. The publicity that surrounded Selfridges' grand opening had caught competitors off-guard. By mid-spring, however, Harrods, Swan and Edgar, Peter Robinson's, and Whiteleys had all found convenient "anniversaries" about which to mount their own Selfridge-style appeals.[15] The most concerted response came from Harrods, whose managing director Richard Burbidge chose to host the store's diamond jubilee during the week of Selfridges' opening. While maintaining Harrods' position as "the shrine of fashion" and "one of the few smart rendezvous acknowledged and patronized by Society," Burbidge used the occasion to sponsor a series of ladies' concerts by Landon Ronald and the London Symphony (Adburgham, pp. 272–274). The following month, he announced plans for an in-store "Theatre of Dress," in which mannequins would parade gowns on a specially constructed stage. By October, Harrods' theatre was ready to host the store's winter fashion show, presenting garments first to select groups of favored clients, then to the public at large. The event was hailed in the *Queen* as "a red-letter day in the annals of the shopping woman" – evidence, it was claimed, of Harrods' ability to wield effectively "the power of money" (1 May 1909, xiii; 2 October 1909, 626). Through the campaign, Burbidge found a valuable ally in George Edwardes, whose Gaiety opened its 1909 season with *Our Miss Gibbs*, a musical comedy that functioned as part of the store's promotional push. A descendant of the shop-girl musicals of the 1890s, *Our Miss Gibbs, or The Girl at the Stores*, catered to a developing sensibility that through the pre-war period had come to demand as much emphasis upon its "shops" as its "girls." Three years earlier audiences had cheered Bantock's *The Girl Behind the Counter* (Wyndham's 1906), with its "shop till we drop" chorus of female consumers prowling about a thinly disguised Bon Marché.[16] *Our Miss Gibbs* completed the process, setting its tale of Mary Gibbs, a shop assistant at "Garrods [*sic*] Department Stores," in an identifiable replica of Harrods' "*Vestibule or General entrance*" with "*Staircases lead[ing] to the upper floors and glimpses of the various Departments*" (LCP, p. b).[17] Prominent among these was a Millinery Division, whose mannequins struck "*fashion plate attitudes*" in costumes supplied by its Harrods' original. Burbidge, who attended a matinée performance, commented upon the "realism" of the effect (Adburgham, p. 274). In production, the

episode was subsumed in a broad celebration of Edwardian consumerism. The play's authors, the team of "Cryptos," made the
point in an initial stage direction in which they insisted that
"photographic reproduction" was less important than creating *"the idea"*
of Harrods, and a sense of *"the luxury which makes shopping a matter of
enjoyment and not 'fag'"* (LCP, p. b).[18] What resulted was a West End
tribute to department store merchandising that placed upon London's most popular stage through the 1909 and 1910 seasons many of
Selfridge's more profitable assumptions about fashion, money, and
female emancipation.

It was to challenge such endorsements that Barker added to his
rotunda debate a Lucile-style mannequin parade, designed to
comment upon the motives and ethics of his exclusively male milliners
(plate 18). In its earliest drafts the play's third-act negotiations were
conducted over a sheaf of fashion-plate drawings distributed by Mr.
Windlesham, the effete manager of the latter-day House of Madras.
As State argues the virtues of modern retailing to a skeptical Philip
and openly cynical Constantine, Windlesham's illustrations are
circulated among the scene's drapery executives. Included are
renderings of a green velvet dress trimmed in buttons and ermine, a
transparent gown of flesh-colored silk, and a "severely soft" outfit,
designed, we are told, for "anti-suffrage" sensibilities. Also represented is a straw hat made from an upended fish basket. The last is
identified as the creation of "la belle Hélène," a Parisian "cocotte"
whose tastes, Windlesham claims, have helped influence West End
fashion. Some time, however, between the play's licensing on
17 January and its first performance on 9 March, Barker decided to
replace Windlesham's plates with live models promenading a
succession of high-fashion hats and gowns. His impetus seems to have
been the egalitarianism that through the decade had extended the
world of haute couture to a large middle-class market. In addition to
Selfridges' grand opening, the debut of Harrods' millinery theatre,
and the appearance of mannequin choruses in popular musicals like
Our Miss Gibbs and Paul Rubens's *Dear Little Denmark* (Prince of
Wales's 1909), the 1909–1910 season had witnessed the general
release of London's first fashion film, a documentary called *Fifty Years
of Paris Fashion, 1859–1909*. The experience this offered to "an even
wider audience" is summarized in the *Bioscope* description of "a lady
sitting in the picture theatre...imagin[ing] that she is in the
showroom of a fashionable modiste with the mannequins walking

18. Madame Hayward's mannequins (upper right) and Mr. Windlesham with the beehive bonnet of "la belle Hélène" (lower left) in "*The Madras House*: Sketched at the Duke of York's Theatre by H. M. Bateman" (*Bystander*, 23 March 1910).

around for her inspection" (Leese, p. 9). Barker may also have been
influenced by the highly topical "Gowning Street Scandal," which
resulted in widespread press censure of Mrs. Asquith, who had
offended home industries by entertaining Poiret's French mannequins at the Prime Minister's official residence (*Sketch*, 26 May 1909,
205). In any event, the addition of a full-scale fashion parade was
facilitated by the failure in mid-February of Seymour Hicks's *Captain
Kidd*, a closing which made available to Frohman's company a
number of London's most accomplished showgirls. Of these, Barker
signed Asta Fleming and Mary Brenda, eking out his entourage with
neophyte Mair Vaughan. The figures of all three approximated the
look popularized by Lucile and her imitators. For the outfits each
would wear, Barker turned to Madame Hayward, a Bond Street
couturière who had designed for a number of society plays in the
period. A rival of Lucile's, Madame Hayward had supplied gowns for
recent remountings of *The Liars* (Wyndham's 1900) and *Lady
Windermere's Fan* (St. James's 1904), as well as more contemporary
works by Sutro, Pinero, Barrie, and Maugham. Cited, like Lucile, for
her exuberant theatricality, she would by 1914 share honors with
both Lucile and Redfern as a defender, against Parisian imports, of
the allure of the specifically English model. A *Sketch* supplement for
that year shows one of Madame Hayward's Junoesque "girls"
descending a fashion ramp in a gown of pale-blue brocade with
draped bodice and a *décolletage* of blue tulle. The effect is clearly
"school of Lucile" (3 June 1914, 10) (plate 19).

For *The Madras House* Madame Hayward agreed to build to
Barker's specifications, realizing in three dimensions effects previously suggested in two. For this purpose, designer Norman
Wilkinson was asked to fit the play's third-act set with a curtained
alcove, "*a platform, a few steps high,*" and a frame of pink lights similar
to those Lucile had introduced at Hanover Square. Windlesham was
accordingly transformed into a "mannequin-driver" shepherding
across the stage "some new models" brought "from Paris only
yesterday" (p. 74). The supposedly French origin of Windlesham's
"models" – women as well as gowns – offered a convenient fiction
under which Madame Hayward was able to mock both period trends
and the house styles of her competitors. Among the half-dozen outfits
she created we can identify the buttons, fur trim, transparent silk,
and straw hat of Windlesham's originals. Yet when promenaded by
"*young ladies of pleasing appearance,*" smiling vacuously or attempting

19. "The Fair British Mannequin: From Madame Hayward's" (*Sketch Supplement*, 3 June 1914).

an effect of "*calculated ... innocence*," her realizations conducted a
visual argument in counterpoint to the deliberations of Barker's
drapers. The ironic Philip, most alive to such nuances, used them to
launch his own attack upon the fashion trade's most flagrant abuses.
When gown number five, Windlesham's dress of green velvet, is
praised by State as "the very thing, no doubt, in which some Peeress
might take the chair at a drawing-room meeting," Philip, eyeing its
buttons and fur, recalls both the sweated labor of Huxtable's
seamstresses, and the anti-pelt campaigns of their activist sisters.[19]
State's peeress, he retorts, might take her chair at a gathering of
either "the Humanitarian or ... the Anti-Sweating League." Gown
six, "grey with a touch of pink," is the "severely soft" ensemble State
had characterized as "an anti-suffrage Platform." Noting the dress's
square neck, Philip impishly suggests marketing the garment in
"suffrage" rather than "anti-suffrage" circles. It is, however, the hat
of "la belle Hélène" that allows Philip full scope for his sarcasm.
Here Madame Hayward chose to present a variation upon the
season's controversial beehive bonnet, a boulevard import much
disparaged by English critics. The previous winter, M. E. Clarke, the
Queen's Paris correspondent, had warned of an impending influx of
"hideous" hats, "enormous erections of coarse straw, flowers, and
ribbons, which make no pretence to line or curve, but merely strive
to be very big, and loud" (27 February 1909, 349). In London,
society columnists Mrs. Jack May and Ella Hepworth Dixon were
likewise alarmed by a proliferation of "gigantic thimbles" and
"inverted pudding basins," beside which "the German invasion-
scare paled in significance" (*Queen*, 20 February 1909, 305; *Sketch*,
31 March 1909, 353). Indeed, Windlesham's claim – that the hat's
origins could be traced to a French courtesan's decorated fish basket
– had been anticipated by a *Sketch* satire showing readers how similar
hats could be constructed from household waste baskets (14 April
1909, 10). Philip, however, is less concerned with the hat's appearance than with the symbolism of its production. Proclaiming
"la belle Hélène" both "a credit to her profession and externally ...
to ours," he reads in her innovations obvious links between
whoredom, fashion, and the mating rituals of West End London. In
endeavoring to sell both herself and the idea of herself, "la belle
Hélène" has entered the realm of what Windlesham calls "*la haute
cocotterie*." In such matters, Philip concludes, it may not be amiss "for
the professional charmer to set the pace for the amateur" (p. 77).

This final point is reinforced by the use Barker makes of the commercialized eroticism championed by Lucile and Poiret. As the play's drapers survey Madame Hayward's creations they find themselves confronted by their own responses to the bodies that both animate and are animated by Edwardian fashion. Most pertinent are the reactions of Major Hippisly Thomas, Philip's friend and London agent for Eustace State. Incapable of either Philip's wit or State's boosterism, Thomas is presented as the fashion trade's quintessential voyeur, neatly placed by State's mangled French as "the mean sensual man" (*l'homme moyen sensuel*). From the outset Barker is quick to distinguish his objectification of women from that of the asexual Windlesham. When Windlesham, "*quite unconscious*" of the "*separate existence*" of Madame Hayward's third mannequin, rearranges her costume in a series of maneuvers that "*seem to involve a partial evisceration of [her] underclothing,*" Thomas objects in a hoarse whisper: "I say, he shouldn't pull her about like that" (p. 76). The point is underscored when Thomas attempts to offer his chair to the mannequin in the "severely soft" gown. Here he is baffled by Windlesham's observation that in the corset needed to give the outfit its shape, sitting is not a possibility. The retort, once again, is both specific and barbed. The long-line corset introduced by Poiret to alleviate the inconveniences of the *Gache Sarraute* had the effect of substituting for the confinement of chest and waist that of the hips and upper legs (Steele, *Fashion and Eroticism*, pp. 224–228). Poiret's quip, already cited, about "freeing the bust" to "shackle the legs" was noted by suffrage writers like Elizabeth Robins, who complained of the appearance of the "hobbled" look at just that moment in history in which women had begun to stride forward towards freedom. Barker's juxtaposition of the Major's "chivalry" with new restrictions placed upon female movement prepares us for both State's self-serving defense of corsets, and Philip's attack upon the offending gown as "a conspiracy in three colours on the part of a dozen sewing women to persuade you that the creature they have clothed can neither walk, digest her food, nor bear children" (p. 90).[20] Similarly charged is Thomas's response to Madame Hayward's transparent dress of flesh-colored silk. In performance, Windlesham's fourth fashion plate becomes a Lucile-style affair of shimmering *diamanté*, "*the most elaborate evening gown that ever was.*" In fact, State's characterization of it as "more likely to be the centre of Emotion than Thought" winks knowingly at Lucile's most popular collection, her so-called "Gowns of Emotion."[21] On its first appearance, however, the garment's wearer miscalculates, making her entrance through the wrong alcove door. Without a backdrop of black velvet or wash of rose-colored light, Windlesham's model appears to "*separate*" from her gown, until, we are told, "*she seems half naked.*"[22] It is a moment reminiscent of Lyttelton's attack upon aphrodisiac evening wear in the fitting-room incidents of *Warp and Woof*. Windlesham, his aesthetic sense outraged, restages the entry. A manuscript note cues the frame of "pink lights" which helps to create what is now described as a "*vision of female loveliness*" (Typescript, Act III, p. 12). The Major, caught between middle-class prudery and a predatory sexuality that threatens to reduce him to the level of Corelli's Carlton lounge loafers, describes the effect as "damned smart." At the same time he suggests that, in England at least, it might be prudent to "have the shiny stuff marking a bit more carefully where the pink silk ends and she begins" (p. 86). Bemused by such shuffling, Philip brings the episode to a close, fixing Thomas's place in the era's commercial and sexual politics: "as long as it's Numéro Cinq, Six or Sept that attracts you…well…so long will Madras Houses be an excellent investment for Mr. State" (p. 95).

The larger issues of fashion and gender raised by such exchanges are explored in a leisurely fourth act that gave Barker some trouble. Indeed, both Bernard Shaw's *Misalliance*, produced by Frohman during the same season, and a brief conclusion Shaw wrote for *The Madras House* itself, have been viewed as attempts to urge Barker on with his story. Shaw's solution was to bring back Miss Yates, rechristened Miss Knagg, for a confrontation with Constantine over their illegitimate child (Dukore, "*Madras,*" 135–138). Barker does, in fact, arrange such a meeting, but wisely keeps it off-stage. What playgoers did see at the Duke of York's in 1910 focused instead upon domestic crises within the Madras family. Set in Jessica's West End drawing room, the episode begins with Constantine's departure. Declaring himself an unreclaimed sensualist distracted by Europe's public flaunting of its women, Constantine beats a strategic retreat back to his harem in "Southern Arabia." The remainder of the scene – almost half its length – consists of a long duologue between Philip and Jessica, in which Barker gathers in the thematic strands of his previous three acts, ranging over a variety of related topics, from surplus women and sweated labor to erotic advertising and the sustained gaze of "the mean sensual man." At its close, Philip reiterates his decision not to go about his father's business, preferring a seat on the County Council to State's offer of a Madras House directorship. Jessica, for her part, begins to sense the relationship of her own smart wardrobe to the ingrained ills of a free market economy. As husband and wife stand together before a blazing fire, the curtain rings down upon their joint affirmation that while sex may be biologically determined, gender is a social construct, and, as such, amenable to change: "Male and female created He them... and left us to do the rest. Men and women are a long time in the making" (p. 137). Coming at the end of an already long evening, the episode was dismissed by society papers as hopelessly "suburban," "nothing but talk, talk, talk" (*Modern Society*, 19 March 1910, 13). Even Max Beerbohm, who found in the rotunda debate "deeper and nimbler thought" than in any comparable scene in modern drama, suggested that viewers might think better of the play if they left after its third act (*Saturday Review*, 19 March 1910, 362–363). Yet if West End critics dwelt upon Barker's talkiness and Frohman's undeniably empty stalls, representatives of the women's movement and labor press found themselves increasingly drawn to the play's unconventional close. Margaret Llewelyn Davies in the *Manchester Guardian* proclaimed it "the greatest blow struck for women's freedom and for the civilization of both men and women in our time" (24 March 1910, 24), while the *Common Cause*, citing Barker's separation of sex and gender, maintained that "all friends of women owe Mr. Barker their most grateful thanks" in laying bare "the conspiracy of society against a woman's self-development and self-expression" (7 April 1910, 734). *Votes for Women*, lamenting poor attendance by drapery assistants who might have benefited from the play's lessons, also praised Barker's final encounter, speaking enthusiastically of the moment "when at last each drops the mask and speaks the truth" (8 April 1910, 439). Parallel comments came from Margaret Bondfield, who in correspondence with Barker talked scathingly of the abuses of the fashion trade. Thanking Barker for the play as a whole, but for its last act "most of all," she hoped that his final distinction between "conventionally provocative femininity" and true "womanliness" might offer practical models for "all women... groping towards freedom for self-expression" (unpublished letter, 25 March 1910). In the end, however, theirs were isolated voices, overwhelmed by lean receipts and a smug popular press that pretended to think that the play's attack upon sexual marketing was a backhanded defense of Constantine's polygamy. Indeed, the *Sketch*, glancing at the drama's repertory roots, waggishly dubbed it the new theatre's "Polygamy for the People Play" (16 March 1910, 309). By the time King Edward's death brought Frohman's season to a premature close, *The Madras House* had received only ten performances. It would not be revived for another fifteen years. Barker, in a private note to Gilbert Murray, confessed that he did not think a play could have been so willfully misconstrued – "even," he added, "by mean sensual men" (Salmon, p. 254).

How ill-prepared West End stages were to receive Barker's work may be gauged by the success at the Royalty Theatre, four seasons later, of Edward Knoblock's *My Lady's Dress*. Produced as part of a program of pieces staged by Barker's former colleagues John Vedrenne and Dennis Eadie, Knoblock's play focused, once again, upon the products and processes of Edwardian fashion. Indeed, at first glance, the work's auspices as well as its theme must have cheered avant-garde playgoers. Vedrenne had co-produced Barker's 1904–1907 Royal Court seasons, joining him afterwards in his brief but unsuccessful attempt to bring repertory theatre to the Savoy. Actor Eadie had been a mainstay of both the Court and Duke of York's companies. At the Court he had created the roles of Hugh Voysey (*The Voysey Inheritance*), Hector Malone (Shaw, *Man and Superman*), Henry Jackson (Hankin, *The Return of the Prodigal*), and Menelaus in Gilbert Murray's adaptation of *The Trojan Women*. At the Duke of York's he had appeared, appropriately enough, as Philip Madras, as well as Will Falder, the shifty-eyed anti-hero of Galsworthy's *Justice*. After the collapse of Frohman's 1910 venture, Eadie and Vedrenne had joined forces, attempting to establish a contemporary but commercially viable drama at the newly redecorated Royalty. In an informal statement of purpose, issued during their third season, both talked of staging experimental works of artistic merit. It was a claim born out by their championing of new drama stalwarts like Galsworthy and Hankin, as well as feminist playwright Edith Lyttelton. Yet in spite of the expectations to which it first played, *My Lady's Dress*, which ran for 176 performances in the spring of 1914, challenges from the point of view of an entrenched orthodoxy both the sexual and sartorial radicalism of Barker's *Madras House*. Cast in the form of a dream vision, revolving about the manufacture and marketing of a single ballgown, Knoblock's play opens in a pre-war boudoir with a society couple debating the costs and purposes of haute couture. The immediate object of their argument – the "dress" of the play's title – is a 55-guinea evening gown ordered by wife Anne from a Bond street modiste.[23] An elaborate affair of silk, sable, lace, and fabric flowers, it is presented as what Anne calls a "destroyer," intended to demolish the defenses of a lecherous lord who holds in balance the career of her husband. The remainder of the play, divided into three acts, called respectively "The Material," "The Trimming," and "The Making," consists of a drug-induced trance, in which Anne is visited by the workers who have produced and marketed her gown. Act I takes us to Lyons and Lake Como, where we find ourselves embroiled in the domestic hardships of the weavers and worm-farmers responsible for its silk. In Act II we are transported, in quick succession, to seventeenth-century Holland, nihilist Russia, and a Whitechapel sweatshop, to survey the lives of those who have supplied the gown's lace, fur, and artificial flowers. Act III, identified by Knoblock as the play's "big scene," takes place in a West End salon, where the dress is paraded in yet another eroticized fashion show, and Monsieur Jacquelin, the shop's proprietor, attempts to bully his models into acts of prostitution. At the scene's close, in what one reviewer called "the biggest thrill" of the season, an abused mannequin stabs the couturier with his own pinking shears. Through the play's otherwise sprawling structure, continuity is maintained by an elaborate doubling pattern that casts the actors playing Knoblock's husband and wife in the lead roles of each episode. A final scene returns us to the boudoir of Act I where we are asked to "reread" Anne's gown in terms of the far-flung suffering that has gone into its making.

The story in its own right was not without potential to disturb or disrupt. The critic for the *Queen* spoke nervously of its creeping socialism (2 May 1914, 894), while the *Lady's Pictorial* warned readers of the challenges to be faced in spending an evening with "a dramatized industry" (2 May 1914, 703). Yet if comparisons were drawn between Knoblock's text and the speculations of historians like H. T. Buckle (*Stage*, 23 April 1914, 22), the piece was, in the end, calculated to comfort rather than unsettle its viewers. A successful author with a keen ear for current debate, Knoblock had capitalized through the decade upon his ability to turn topical issues into spectacular entertainment. In *Kismet*, an oriental fantasy staged by Oscar Asche in 1911, he had built profitably upon English obsessions with Asiatic sexuality. Set in the seraglio of a Near Eastern despot, the piece included a scene in which "nude" harem girls splashed about in an on-stage pool. *Milestones*, written in collaboration with Arnold Bennett, premièred at the Royalty the following year. Its portrait of three generations of an English family made palatable the cultural distances between Victorians and Edwardians by reducing them to a succession of period styles. With an initial run of 607 performances, it proved one of the era's most durable hits. Like its predecessors, *My Lady's Dress* was conceived as commercial spectacle, and produced as a display vehicle for its performers. Eadie himself assumed the work's multiple male leads, while its principal female roles were allotted to Gladys Cooper, said to be the most photographed woman in England. Indeed, the presence of Cooper, a former Gaiety Girl and Helena Rubenstein model, became central to the play's meaning. Engaged largely for what the fashion press called "her talents as a clothes horse" (Morley, p. 150), her several appearances as both Anne and the various women who worked on Anne's gown encouraged viewers to see the play's action as a sartorial pageant, moving confidently from the rustic uniforms of its initial acts to the couture house collection exhibited in Act III. Knoblock, who confessed to weaknesses for stage realism and social extravagance, managed to work both into his text. For his opening scenes he had purchased, on site, garments actually worn by village workers in Italy and France. Even the loom used in scene iii was acquired, he tells us, from a Lyons workshop similar to its stage counterpart. For his Whitechapel episode, in which Cooper played a hunchbacked flower-maker, Knoblock produced "a white rather soiled apron" that "had already seen a year of service in a factory." When his action turned historical, dipping back two centuries to the Holland of Hals and Terboch, he instructed theatrical costumier J. L. Nathan to copy garments from old masters in the National Gallery (*Vanity Fair*, 7 May 1914, 13, 46). The point of such verisimilitude was to suggest a Darwinian push from peasant to peeress that culminated in the "real" evening gowns promenaded in Act III at Monsieur Jacquelin's. For this Madame Ospovat, a Mayfair couturière practiced in stage work, was asked to provide the only saleable items of the evening, five ballgowns meant to anticipate without irony or comment the fashions of the coming year. The effect was to complete a visual progress that tugged against not only the lessons of Barker's *Madras House*, but the rich tradition of seamstress iconography with which the play pretended kinship. How far it allowed Knoblock to undermine even the tentative liberalism of Hood's "Song of the Shirt" or Redgrave's *Sempstress* is revealed at the work's close, when Anne, in a rationalization worthy of Lyttelton's Poppy Price, resolves to wear her new dress to remind her of those who have sweated to produce it.

In his opening acts Knoblock eased the consciences of his viewers by separating the misery involved in his gown's making from the process of its production. In plays like *Warp and Woof* and *Miss Tassey*, the brutalization of drapery workers had been presented as a consequence of patriarchal capitalism, suffering imposed by a callous and indifferent industrial system. For Knoblock such hardship was casual, a sentimental and often picturesque accompaniment that ran parallel to, but was independent of, the business of haute couture. In Act I we witness the destruction of a crop of silkworms, and the consequent ruin of the young couple entrusted with its care. A following scene documents the case of a consumptive weaver whose loom-work, completed by his wife, no longer meets trade standards. In both instances the fate of Knoblock's characters is determined not by their occupations but by their participation in what the author calls "universal" passion. The silkworms, it turns out, die when a jilted lover exposes them to an unseasonable frost, while the weaver is saved when a compassionate colleague agrees to substitute his work for that of the weaver's wife. The pattern is extended in Act II, as we watch the assembly of the gown's trim. The lace-making of an opening scene provides a comic interlude in which an heiress escaping a foolish suitor disguises herself as a shop assistant. A companion piece shows a Russian trapper compelled by his wife to sell a particularly fine pelt he had hoped to save for their son. As in Act I, the trades of these figures are incidental to their fortunes. The closest we come to the ambience of "seamstress drama" is in Knoblock's Act II replication of a Whitechapel slum. Here Annie, a cockney flower-maker, works into the night making decorations for a Bond Street modiste. The hard conditions of her employment are clearly meant to suggest the worlds of Theodosia Hemming and Diana Massingberd. Yet while the accidentals are familiar enough – "*a dingy dark room ... covered with a muddy brown paper,*" a solitary lamp, a vast table strewn with "*countless pieces of coloured cloth*" – Annie's decision, before the scene is out, to seek refuge at a local orphanage is due entirely to the selfishness of her family. In brief, while Knoblock's workers undoubtedly suffer, the author effectively blocks any attempt to link their oppression to their work. In fact, not only is the fashion industry exonerated of wrongdoing, but the clothing incidents about which each scene is built are often directed against the workers themselves. Indulging in conventions of misogynistic satire that stretch back to Juvenal and Persius, Knoblock seems especially bent upon demonstrating the pride, greed, deceit, and vacuity of the women associated with Anne's dress. The silkworms in Act I perish because a young wife flirts with a vindictive pedlar. In the end her livelihood and that of her husband is sacrificed for a headdress, kerchief, and pair of gold earrings. The weaving episode argues, against all evidence, for the inferiority of women's handicrafts, while the trapper's wife is condemned as unfaithful and mean-minded. Even Annie, who cuts off her hair to finance the wedding of an ungrateful sister, becomes an emblem of snivelling dependence. Her decision, and final retreat to a state home, follows a passage in which she despairs of ever finding herself a husband. To liberal critic Richard Fletcher such stuff smacked of "anti-suffrage" diatribe. In a lengthy and often caustic review for *Vanity Fair* he summed up his objections to what he termed Knoblock's "gallery of minxes" by suggesting that the play might have been more appropriately titled "woman the parasite" (7 May 1914, 12, 48).

It is, however, in his third and final act that the full scope of Knoblock's agenda becomes clear. Set in the salon of Monsieur Jacquelin, an upstart couturier modeled loosely upon Paul Poiret, the episode attempts to reclaim for the fashion world some of the ground it had lost in Barker's *Madras House* rotunda.[24] The act opens in an outsized Adam room, created by architect Max Ayrton to serve as Jacquelin's inner sanctum. It is here that Anne brings the port-faced Sir Charles to tease him with the gown she intends to wear to his dinner party that evening. When the curtain is raised a mannequin show is already in progress. From an up-stage alcove, hung with the now obligatory black drapes, comes Messaline, "*a very tall striking girl*" in a *décolleté* outfit called "Danger Ahead." She is followed by models Trottinette and Psyche. The former, "*a petite Frenchy girl*," wears "Red Mullet," "*a glittering pink and red evening frock.*" Monsieur Jacquelin, we are told, is naming "a lot of gowns after dishes this season." Psyche, an Eastender with a broad Cockney accent, pauses significantly before Sir Charles. Her dress, described as "*a perfect, classic gown*," is called "Pagan Maid." The sequence of models and garments, as well as the interjections of Sir Charles, who wonders "how many more of these young women have they got in stock?" (p. 329), draws upon the practices of some of the era's most controversial designers to create an episode both topical and titillating (plate 20).[25] Indeed, the best informed in Knoblock's audience may have known that Messalina was a pet name Poiret had used for his mannequin Andrée, while the practice of calling gowns after gourmet dishes glanced back to the same designer's "Sorbet" tunic of 1912 (Mackrell, pp. 42–43).[26] Lucile, in turn, is suggested by the provocative names given to the remaining gowns, including Anne's *pièce de résistance*, the outrageously dubbed "Take Me." Also reminiscent of Lucile is a table at which Jacquelin's male callers are invited to paw through "*samples of delicate underwear.*" An extension of her Rose Room tactics of the nineties, the exhibit includes a locked bureau, in which we learn "much naughtier" items are kept for a "special clientele." Yet while the scene's blatant prurience masquerades as social comment, Knoblock is careful not to let moral indignation interfere with either the comfort of his viewers or the sales opportunities of his designer. Madame Ospovat, who had come to the play from dressing the "society ladies" in Eleanor Gates's *Poor Little Rich Girl* (New 1913), was given a free hand to create both Anne's black-and-white entrance gown, and the items worn by each of the scene's five mannequins. Unlike Madame Hayward who, in costuming Barker's rotunda parade, had to build to her playwright's designs, she was not obliged to submit either individual gowns or broader fashion trends to the corrosive scrutiny of cultural analysis. Indeed, the ensembles she created, in concert with milliner Michée Zac, functioned as such items traditionally functioned in society drama and musical comedy, offering West End playgoers a prospectus for the new season. Not surprisingly the novelties exhibited, from Messaline's "long overdress of cloth of silver" to Trottinette's "exquisitely draped gown of cerise mousseline de soie," attracted the attention of society and fashion critics, who had maintained a discreet silence in the face of Barker's *Madras House* collection. Outfits were sketched by May Nisbet for the *Pall Mall Gazette*, painted by Royal Academician John Collier, and described at length in the "Frocks and Frills" pages of *Play Pictorial* (24:145, 78–79). Perhaps, though, the scene's reception is best summed up in a *Bystander* spread that appeared the following fall. Presenting readers with a photographic sampler of Jacquelin's mannequins in their Ospovat gowns and Zac head-dresses, an anonymous writer declared Knoblock's

20. The mannequin parade from Act III of *My Lady's Dress* (*Play Pictorial*, 1914, 23:145).

work "A Play that is Playing – to Crowded Houses – the Part of a Guide to Autumn Fashions" (14 October 1914, 59).

The implications of such responses are clear enough. If Knoblock had advanced in his initial acts what amounted to an apologia for trade abuse, his couture house episode proclaimed the innocence of the gowns themselves. No matter how calculated their display or provocative their effect, freedom from blame could be established if, as Knoblock maintained in a post-production interview, one insisted upon the "exceptional" nature of Jacquelin's shop (*Vanity Fair*, 7 May 1914, 46). As a result, where Barker had shaped social indictments out of fashion statements like the beehive hat of "la belle Hélène," Knoblock's mannequins confront, not a questionable system, but a wicked couturier, played by Eadie as a slick, mustachioed villain. Jacquelin himself, it is argued, may be a despicable bounder, but his "creations" – and therefore the products of Mesdames Ospovat and Zac – can be purchased and worn with a clear conscience. The method is seen to best advantage in Jacquelin's presentation of Anne's title gown, the visual climax towards which the entire play builds. The outfit itself makes two entrances. It is first carried on by a shop assistant, a maneuver that permits Anne to review the silk, lace, sable, and fabric flowers assembled in the previous acts. Then, after Anne is hurried off-stage, allowing 90 seconds for an essential costume change, the dress reenters worn by Cooper as the mannequin Anita. Playing to Sir Charles in a now empty showroom, this newest and most alluring of Jacquelin's models, "*poses on the platform*" before making her way "*down the steps slowly in the 'mannequin' fashion.*" Sir Charles, distracted from the négligée table, grunts and "*ogles her eagerly.*" Before the scene is out he will, in the coded argot of the period, ask if she "sups." Through the encounter, we might note, the features of Madame Ospovat's gown, described as both "Merovingian" and "the very latest scream," go unremarked – including the fur and the kind of blinding detail work that had roused Philip's ire in the *Madras House* pavilion. The emphasis falls rather upon Jacquelin's personal baseness, as he attempts to ingratiate himself with Sir Charles by literally prostituting his model. Indeed, Knoblock's narrowing of terms defeats any attempt to see prostitution as Barker's broad metaphor for the fashion trade itself. Instead we cross into the realm of melodrama, both in the act's "thrilling" conclusion and its insistence upon grappling with specific cases rather than general principles. In a second scene played, to the discomfort of the Lord Chamberlain's Office, on the far side of the mannequins' curtain,[27] Jacquelin reads Anita his own lecture on the economics of surplus women: "As long as there's a glut of you females in the market, we've got the whip hand. And I for one won't let go the whip" (p. 348). Anita's response brings the scene to an appropriate close. Brandishing a pair of dressmaker's scissors, she stabs her oppressor, Polonius-style, through the arras. The moment, captured by theatrical photographers Foulsham and Banfield for the *Play Pictorial* (plate 21), elicited comments about Anita as feminist rebel. Yet the fraudulence of the image is suggested in a *Punch* cartoon by George Morrow, the reactionary artist responsible for Grundy's *New Woman* poster of 1897. During the first run of Knoblock's play, militant suffragette Mary Wood had slashed John Singer Sargent's portrait of Henry James at a Royal Academy opening (*Illustrated London News*, 9 May 1914, 747). Dovetailing the incident with John Collier's painting of Gladys Cooper as Anita – exhibited at the same Academy show – Morrow transformed Knoblock's mannequin into a clench-fisted radical armed with a demonic hat-pin. In so doing, however, he recast Cooper's features as those of a gaunt, mannish spinster (*Punch*, 13 May 1914, 377). The joke, such as it was, lay in the sympathy the play shared with traditional caricatures of feminist protest.

What audiences did take away from Knoblock's work was the reassuring spectacle of "several of the most beautiful women in London" wearing a succession of increasingly smart gowns. In fact, Vedrenne boasted of selling boxes as late as 10.00 p.m. for those who wished to see only the work's couture house parade. He likened the episode's after-dinner drawing power to that of the trial scene in *The Merchant of Venice*. Cooper, in such company, was first among equals, her status as fashion armature applauded by both popular and society critics. Even Somerset Maugham, looking back from the perspective of some four decades, commented upon the play's curious after-image: "The only recollection I have...is that [Gladys Cooper] wore a number of pretty frocks and looked even more beautiful than I remembered her [in her Gaiety roles]" (*The Sunday Times*, 19 July 1953, 9). What the fashion press had initially identified as the work's "socialistic tendencies" became a comforting backdrop, reminding patrons that haute couture participated benignly in what Knoblock, drawing once more upon drapery metaphors, called "the tragedy, comedy, and pathos [that] are all woven into the universal

21. Anita (Gladys Cooper) stabs the couturier Jacquelin through the curtain in Act III of *My Lady's Dress*.

fabric." The play's moral, a complete reversal of Jessica Madras's vow to rethink her wardrobe, is contained in Anne's final decision to wear her new gown to Sir Charles's society function. Its sensuality and ostentation, she reasons, will help to remind her of those less fortunate than herself.

Eadie, attempting to make the best of the situation, continued to behave as if he had produced a truly radical work. Speaking from the stage on opening night, he even likened the sweated labor that went into luxury dressmaking to the behind-the-scenes efforts of theatre tradesfolk, who worked "invisibly" on dramatic performances. The appeal, however, was not to all tastes. John Palmer, who had succeeded Max Beerbohm as drama critic for the *Saturday Review*, put the matter most succinctly. Condemning Knoblock for the "mangling of a great idea," and the production itself as "a cheap advertisement of [its actors'] versatility," he concluded by asking, with some incredulity, "What has happened to Mr. Dennis Eadie?" (2 May 1914, 565–566). A. A. Milne recorded similar objections in a *Punch* parody called *My Lord's Dinner*. Catching the cynicism of his copy, Milne offered readers a late-supping lord who falls asleep after a performance of Knoblock's play. Haunted by the "whitebait jockeys" and "macaroni-makers" who have put his meal on the table, he decides, upon waking, "not to eat so much in future." As he does so, he devours what a stage direction informs us is "*his fifth egg*" (29 April 1914, 326–327). For the majority of Knoblock's patrons, however, Anne's decision to combat social oppression by dressing well produced a collective sigh of relief. The play ran through the remainder of the season, being interrupted not by the outbreak of war, but by the temporary indisposition of Cooper. Its resumption the following fall was justified by one critic who reminded readers that "women, after all, must wear some clothes, even in war-time" (*Bystander*, 14 October 1914, 59). In restoring Eadie's Royalty stage and progressive intentions to the world of product advertising, Knoblock, once again, demonstrated his ability to gauge and exploit the sensibilities of his time. If the popularity of *My Lady's Dress* represented a setback for Barker's notions of repertory theatre, Knoblock's relationship to both his subject-matter and public suggests a parallel defeat for drama as a mode of cultural inquiry. Indeed, the implications of the play's success may be read in the post-war histories of both Barker and Knoblock, as well as those of their fashion trade counterparts. After the failure of Frohman's Duke of

York's season, Barker effectively ended his career as a professional dramatist. He continued to write, but reserved scripts for an ideal theatre that had not yet been called into being. Lucile found new markets in the cinema, where during the war she developed the so-called "fashion serial," adventure films like *The Strange Case of Mary Page* and *The Adventures of Dorothy Dare*, in which "action was stopped at intervals to describe the [heroine's] gowns" (Leese, p. 11). She also became principal designer to Florenz Ziegfeld, creating wardrobes for six successive *Ziegfeld Follies*, a number of which featured her own supermodel Dolores. Knoblock, together with Elinor Glyn, turned to screenwriting, working in both London and Hollywood. His flair for extravagant costume-pieces culminated in scenarios for Douglas Fairbanks's *Three Musketeers* (1921) and *Thief of Bagdad* (1924). Glyn, to the end a dazzling packager of modish eroticism, managed to outdo her colleagues. In a 1928 Paramount adaptation of her own *Cosmopolitan* short story, she popularized what she called the concept of "It" – or sex appeal – creating a touchstone of twenties sexuality out of a boyish, red-headed typist named Clara Bow.

CHAPTER 5

The suffrage response

To Lucile, the women's suffrage movement seemed "a huge joke."
Her head stuffed with images of stone-throwing spinsters, she
confessed to picturing the radical Mrs. Pankhurst as a "big, strong,
aggressive, dictatorial person." To be sure, Emmeline Pankhurst,
frustrated by the Fabian tactics of the law-abiding National Union of
Women's Suffrage Societies (NUWSS),[1] had, in 1903, helped to
found the Women's Social and Political Union (WSPU). The
organization was committed to highly public, confrontational, and
increasingly violent tactics, which Lucile termed "nonsensical" and
"undignified." Still, Lucile was delighted to receive a society
invitation to meet this "fighting suffragette" at Lady Cowdry's Dun
Edit Castle. She recounts in her memoirs how, while awaiting her
introduction, she fell into conversation with "a dear little woman ...
very simply dressed." Lucile took the opportunity to paint a lurid,
"almost abusive" portrait of Mrs. Pankhurst as "a powerful
masculine type of woman." To which, she records, "the gentle
woman beside her smiled and said, 'I am Mrs. Pankhurst!'" (Duff
Gordon, pp. 106–107). A curious meeting, this, of the new century's
most accomplished shaper of fashionable ladies and the period's
preeminent maker of feminist women. True to form, Lucile concludes
the episode by boasting that "they never made a suffragette of me."
In her eyes, in spite of Mrs. Pankhurst's surprising gentility, and what
WSPU supporters termed her "perfect dress sense," fashion and
politics could not meet. In this, moreover, Lucile was not alone. To
their opponents, in the face of abundant evidence to the contrary,
Edwardian feminists remained "masculine women ... with short hair,
billycock hats, and other articles of masculine attire," such attributes
cited, in turn, "as another argument against giving women the vote"
(*Votes for Women*, November 1907, 13). Big boots, cropped hair, ties,
collars, blue spectacles, and murderous umbrellas, were, off-stage as

well as on, a convenient shorthand for the unnatural woman, a would-be man who, like "real" men, had no fashion sense (plate 22).[2] According to such arguments, a woman's desire to participate in public life meant intruding herself into male territory, a trespass accompanied by a rejection of femininity and consequent assumption of what were agreed to be "male" characteristics, signaled most immediately through dress.[3] Furthermore, as ideals of fashionable womanhood shifted through the period from "massive daintiness" (Gernsheim, p. 85) to what might best be described as a kind of slender youthfulness, anti-suffrage iconography adjusted in response. As art historian Katrina Rolley has observed, "when the ideal woman is voluptuous the caricature must be skinny, and when the 'real' woman is slender, the suffragette is fat. She remains masculine, since masculinity is always in opposition to femininity" (67).

Yet despite such taunts, Edwardian feminists did not wish to be men. Nor did their vision of a new millennium include the dissolution of the sexes into a common gender. For while they fought for equal legal and political rights, a major tenet of the suffrage campaign was the belief that society as a whole needed woman's distinctive (often, it was argued, morally superior) voice. Putting a new spin upon the Victorian notion of "separate spheres," feminists insisted upon the value of complementariness, seeking, in the process, to secure their differences from men. Under the circumstances dressing fashionably became a political act. Indeed, through the period the most militant champions of women's rights deliberately embraced modishness as a means of providing a living retort to the labels hung upon them by hostile witnesses. They hoped, moreover, in the words of social historian Lisa Tickner, that "as active agents they need not passively endure the gaze of on-lookers who were curious or perhaps indifferent. They could invite it, respond to it, work with it and then move on." The result, Tickner argues, was that "their bodies were organized collectively and invested politically and therefore resistant to any simply voyeuristic appropriation" (p. 81). Of course, presenting themselves as a spectacle in order to create distance from their viewers did not guarantee control over the meanings thus generated. That said, Martha Vicinus's conclusion that because suffragettes "encroached upon male space, they could not effectively prescribe the desired response to their femininity" (p. 264) seems unduly deterministic. Without underestimating the difficulties involved, suffrage feminists worked to educate their observers. And for

22. "The Suffragette Nails her Colours to the Mast." Anti-suffrage postcard.

the most part they used the vocabulary of fashionable dress, the assumption being that whatever was modish would, by virtue of its modishness, be accepted as both feminine and womanly. There is, for example, surprisingly little concern with dress reform in suffrage literature. To have strayed too far into the camp of "rational dress" would, it was argued, have endangered a collective good for the lesser goal of individual comfort. The position is nicely summed up in a 1911 obituary for Victorian dress reform advocate, Lady Harberton:

She was a genuine dress reformer in her day, and not one of the modern humbugs who swagger about in "harem-skirts" with a music-hall pretence of being "advanced," because the vulgarer newspapers have found copy in it. Lady Harberton really tried to inaugurate the fashion for comfortable clothes and it almost seemed as if the bicycle might make them possible. But the chance slipped by and modern women are too busy with a great reform to make themselves conspicuous in a minor matter. (*Common Cause*, 11 May 1911, 74)

In brief, suffrage feminists opted to dress "conventionally" in unconventional circumstances. The main thrust of their argument remained women's right *as women* to occupy space previously occupied by men alone. They were aware, of course, of a reciprocal power to define (and contain) their actions as "indecorous and unwomanly" (*Sketch*, 13 January 1909, 24). Still, in the optimistic rhetoric of the WSPU's newspaper, *Votes for Women*, many considered the battle singularly winnable, even partly won: "Suffragette of the shorn locks, billycock hat, ill-fitting skirt, masculine habit, collar and tie – Beloved of the Caricaturist – where art thou? Vanished with the back numbers, if ever thou didst exist? Behold the present-day Suffragette pondering fashions side by side with political problems, for she is an essentially up-to-date being" (7 July 1911, 7).

In fact, so concerned was the WSPU with the appearance of its members that it adopted what Cicely Hamilton called a "costume-code." "A curious characteristic of the militant suffragette movement," Hamilton notes, "was the importance it attached to dress and appearance, and its insistence on the feminine note... All suggestion of the masculine was carefully avoided." This "was due," Hamilton maintains, "to a dislike of the legendary idea of the suffragette as masculine in manner and appearance," adding that "many of the militants were extraordinarily touchy on that point." The explanation, however, runs deeper than personal sensitivity. For the suffragettes (and their opponents) dress was a battle-ground. That "the outfit of a militant setting forth to smash windows would probably include a picture hat" (Hamilton, *Life Errant*, p. 75) was evidence of a sartorial stance that proclaimed a political message. It was not so much that "suffragettes attempted to keep the privileges of social distance by retaining women's traditional clothing" (Vicinus, p. 263) as that they attempted to articulate an ideology through their manipulation of fashionable dress. Sites of physical aggression, their dressed bodies also functioned as figurative fields of combat, a point underscored by the struggle of suffragettes to wear their own clothes in jail (signifying political prisoner status) rather than the "voluminous mustard-coloured woollen skirt, the tight bodice of the same colour and material, an enveloping apron patterned with broad arrows and, with all these, the mob cap that was apparently made in only one size" (Richardson, pp. 102–103).[4] In response to the symbolic implications of their appearance, one angry male proposed that as a solution to these "brawling women," magistrates be granted the power to have their heads shaved, since "no woman... emerg[ing] from the police-court bald as an egg, would dream of becoming a hooliganess" (*Sketch*, 17 April 1907, 29).[5] It was a proposition dramatized in *The Suffragette's Redemption*, a one-act anti-suffrage play by Inglis Allen (Royalty, Glasgow 1909) in which the recalcitrant husband of the piece concludes that the movement could not survive if prison authorities regularly shaved suffragettes' heads.

In the face of such tactics, Edwardian feminists tended to sacrifice what fashion theorist Valerie Steele has called "personal self-image" to the quite different demands of a "self-for-others" (*Fashion and Eroticism*, p. 46). This is not to suggest that they took no pleasure in how they looked, only that the emphasis invariably fell on how that look was read by others. Suffragette Evelyn Sharp, responding to the rotunda debate in Granville Barker's *Madras House*, took particular exception to a passage in which grand couturier Constantine Madras maintained that fashionable ladies, "encouraged to flaunt their charms on the streets," are "proud if they see busmen wink... Proud ... if they see a cabman smile" (p. 95). Without denying that they displayed themselves to particular ends, Sharp argued, in a piece called "Dress and the New Drama," that "smart" women no longer dressed to stimulate men's appetites but rather for what she, aware of the resonances of the term, called "the platform" (*Manchester*

Guardian, 22 March 1910, 16). An illustration of such chic suffragism is offered in an account Sharp provides of the savvy "combination of politics and millinery" that swirled about the hat stall at the WSPU's Women's Exhibition of 1909 (plate 23):

"What I want to know," said the lady in front of the glass, "is this: How long is this absurd Government going to hold out?" "It can't hold out. There's another by-election in West Edinburgh, I hear," said the holder of the hat stall, producing a burnt straw trimmed with purple and green flowers [the colors of the WSPU]. The conversation was a little intermittent, of necessity. "I can't wear burnt straw," said the other lady, waving it away. "Do you think you could do anything to this one to keep it from lopping over one ear? I met a man who knows Asquith yesterday, and he said –" "A bandeau would do it," interrupted the saleswoman, diving suddenly under the stall. "Do tell me what he said," she added when she emerged; and for the next minute or two I confess that the hat occupied a secondary place in the conversation. It resumed its rightful position, however, when the buyer asked, anxiously, if it would do for Sunday in Hyde Park. "Oh, yes," answered the seller, confidently. "I'm sure nothing would make it come off." This might puzzle some people who associate Sunday in Hyde Park with a band and a church parade; but nobody within hearing was puzzled. We all knew what it meant to stand on a lorry on a windy day, and most of us had listened in public to the lady who could not wear burnt straw. (21 May 1909, 688)[6]

If, however, picturing feminists as both politically astute and well dressed was a rebuke to the specter of masculine womanhood, it had the effect of generating an alternative form of anti-suffrage iconography, one that refused to grant serious purpose to a fashionably clothed woman. In a 1906 *Punch* sketch, for instance, two smart young ladies engage in "a duologue on hats," interrupted by one urging the other to canvass for the Conservative Party. Unfortunately zeal outruns ability and the new recruit finds herself campaigning for the Liberals. The scene ends as she laments that "We were talking sensibly about hats at the time, and I told you I didn't understand canvassing. Whereas, hats, now –" (31 January 1906, 86). As the piece closes they are back to "handling a topic they really do understand."[7] An episode from Wilde's *Ideal Husband* had explored similar terrain, as the dandiacal Lord Goring insisted, to Lady Chiltern's "mock indignation," that bonnets *must* be on the agenda at meetings of the Women's Liberal Association. Twelve years later in George Dance's anti-suffrage musical, *The Suffragette* (Clapham 1907), supporters of the cause were still being wooed from politics

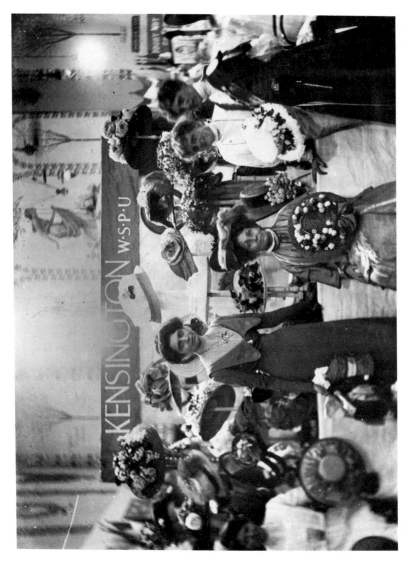

23. The hat stall at the Women's Exhibition at the Princes' Skating Rink, May 1909. The seated figure at the center is Emmeline Pankhurst.

with visions of female finery. Indeed, it became a recurring refrain in the popular and society press that suffrage events were but thinly disguised opportunities for women to admire one another's wardrobes. In *A Woman's Vote*, an anonymous anti-suffrage comedy written for performance at the Corn Exchange, Thrapston, in January 1909, Miss Mashers, a magnificently hatted suffrage worker, is disappointed to learn that newspaper accounts of a suffrage trial do not include dress descriptions, but merely observe that the accused all dressed charmingly, wearing picture hats that obscured them from view. The play closes with the announcement of the impending marriage of a suffrage colleague, the "cause" lost in a flurry of conversation about frocks and fripperies. As late as April 1914, what the *Evening Standard* dubbed a "Clothes and the Woman" controversy broke out in response to a *Times* correspondent's insistence that "men cannot imagine a woman dressed as women have seen fit to dress for the last few years, being competent to take any serious or worthy part in the work of the world" (14 April 1914, 8). Speaking for many in the movement, Marthe Troly-Curtin bitterly complained that "There is no satisfying men. Some say, 'If you want the vote you must deserve it by outward wisdom: the width of your clothes will be an index to the breadth of your mind'; while others would welcome strait-jackets as a uniform for Suffragist leaders" (*Sketch*, 22 April 1914, 82).

Because suffrage feminists did not view themselves as purely oppositional, but struggled instead for places within a system they wished to emend, they found themselves in a dilemma. It they did not dress "well" they were dismissed as unsuccessful women; if they did, they were condemned as "conventional" ones, incapable of thinking beyond their bonnets. They saw themselves, in the words of one *Votes for Women* columnist, steering between the Scylla of the "dowd, caring nothing for dress, and having neither the wit nor the taste to be becoming" and the Charybdis of "that woman [who] finds a full field for her intellectual activity in choosing frocks" (5 November 1909, 87). It was, moreover, a matter complicated by the attempt of a number of Edwardian feminists, including Sharp, Hamilton, and Christabel Pankhurst, to separate femininity from eroticism, a distinction Margaret Bondfield had drawn in her 1910 letter to Granville Barker about the differences between "conventionally provocative femininity" and "true womanliness." They wanted their dress (and appearance) to signify a womanliness that did not

covet "the cabman's wink." Even while Lucile and her colleagues
were successfully harnessing the commercialized sexuality of the
couture house parade, such feminists sought to break the link
between eroticism and salesmanship. Culturally contained and
explained according to sexual function, they attempted to make an
end-run around sexuality, consciously rejecting sex as a means of
selling their message. They accordingly spurned the "advice" of
Marie Corelli who, while condemning the institutionalized prurience
of Edwardian fashion shows, could, in a tract called *Woman or
Suffragette?*, echo Granville Barker's *Madras House* entrepreneur,
Eustace State, in endorsing a woman's prerogative to "dazzle and
conquer":

> A charming woman likes to make the most of her charm, – and she is
> perfectly justified in looking as lovely as she can by natural and hygienic
> means. She knows that a sweet, wholesome, lovely, womanly face and form
> must needs create a sweet, wholesome and lovely influence. Indeed, I am not
> at all sure whether, if a bevy of dainty, beautiful, exquisitely dressed women
> were to quietly enter the Lobby of the House of Commons, and there plead
> with tuneful eloquence and reasonable dignity for their "suffrage," they
> might not so bedazzle and bewilder the members as to cause these gentlemen
> to lose their heads entirely, – even to the extent of granting them anything
> and everything on the spot! (pp. 37–38)

Corelli's "natural" woman – a woman *because* she is not a suffragette
– is an adept practitioner of the much-touted "indirect influence"
that anti-suffragists maintained was the only "influence" women
needed. According to Corelli, there were no "pretty women among
those who clamour for their 'rights'… because every pretty woman
knows she has every 'right' she can ever want, – the right to govern
man completely and draw him everywhere after her like a steel filing
drawn by a magnet" (p. 38). Reviewing the Women's Coronation
Procession of 1911, a massive show of strength for the suffrage cause
extending over 7 miles,[8] a like-thinking *Tatler* correspondent maintained that "Twenty pretty girls suitably arrayed would have been
far more effective and far less trouble" (28 June 1911, 372–373).

In its crudest form it was a position reinforced by stage caricature,
the "feminine" suffragette – like Grundy's "feminine" New Woman
of the previous decade – portrayed as a creature at war with her own
essence. In Edward Knoblock's comic fantasy *The Faun*, produced at
the St. James's Theatre in the summer of 1913, a year before the
completion of *My Lady's Dress*, viewers were assured that pretty

suffrage worker Lady Alexandra Vancey, described in a stage direction as a "*modern type of woman, [but] not masculine*" (p. 118), merely required the awakening of her own better self to forsake politics for more "womanly" goals. When a satyr in a leopardskin arrives to release the unconscious desires of Knoblock's characters, Lady Alex, to the accompaniment of an off-stage thunder clap, falls into the arms of a manly admirer. Yet while it is easy enough to smile at such stuff, even politically astute writers like Elizabeth Robins found it difficult to determine how fashionable suffragettes would be read in performance. In *Votes for Women!*, produced in 1907 as part of Granville Barker's final Royal Court season, Robins had created, in the figure of Vida Levering (played by Edith Wynne-Mathison), the English stage's first sympathetically drawn "smart" suffragette. Initially presented as an elegant weekender accepted in society circles, Levering appears as both a radical feminist, defending the actions of WSPU extremists, and an impeccably dressed lady, whose hand is actively sought in marriage. Herself aware of the power of clothes, and the protection offered by fashionable dress, Levering speaks pointedly of the predatory gaze men direct at women whose costumes declare them social inferiors. In Act I Levering is displayed in a provincial drawing room, in Act II on the speaker's plinth at a Trafalgar Square suffrage rally. In both instances she is a model of Edwardian deportment – well groomed and handsomely outfitted, down to the monogrammed handkerchief that will play its part in Robins's unfolding plot. Yet while Levering, a conscious attempt to challenge on stage the iconography of the mannish suffragette, offered well-disposed viewers a positive and attractive alternative, a distinct minority registered confusion at the significance of her look. The *Times* reviewer, for one, found himself wondering whether Robins's heroine was, at heart, "yearning to be married." Why else, he asks, would she "take such care to make the best of her good looks and pretty figure and wear such charming frocks? Is it to please other women?" (10 April 1907, 5). Echoing Corelli and anticipating the *Tatler*'s account of the Coronation Procession, he assures readers that "the cause would make much more headway than it does if all its advocates were as fair to look upon, as agreeable to hear, and as beautifully dressed" (5). The critic for the *Clarion* responded in kind, simply shuffling bodies in deference to his paper's proletariat clientele. Dismissing Levering as conventionally patrician, he champions instead the play's working-class platform speaker Ernestine

Blunt, a composite figure Robins had modeled in part upon Christabel Pankhurst. "Pretty little Dorothy Minto," who assumed the role "in neat shop-girl attire," was praised accordingly as "a sweet and comely maiden." Attention was particularly drawn to the sensuality of "a wisp of nut-brown hair straggling in attractive carelessness from under her toque." Enumerating the many charms that "nearly converted us all," he concludes by informing *Clarion* readers that nothing could have answered the attacks of the Yellow Press more tellingly than "the deprecatory and appealing smile with which" – while referring to herself as a "female hooligan" – she "fill[ed] the air as with a fluid caress" (19 April 1907, 3).

Refusing to be dismissed as failed women or patronized as "pretty" ones, feminist playwrights used the stage to fight back. In June 1908 Cicely Hamilton and Bessie Hatton established the Women Writers' Suffrage League (WWSL), an organization that vowed to "use the pen" to secure the vote (*Suffrage Annual*, p. 137). Elizabeth Robins served as its first President. Later that same year, Hamilton and Robins both became founding members of the Actresses' Franchise League (AFL), a society committed to casting "the speeches and pamphlets of the earlier Suffrage societies in[to] Dramatic form" (*Suffrage Annual*, p. 10). Under the directorship of Inez Bensusan, the group established a playwriting division to promote the production and publication of suffrage scripts. Among the pageants, duologues, and farces staged during the League's first season was a series of one-act plays by Hatton, Gertrude Jennings, and Bensusan herself that, like the shop dramas of Lyttelton and Baker, focused upon the relationship between a woman and her clothes. In Bensusan's *The Apple* and Hatton's *Before Sunrise*, suffrage sympathizers were reminded of the manner in which women had traditionally been contained and controlled through dress. In the former, presented at a Royal Court matinée in March 1909, protagonist Helen Payson finds herself sexually exploited by her employer and "passed over" by her family, which distributes her share of a small legacy to her pampered brother, the "apple" of the play's title. The predicament of women in Bensusan's world is realized in a subtle and compelling "clothes incident." As the play opens Ann, Helen's unemployed sister, is shown at work on a gown that will enable a third sister, Norah, to attend a society ball. When Helen attempts to assist, using Ann as dressmaker's dummy, Ann finds herself tangled in Norah's finery. Unable to extricate herself, she is, as Bensusan's stage directions make clear, trapped by the clothing itself. In Hatton's *Before Sunrise*, performed at the Albert Hall Theatre in December of the same year, a sympathetic bluestocking, anatomizing "the false conditions" under which women live, talks explicitly of the ways in which "our minds are enveloped in moral stays, just as our bodies are pinched and tortured to take on an unnatural and ugly shape" (p. 64). In *A Woman's Influence*, written for the WSPU Women's Exhibition of 1909, Jennings offers a more positive alternative, combining dress issues with an attack upon the suffragette's bane, the doctrine of "indirect influence." The play's villainess, Mrs. Aline Perry, is presented as "*a pretty babyish little woman ... very well-dressed,*" who deliberately uses her erotic powers to wheedle a man first to political action and then, when she realizes that her own financial interests are involved, political inaction. A suffrage take upon Corelli's ideal "charmer," Jennings's "woman of influence" stands condemned beside the play's heroine, a "*grave, beautiful*" worker for women's rights, and the latter's assistant, "*a pleasant, comely young woman, with very neat hair and a decided manner*" (p. 69). Assured without being masculine, committed without being hysterical, well dressed without being seductive, these are models for feminist action, their virtues underscored by juxtaposition with the dubious antics of a stage coquette.

By 1910, theatrical proselytizing had become so effective that Edith Craig, founder of the Pioneer Players and member, she boasted, of ten suffrage societies, urged co-workers to "write suffrage plays as hard as they can," citing the manner in which such pieces managed to "get hold of nice frivolous people who would rather die sooner than go in cold blood to meetings" (*Votes for Women*, 15 April 1910, 455). It was, however, in the commercially produced dramas of Emily Morse Symonds that suffrage positions on women and dress reached their broadest public. A member of the London Women's Suffrage Society and the Women Writers' Suffrage League, Symonds, who wrote under the pseudonym George Paston, was an established author whose œuvre included popular biographies of Lady Mary Wortley Montague and Alexander Pope, as well as novels of contemporary life such as *A Modern Amazon* (1894) and *The Career of Candida* (1892). Her first full-length drama, *The Pharisee's Wife*, had been produced by Granville Barker at the Royal Court in July 1904. Praised for its "unfeminine" scope – it "tackled a large subject in a serious spirit" (*Saturday Review*, 16 July 1904, 75) – it was faulted, as were Barker's own works, for its avant-garde talkiness. Symonds, however, was also attacked for questioning and transgressing gender boundaries. Even her decision, shared by a number of sister writers, to call herself "George" provoked Max Beerbohm, in a generally favorable review, to digress upon the downfall of a once "manly" name:[9]

> Especially must it irritate gentlemen, who having been baptized George, must either shed the name or be ever dimly associated with womanhood by their readers ... If Mr. Meredith were writing "Richard Feverel" to-day, he would presently burst on the world as "G. Meredith." Otherwise, everyone would suppose him to be a lady. Even after we had read the first few pages, and had discovered quite certainly that this new George must be an authentic man, we should always be hampered by a vague, subconscious vision of him as a very remarkable lady. (*Saturday Review*, 16 July 1904, 74)

Yet if a name could be said to make or mar a man, what was it that made a woman? It is a question that Symonds went on to explore in two plays dealing exclusively with gender and dress. The topic is initially broached in *Clothes and the Woman*, a three-act comedy performed by the Pioneers in May 1907, as part of Norman McKinnel's second subscription series at the Imperial Theatre.[10] The piece was subsequently revived in Manchester by Annie Horniman, first at the Midland Hotel Theatre that October, then, in 1908, at the Gaiety, where, according to critic Rex Pogson, "it ensured the financial success" of the season (p. 35). The reasons for the play's popularity are not far to seek. In an action that anticipates *Diana of Dobson's*, without raising that play's unpleasant questions about labor conditions or trade abuse, Symonds charts the sartorial progress of Robina Fleming, an emancipated "bachelor girl" who supports herself by hack writing. We first encounter her as "*a work-a-day woman in an old and comfortable working costume*" consisting of "*loose slippers*," a "*shabby leather belt*," "*a short mud-coloured skirt*," and a "*loose baggy drab coloured blouse which does not match*." She is "*sallow*" of complexion, wears "*goggles*," and "*has her hair brushed back from her forehead, and twisted up into a hard knot in the nape of her neck*" (p. 7).[11] Initially played by Edith Wynne-Mathison – who in May 1907 was simultaneously appearing as Robins's Vida Levering – Robina is an obvious candidate for a traditional make-over. So much so that Symonds insists in an initial aside that "*Robina looks no plainer than the average woman would look in such attire*" (p. 7) – later informing us that a modish rival "*prettily dressed in a fluffy-flowery frilly style ... looks as pretty as the average English girl of twenty should look in such attire, but not prettier*" (p. 15). The two comments, suggesting the extent to which the play's women are viewed as sartorial constructs, become Symonds's text for an elaborate object-lesson that takes Robina first into the world of haute couture, and then, after a return to the "shabby old clothes" of Act I, to an agreeable middle ground, upon which she rejects both the sensuality of the fashion plate and the negligence of the dowd.

The agent for Symonds's metamorphosis is Mrs. Desmond, a widowed school chum of Robina, who is "*not only a woman of fashion,*" but one who – like Wilde's dandy *raisonneurs* – has "*acquired a touch of social philosophy.*" Observing that men "wouldn't look at Venus if she wore a dun coloured shirt and bald forehead," Symonds's clothes philosopher arranges for Robina a "face treatment" with an improved "colourless fluid," a 2-guinea manicure, a co-ordinated toilette of veils, openwork stockings, slips, petticoats, gloves, a hair "transformation piece" from a Bond Street emporium, and, above all, £300 worth of Parisian frocks and hats. If the alteration cannot be worked by "clothes alone," Robina is assured, it "can be done by clothes *and* the woman" (p. 22). Indeed, punning upon Robina's professional push, she insists that "cheek" will be "called chic in a Paris hat." The fruits of such labor are displayed in Act II, set in "*a pretty garden room*" in Mrs. Desmond's Pangbourne residence. Here, to the accompaniment of an off-stage band, Robina appears in two extravagantly modish outfits. In the first, "*a very smart and audacious-looking gown ... she conveys the effect of a very chic and brilliant French-woman among a group of average well-dressed but rather ineffective Englishwomen*" (p. 25). In the second, an evening dress "*of soft but brilliant colouring, which should have diamanté or jewelled trimming,*" she is praised as an "orchid" and worshiped as "a miracle." The effect of both ensembles is registered by the response of three former male acquaintances. For each the "pal" they had known as "old Bobbins" disappears behind the tulles and *diamanté* of Mrs. Desmond's purchases. Robina, moreover, has learned to "play ... up splendidly to [her] clothes." Employing a repertoire of seductive mannerisms, as she toys with her fan, flowers, and cigarettes, she explicitly attributes her altered conduct to her new gowns, confiding afterwards that she could have never "behaved decently ... in those frocks" (p. 50). Outshining her rivals, at least one of whom is dressed by Poiret, Robina champions what she calls the cause of "clothes –

backed by brains, impudence, and a ready tongue." By the scene's end, condemned by a disappointed lover as "a vain, heartless, frivolous, little baggage," Robina has accumulated a roomful of suitors. Among her conquests are numbered, appropriately enough, a journalist turned fashion writer, and a fashion-plate artist determined to draw "figures" rather than "bodies." Her defense for turning the heads of such "silly asses" is the manner in which men have chosen to see women. "Could I have won the game if men hadn't been – what they are?" she asks a fourth superannuated admirer: "I was the same woman before I began to masquerade. But did any man admire me then – much less love me?... You only love with your eyes – you never look beyond the pretty frocks, the rosy cheeks, the shining hair" (pp. 56–57).

Yet Symonds is unwilling to close the play with either the cynicism or celibacy implied by the outburst. In Act III we find Robina back in her Doughty Street lodgings "*dressed exactly as in Act 1.*" Here, bolstered by the support of a female colleague, who assures her that "how she looks" makes no difference at all, she commits herself to two social experiments. For the first, she summons before her the well-dressed Ethel Warrender, and Ethel's fiancé, fashion artist Claude Goring, now obsessed by Robina herself. In a spirit of female camaraderie, Robina, who "*places herself at Ethel's side*" lectures her rival on female independence. In the demonstration that follows, Robina presents Claude with "the essential part" of herself, removing from a cupboard a dressmaker's dummy attired in the hairpiece, curls, gown, and hat she had worn through the previous scene. Pursuing Claude down-stage "*with the dummy*" she informs him of the lessons to be learned when a "woman ... [is] actually taken to pieces before his eyes" (p. 54). At this conclusion, we are told, Ethel "*smiles faintly.*" Robina's second lesson is conducted for a more sympathetic admirer, a physician who professes not to have been taken in by her Act II masquerade. Yet while Dr. Lomax, who offers marriage, continues to deny the efficacy of "dressmaker's magic," he must face Robina's accusation that while he had known her "for a good many years" he "never wanted to marry" her until he "saw [her] in make-up – playing a part." His response, which stresses process rather than product, enables Symonds to articulate the play's central theme. When Robina looked like "Old Bobbins," the doctor confesses, he found it hard to realize that she was a woman. "For a woman's toilette," he explains, "is a part of her ritual. It is to her what his vestments are to a priest, his form to a sportsman, his style to the author." When Robina replies "Then, if the style is the man – ?" Lomax completes the phrase: "The clothes are the woman... For the first time I've seen you practising your ritual, and it opened my dull eyes to the fact that my old pal was a woman" (p. 58). What follows is the scene's second deconstruction, as Robina reenters in "a simple but well cut and becoming... skirt and white lawn or muslin blouse" (LCP, Act III, p. 22), placing herself between the dressmaker's dummy, now dubbed "the fascinating Miss Fleming," and a chair upon which she props up the muddy skirt and dun blouse of "old Bobbins." The play's lesson, its appeal both broadened and diluted by the pairing-off of Robina and Dr. Lomax, is stated at its close. An emancipated woman can reject the extremities of fashion without becoming an object of ridicule. For Edwardian feminists the point was underscored by the resemblance of Robina's "well cut and becoming" final ensemble to the white blouse and skirt combinations recommended in the suffrage press.[12]

The more militant implications of *Clothes and the Woman* are explored in *Tilda's New Hat*, a one-act comedy staged at the Royal Court in November 1908. First performed under the auspices of the Play Actors, a group that included on its Council both Hamilton and Bensusan, as well as AFL member Winnifred Mayo, the piece soon recommended itself to West End managements. In January 1909 it was revived at His Majesty's as a curtain-raiser for Shaw's *The Admirable Bashville*, and the following season at Wyndham's and the Prince of Wales's, where, in the company of Monckton Hoffe's *The Little Damozel*, it enjoyed a run of ninety-eight performances. A discourse on dress that plays ironically with Hamilton's observation that woman "is not woman at all – until man has made her so" (*Marriage as a Trade*, p. 20), the work's radicalism is cloaked in efficient good humor. Symonds's protagonist, Tilda Fishwick, is, like Robina, an independent woman. Here, however, the resemblance stops. A "*dark, showy-looking girl*," who earns her keep in a jam factory, Tilda lavishes most of her salary upon personal adornment. Her first appearance is made in "*a fawn skirt*," "*a bright blue satin blouse, very fussily made, with a large cape collar of white crochet lace*," "*a string of big pearl beads*," and "*a large gilt brooch*." Sporting the latest in smart coiffures, her "*black hair [is worn] puffed out over her ears, coming low on her forehead in a large fringe or three sausage curls*." When the curtain rises, she is discovered "*pinning black ostrich feathers*" into the "*huge*" – and in 1908 very modish – "*black velvet ... hat*" of the play's title (pp. 7–8). For Tilda, however, such attire is a badge of personal independence. Symonds makes as much clear in an opening exchange with Mrs. Fishwick, as Tilda contrasts her own broad-brimmed hat with the "*nice chip bonnet trimmed with ribbon and tied under the chin*" that had been for her mother a mark of domestic service (pp. 7, 9).[13] Yet Tilda's central struggle is not with Mrs. Fishwick, but with the sentimentally named Daisy Meadows, who blames Tilda for alienating the affections of Walter Emerson, a Cockney printer who plays "Rowmeo" in local theatricals. "*Very plainly but tidily dressed in a dark skirt, with a cotton or flannelette shirt ... [and] a flat hat, simply trimmed with ribbon*" (p. 17), Daisy levels specific charges against the particulars of Tilda's wardrobe – especially her "hat and feathers," "dressy blouse," and "padded hair." Tilda's response is to play Mrs. Desmond to Daisy's Robina, outfitting her in a manner designed to win back the erring Mr. Emerson. In the process of remaking Daisy, Tilda, however, begins to take on the externals of Daisy herself. Replying to Daisy's " – if I had a hat like that – ," Tilda puts her own hat upon Daisy's head, agreeing to lend it to her while she refashions Daisy's own. What follows is an exchange of blouses, and even coiffures, as Tilda uses her hair frame to roll Daisy's curls forward, and, in an attempt to show Daisy the drabness of her former style, "*flattens her [own] front hair back, leaving her forehead bare,*" likening the look to popular caricatures of protesting suffragettes:

This is how *you* walk out with a chap. Fit to scare the motor-buses. Ever see a suffragette after a kick-up with a policeman? The latest fashions for 'Olloway, the new winter health resort. Votes for women! (p. 21)

The ritual prepares us for a theatrical double-take as the returning Mr. Emerson first mistakes the redressed Daisy for Tilda, then, realizing his error, elects to "walk out" with Daisy in Tilda's clothes rather than Tilda in Daisy's. At the play's end, Tilda, unlike Robina, is offered no consolation in romance. Her triumph resides in her ability to live in a world without "Rowmeos," and the kinship she finds with both Daisy and her own mother. The curtain, which descends upon Tilda and Mrs. Fishwick dancing and singing music hall refrains, is raised for a reprise, in which Tilda appears "*still dancing*" while her mother "*looks on admiringly.*" It was a moment, the *Sketch* declared, that seemed to put "the whole theory of the solidarity of women ... into dramatic form" (18 November 1908, 191).

The lesson of such plays was not lost in the wider theatre of suffrage politics, as activists conducted a parallel campaign by exercising their power as fashion consumers. In 1908, dress columns had begun to appear in the WSPU's *Votes for Women*. That the most militant of suffrage publications should feel the need for such features suggests how fully sartorial argument figured in combating the notion of civil disobedience as itself unwomanly. The law-abiding "suffragists" of the NUWSS, as we shall see, determined not to admit fashion columns to the pages of the *Common Cause*. In their more moderate publication, they feared, clothes-consciousness might be open to misinterpretation. In both instances the decision reached was informed by a desire to assure onlookers and members alike that "womanliness" and political commitment were emphatically joined. For that reason no dress column that did appear in the radical press was free from editorial comment. Advocating a politicized modishness, suffrage fashion writers championed a look both smart and militant, a combination made possible by the decision of suffrage societies, as of 1908, to proclaim their numbers by dressing in distinctive colors. Once again, the WSPU led the way, requesting members in the spring of that year to affirm their allegiance by wearing purple, white, and green, seasonal shades whose selection was rationalized after the fact by the assignment of allegorical significance.[14] Other groups followed suit, the NUWSS adopting red, white, and green, the WFL green, gold, and white, the WWSL black, white, and gold, and the AFL white, pink, and green. Trimmed in such colors, suffrage dress, complemented by the banners and ceremonial paraphernalia of each society, became an essential tactic of the street pageants and public demonstrations that were the movement's most visible means of declaring its support. They appeared to particular advantage in the 1911 Coronation Procession, a collaborative effort of the WSPU and NUWSS that attracted more than 40,000 participants. On that occasion, the contingent from the Actresses' Franchise League was photographed wearing the requisite scarves in League colors fastened across white gowns. Carrying poles with green and white streamers, the group marched beneath a pink and green banner displaying the traditional masks of comedy and tragedy.[15] The effect is at once both feminine and militant (plate 24).

Indeed, the simultaneous appearance of "colors" and fashion columns may not have been coincidental. From the anonymously

24. The Actresses' Franchise League at the Women's Coronation Procession, June 1911.

penned "The Suffragette and the Dress Problem," which appeared in the 30 July 1908 number of *Votes for Women* (348), virtually every dress article to appear in suffrage publications spoke of the impact of current fashions when carried out in "the colors," as well as the meanings such garments acquired when worn by womanly women. Even evening wear was not exempt. In the eyes of a fashion critic for the *Suffragette*, the newspaper which, in the fall of 1912, replaced *Votes for Women* as the official organ of the WSPU,[16] such garments too had their educative function. After urging the claims of certain furs, reduced from 100 to 70 guineas, the columnist asks her obviously moneyed readers to "imagine a drapery of [WSPU] purple velour falling with négligé grace into the new square train, over an underdress of chiffon-veiled silver lace" (1 November 1912, 38). The *Vote*, published by the radical Women's Freedom League, for two seasons debated whether or not to include fashion coverage. In an initial editorial an attempt was made to establish a dress policy. Readers, addressed as "the increasing class of educated women who have intellectual, industrial, or public interests," were informed by Cicely Hamilton and Marion Holmes that the paper's priorities were "not quite" those of "the reader to whom the ordinary fashion article addresses itself." Its concern would be rather with "the busy woman, part of whose business it is to be suitably dressed," and who "would welcome articles that did not describe the extremest and most ephemeral fashions, but that really helped to make her task easier" (8 September 1909, 1). When in the spring of 1911, regular fashion columns began to appear, they took the form of shopping excursions narrated by house author Louise Thomson-Price. Developed from occasional shorter pieces that had puffed certain of that paper's regular supporters, Thomson-Price's column used the *Vote*'s rota of advertisers as a consumer guide. Motivated, cynics might suggest, at least partly by self-interest, the first stop on Thomson-Price's shopping odyssey was Madame Louise's millinery emporium where readers were urged to purchase the WFL hat the writer had herself designed.[17] Yet even here we are never far from political calculation. A black straw *chapeau* trimmed with a cockade of green, white, and gold, the item was bought, Thomson-Price assures us, by her (fictional) anti-suffrage shopping companion whose conversion to the cause would be documented in a later column: "That the wearing of our colours first set her thinking on the Suffrage question, however, proves that a Suffragette's shopping day – in the company of an 'anti' – may be wrought with other possibilities besides those of supporting *Vote* advertisers" (3 June 1911, 75).

Yet supporting suffrage advertisers was central to the purpose of such features. There is not a single piece on fashion that does not fail to make the case for patronizing advertisers; conversely there are virtually no columns that praise an establishment that did not advertise with the paper in question.[18] In fact it could be said that the genesis of such columns lay in a desire to offer additional copy to regular advertisers who provided a major source of suffrage revenue. Every suffrage paper published "shopping guides" that were little more than lists of such advertisers, as well as recurring reminders to patronize only those establishments. Indeed, so vital was advertising income that the *Vote* announced a contest in 1910 to award prizes to those readers with the most receipts for goods purchased. The moderate NUWSS progressed through the period from requesting *Common Cause* readers to "please support our advertisers" to urgent appeals to "deal exclusively with them." In a more bellicose mood, the WSPU, in an editorial called "Whet Your Weapon," implored *Votes for Women* readers to approach shopping with the precision and single-mindedness of a military campaign:

Many of the most highly reputed firms advertise weekly in the columns of *Votes for Women*. These firms are not philanthropic societies. They are business firms, run on sound business lines. If they find it pays them to advertise in *Votes for Women* they will advertise – if they find it doesn't, they won't. The more money that flows into the coffers of our advertisement department the better our paper can be made, the wider its circulation becomes, the further its influence reaches. Therefore, let every woman who believes in this cause never enter a shop that does not advertise in *Votes for Women*, and let her deal exclusively with those firms who do, and inform them why. (2 June 1911, 579)

Nor were those firms that did advertise in the suffrage papers slow to respond to the needs of new markets. *Votes for Women*, once more, pointed the way. In its first dress column it puffed the paper's dress advertisers, but in such a way as to promote its own interests. Urging the claims of the dressmaker Madame Elizabeth, it alluded to "a particularly pleasing frock in white Ramie" with the proviso that it "could be carried out in any colour – e.g., purple (one of the Union colours)" (30 July 1908, 348). But perhaps the WSPU was only exploiting the idea of Messrs. Nicolson, drapers in St. Paul's churchyard, who in June 1908 had put on window display a range of white dresses arrayed in WSPU colors (*Votes for Women*, 18 June 1908, 247). Other firms responded with alacrity. So much so that by October 1908 *Votes for Women* could proclaim that "one cannot walk down Bond-street and the neighbourhood without being struck by the fact that our colours are evidently going to be the leading shades in autumn and winter fashions. Almost every shop window is showing purple hats and green hats, purple ties and green ties, purple cloth gowns and green cloth gowns in endless variety" (1 October 1908, 5).

By virtue of their organized buying power, suffrage feminists clearly influenced the look of goods sold, as manufacturers and retailers fought for a large and lucrative market. At the same time advertisers were quick to target specific suffrage needs, urging upon feminist consumers the merits of their own products. Big stores like Swan and Edgar, William Owen, Burberrys, Peter Robinson's, Derry and Toms, and, of course, Selfridges, supplemented regular advertising with extraordinary notices coinciding with major suffrage events. Hats, coats, skirts, gowns, and even corsets were marketed in this manner. For the 1911 Coronation Procession, for example, William Owen featured "White Attire for Processional Wear" and Peter Robinson's illustrated white walking costumes "For the Great Demonstration;" Derry and Toms informed members that "During the next few days we shall be exhibiting in one of our windows hats and toques made in the colours of the various organizations in connection with the Woman Suffrage movement," adding that "this should be a unique opportunity for purchasing suitable millinery for the great Procession." "For the Pilgrimage" organized by the NUWSS in June and July 1913 Swan and Edgar offered "Serviceable Attire at Moderate Prices" including "hats trimmed with ribbon in N.U. colours," while Burberrys urged the claims of "The Burberry – the Ideal Coat for the Pilgrimage." Yet while it is apparent that the wide range of fashion advertisements in suffrage papers contributed to the making of a suffrage look, suffrage supporters responded by claiming the look as their own, advertising both it and their control over the merchandisers who helped supply it. To members of the WSPU, *Votes for Women* insisted:

white is especially dear, so much so that the casual passer-by may be heard to remark, "Oh! they're suffragettes, look how they're dressed," when he meets ladies clad in white. The man in the street is right; whenever or wherever she can, at processions, demonstrations, meetings, homely or gala occasion, the suffragette is there, bright as a new white pin. So to her, more than to the average woman, comes an interest in white sales and more especially in the sales of firms whose names appear in our advertisement columns. (27 January 1911, 282)

Similarly, Swan and Edgar might undertake to supply blouses, dresses, coats, and skirts in the gray, white, black, or navy that organizers determined would best display National Union colors on the 1913 Pilgrimage, but in the event the NUWSS put on such garb to "'advertise' ourselves, our objects, and our methods. Here is a giant advertisement, which all the country will hear of and see" (*Common Cause*, 13 June 1913, 151).

Any doubts about the true allegiance of suffrage shoppers were dispelled by the window-smashing campaign of March 1912, when WSPU members attacked the property of regular advertisers like Swan and Edgar, Burberrys, D. H. Evans, T. J. Harries, A. Stedalls, Regal Corset, Frederick Gorringe, John Barker, and G. Cozens. They broke windows, according to an explanatory Women's Press handbill, because they held voting store owners responsible for the acts of Members of Parliament. Insisting upon the political influence of businessmen, the handbill reminded them of the reciprocal influence of feminist consumers: "You can get on very well without Mr. Asquith or Mr. Lloyd George, but you can't get on without the women who are your good friends in business" (Atkinson, p. 110). With refreshing candor, the business community seemed to agree, continuing to seek suffrage custom in spite of the movement's increasingly vexed relationship with the law. Each of the above concerns continued to pour advertising revenues into the coffers of the WSPU through its various publications which, after 1912, included the proscribed *Suffragette*. In 1913 the linen and handker-chief manufacturing firm of Robinson and Cleaver, anxious lest consumers boycott "those firms which had had the temerity" to bring damage actions for broken windows (*Common Cause*, 13 June 1913, 151), went so far as to take space in both *Votes for Women* and the *Suffragette* in order to apologize for writs served on its behalf. The firm was allowed to claim, apparently with Mrs. Pankhurst's approval, that "we were not personally responsible, but that owing to the conditions of our Insurance Policy, we had no option in the matter and were unable to prevent our name being used" (*Votes for Women*, 18 October 1912, 38; *Suffragette*, 18 October 1912, 5). Even after the government tried to stop publication of the *Suffragette*, issuing writs in the spring of 1913 against its printer, the Victoria

House Press, and members of the editorial board for conspiring maliciously to damage property, London's largest stores continued to advertise.[19] Thus we find a publication under threat of suppression supported by, among others, Selfridges, Debenhams, Jaeger, William Owen, Peter Robinson's, D. H. Evans, and T. J. Harries.[20] In the summer of 1914, with Emmeline Pankhurst in prison, Christabel running the WSPU from exile abroad, and the publication and distribution of the *Suffragette* disrupted by police action,[21] Selfridges continued to advertise "Mannequin Parades exhibiting the latest fashion in ladies' bathing dresses" – admission, it specified, for women only. Indeed, Marshall and Snelgrove, declaring that "a woman's position depends upon her distinction, while her taste is judged by the clothes she wears" (10 April 1914, 426), did not begin to buy space in suffrage publications until the WSPU's so-called "argument of the stone" had begun in earnest.[22]

Whether the big stores actually supported the extension of the franchise to women is another question. Indeed, apart from Selfridges, a special case to which we shall return, most seemed content with an alliance based upon mutual convenience. Preferring profits to politics, each continued to defer to a large suffrage clientele while remaining indifferent (or hostile) to the movement and its ends. Suffrage societies, for their part, were happy to receive advertising revenue, finding their own ways to profit from an emerging consumer culture. If they preferred to buy rather than boycott, suffrage sympathizers were still discouraged from shopping where there was no chance of gain. Aware, moreover, of the potential "tyranny" of fashion marketing, with its created and manipulated "demands," they looked forward to what one correspondent characterized as "the day ... when woman, with a final spear thrust, [might] drive the tyrant Fashion from his lair, and claim her right not only to a voice in making the laws she has to keep, but also in the fashion of the clothes she has to wear" (Swift, 143). For smaller concerns advertisement in suffrage publications was less fraught. "Smart's Invisible Hooks and Eyes" were, their testimonials tell us, the "patented invention and property of two members and supporters of the Women's Social and Political Union" (*Votes for Women*, 2 July 1908, 285). Miss Bassnett was a suffragette specializing in fine needlework (*Votes for Women*, 27 August 1908, 412); Clara Strong, a "Suffragette Milliner" who trimmed hats in WSPU colors (*Votes for Women*, 4 February 1909, 319); Jane Harding, a WFL dressmaker who urged readers to "support...fellow suffragettes" (*Vote*, 8 May 1914, 43); and Violetta, a ladies' tailor proud of her NUWSS affiliation (*Common Cause*, 27 June 1913, 197). For each, and they are typical of the movement's small business advertisers, commerce and politics went hand in hand, as Edwardian feminists profited by catering to one another.

On the stage such alignments were celebrated in a succession of suffrage dramas, in which female fashion entrepreneurs were presented as emblems of a politically correct and financially secure womanhood. In Cicely Hamilton and Christopher St. John's *How the Vote was Won* (Royalty 1909), the most popular of suffrage comedies, the reactionary Horace Cole is converted to the cause by the inconvenient arrival of a succession of self-supporting female relations, each of whom demands food and lodging. Among his visitors, who include an "authoress" and a music hall chanteuse, is Madame Christine, an affluent modiste who runs "*a profitable dressmaking business in Hanover Square.*" She is, we are told, "*dressed smartly and tastefully, age[d] about forty, [with] manners elegant, smile charming, [and] speech resolute*" (p. 29). In one of the few surviving photographs of suffrage drama in performance, Madame Christine appears clad in a fashionably long fur stole and muff. Her light gown is trimmed in what one assumes to be purple and green (plate 25). Again, in Elizabeth Baker's *Edith*, a one-act comedy first performed as part of a matinée entertainment hosted by the Women Writers' Suffrage League at the Prince's Theatre in February 1912, the "handsome woman" of the play's title "humanely" runs a successful chain of millinery stores. In both cases, trade in female finery allows women the opportunity to deal successfully and exclusively with one another. When, on the other hand, such businesses are represented as being run by men, suffrage playwrights fall back upon the traditional iconography of the stage seamstress. In Alice Chapman's *At the Gates*, performed at an Albert Hall meeting in December 1909 – while Chapman herself was serving a prison term for suffrage agitation – a suffragette holding a vigil outside the House of Commons meets a sweated seamstress. A victim of domestic violence as well as trade abuse, the play's drapery worker retains her function as an all-embracing symbol of man's tyranny over women. Such oppression can be ended, the play argues, only when women take power and use it to help one another. Accordingly, while there is no evidence of a concerted effort to investigate the employment conditions of those

25. Madame Christine (far right) in *How the Vote was Won* (*Sketch*, 17 November 1909).

establishments that took space in the suffrage press, each publication assured readers, in general terms, of the probity of its advertisers. Occasionally, we find articles referring more specifically to labor practices. The *Common Cause*, for instance, in a column entitled "Our Advertisers," praised the behind-the-scenes operations of Debenhams (26 January 1911, 691),[23] while the *Vote*, a paper more specifically concerned with women in industry, ran occasional notices praising the working conditions of selected dressmaking establishments (i.e. The Goodwill Outfitting Society, 3 January 1913, 165; Gretta's, 10 February 1912, 189) while urging shoppers to avoid products produced by sweated labor: "We can refuse to buy ready-made clothing which the salesman will not vouch for as being made under conditions favourable to the worker" (10 September 1910, 238).[24]

One immediate advantage of the rapprochement reached between suffrage supporters and fashion retailers – both large and small – was the authority the alliance lent to Edwardian feminists in turning the tables upon anti-suffrage opponents. In both the drama proper and the politicized street theatre of the movement, suffrage sympathizers were able to paint an opposition either unmodishly out of date or gauchely overdressed. During the Pageant of Women's Trades and Professions, held on 27 April 1909, dressmakers, milliners, and fashion designers marched in a block, the designers carrying aloft "two poles, contrasting a crinoline with a contemporary sheath gown, and a motto... [that read] 'the old order changeth, yielding place to new'" (Tickner, p. 102). Five years later, a *Votes for Women* title-page cartoon could still pointedly show a male "Liberal Party" caught between an "anti-suffragette" in Victorian crinolines and "Modern Suffrage," a smart young woman clad in a stylishly tailored sheath dress and coat (23 January 1914, 247). When suffrage opponents were not presented as hopelessly outmoded, they were derided as fashion's slaves, faulted for their "unexamined" appearance. In *An Allegory*, written by WSPU organizer Vera Wentworth, and first staged at the Rehearsal Theatre on 25 April 1911, an emblematic "Woman" makes her way along a dusty and overgrown road, strewn with sharp stones, towards a utopian "City of Freedom." She wears, round her neck, ankles, and wrists, chains placed there by "Prejudice" and locked by "Convention." Midway on her journey she encounters a second "Slave Woman," who, however, wears a multi-colored dress and extravagant coiffure. "*Her feet are not bleeding and travel-stained like her sister's,"* we are told, *"but are small and white, and her sandals are studded with precious stones. She is chained almost from head to foot, but the chains are jewelled"* (pp. 95–96).[25] Although "Slave Woman" at first denounces Wentworth's protagonist, insisting that "No man will look at thee who sees thy feet and garments," she eventually chooses to follow her to the "City of Freedom." Extravagantly fashionable clothing is here made to stand for a sensual (and male-defined) modishness that hardens the hearts of well-to-do ladies. As "Slave Woman" learns from her suffragette mentor, "All women's chains are not jewelled ... Some are chains of iron, which drag upon their limbs until they die" (p. 96). Fashionability in such a context is reconfigured as a by-product of patriarchal control, in feminist eyes just another variant on prison dress.

What distinguished fashionable suffrage supporters from fashionable anti-suffragists was, they claimed, their attitude towards dress – "the ways" Rolley suggests "in which the Cause altered a woman's relationship to her clothes" (57). If anti-suffrage dress could be said to betray male ownership, feminists' clothes stood for female camaraderie. "Antis" dressed for men, feminists for the women's cause. The fashion columns of the suffrage press were invariably at pains to portray suffrage supporters as busy women who shopped efficiently for a look that aided their work, one that "combine[d] perfect cut and fit with good taste and suitability" (Swift, 143). When suffragettes "start on a shopping expedition," the *Vote* accordingly punned, they "really mean business" (6 May 1911, 22). In practice, however, the distinction between a well-dressed suffrage opponent and a fashionable fighter for women's rights was not always easy to draw. Thus, when in 1913 the *Common Cause* mooted the possibility of incorporating a dress column to show its readers "how to clothe themselves in such a way as to add to the beauty and dignity of life" (8 August 1913, 309), a number of correspondents objected that it would "lower the tone of the paper" (15 August 1913, 326) or, in the eyes of one (male) contributor, lend the publication a regrettably "one-sex" character (22 August 1913, 343). Proponents argued a more conventional suffrage line, urging that "an attractive appearance is a valuable asset in any business purpose" (15 August 1913, 326) and "that it is advisable for those who are prominent in the Women's Movement to dress sensibly yet beautifully – which does not mean extravagantly" (22 August 1913, 343). Perhaps, though, the case for suffrage dress columns was most effectively put by working-class suffragist, Ada Nield Chew, in a lengthy letter printed in the *Common Cause* in the fall of 1913:

Nobody can possibly be more bored than I am by the pictures and dress articles which fill so many pages of women's papers and "Woman's Realm" columns of the newspapers... Yet a badly dressed woman (though I can never tell what is wrong with her) is an eyesore; and I really suffer when I hear, as I did the other day, that "you can always tell Suffragists by the way they are dressed" (it was a very friendly man who spoke, and I am told that he meant what he said). And when he added: "There's Mrs. Chew, for instance – her hat's never on straight!" he voiced one of my life-long trials. If your "Dress" articles could be written by one of those clever people who never spend much money, but whose clothes "belong"; and who know just what would suit one woman, and would look hateful on another... it would be a boon and a blessing to many well-meaning but stupid Suffragists who don't know how to dress... And if some advice could be given as to how to keep one's hat straight; how to look and feel warm in winter without swathing oneself in dead animals' skins; what kind of gloves will stand a few weeks' hard wear, and keep tolerably clean for longer than a day or two; what (if any) boots or shoes will remain watertight when one must trudge country districts in autumn and winter, etc., etc., not only would the articles result in an army of Suffragists who would prove their good sense by their attire, but in the easing of the burdens of some of them, who have quite enough worries without the uneasy certainty that, though they spend, perhaps, more than they ought on dress, yet that they are no credit to the cult of the "new woman." (5 September 1913, 372)

In the end, the *Common Cause* chose not to publish such columns, convinced that it would be unable to maintain an acceptable distance between fashion and frivolity. Yet Chew's plea for a well-dressed "army of Suffragists" was answered the following year by the appearance of an outfit best described as a product of the volatile alliance between suffrage image-makers, fashion marketing, and political theatre. Apparently swayed by the success of the WSPU's earlier dress-code, the larger, more moderate NUWSS announced in March 1914 the adoption of a preferred uniform for its Active Service League.[26] Defended as "cheap, serviceable, and simple," the outfit consisted of "a dark green coat and skirt, white blouse, red tie, [and] soft green felt hat" (13 March 1914, 958). Smartly cut, and illustrated in conformity with current conventions of fashion-plate art – slender, elongated torso and limbs – it was available exclusively through the West End offices of Swan and Edgar (plate 26).

26. Swan and Edgar's advertisement for the NUWSS's Active Service League uniform (*Common Cause*, 15 May 1914).

We have reserved for last a consideration of Gordon Selfridge, whose unique relationship to fashion, theatre, suffrage, and consumerism raises larger questions about cultural production and dress debate in what Selfridge himself called a "pre-eminently commercial age." Indeed, through the pre-war period Selfridge might have claimed, as Wilde had in the 1890s, to have stood in symbolic relations to the art and culture of his age. An economic buccaneer who befriended writers like Granville Barker and Arnold Bennett, a champion of progressive causes who saw 3,000 years of commercial history culminating in his own department store, Selfridge had by 1909 come to believe in retail marketing as "a great force at work altering the bad not because it is bad, but because a bad thing is an uneconomic thing" ("Callisthenes," vol. II, p. 41).[27] As an early supporter of women's rights, Selfridge had both underwritten the publication of the *Suffrage Annual Who's Who*, and flown from his store the WSPU colors on the occasion of Mrs. Pankhurst's first release from prison (Atkinson, p. 27). During the incendiary campaigns of 1914, he would buy space in the *Suffragette* and *Votes for Women*, not to sell products, but "out of compliment to many … customers who have expressed a wish that [his] House should be represented among advertisers" (*Votes for Women*, 13 March 1914, 370). For its part, the suffrage press was quick to reciprocate, celebrating Selfridges' first year of business by informing supporters that:

no firm has been quicker to seize the possibilities of the Suffrage movement than Selfridges. At the great establishment in Oxford Street a large amount of goods is being specially prepared to meet the demand for articles in the colours. Thus, there is a promise of blouses in a silk which is being made with the familiar purple, green and white in delicate stripes. Ribbons and badges are also being got ready. In the meantime there are some dainty wrist bags, in which kid is broken by stripes of suede in heliotrope and green. (*Votes for Women*, 14 January 1910, 247)

Yet allowing Selfridges to "seize the possibilities of the Suffrage movement" was not without its costs. As Granville Barker attempted to show in the cautionary figure of Eustace State, placed upon the Duke of York's stage later that same season, Selfridge's "romance of commerce" meant, in practical terms, imposing upon a large, middle-class clientele the manipulative practices of couture house marketing. In this sense *The Madras House* proved prophetic, not only documenting Selfridge's 1910 policies, but pointing the way to future innovations. State's pamphlet on behalf of corsets, for example, anticipates by two years Selfridge's own decision to go into print to defend "new figure" foundation garments against the attacks of artists John Collier and Marcus Stone ("Callisthenes," vol. I, p. 59). In the spring of 1912, moreover, Selfridges, like its *Madras House* prototype, introduced in-house mannequin parades, constructing "a low stage ... round the light wells on [its] Second Floor" upon which "wonderfully gowned women and girls stroll[ed] nonchalantly to and fro ... display[ing] the fashions of Paris and Vienna." The remainder of the floor was transformed, we are told, into one "big auditorium" ("Callisthenes," vol. I, p. 82). Indeed, Selfridge, who spoke of his Oxford Street premises as a vast "store stage," exploited the techniques of theatrical display as fully as had Lucile or Poiret – or, for their own quite different ends, the suffragettes. Maintaining that "business, rightly considered, is a play," he lured Percy Nash from his post at His Majesty's to join Selfridges in an executive capacity, arguing that retail sales must be entrusted to those "who study a [store] window with the same care that the stage manager or scenic artist studies his stage effects" (Selfridge, p. 377).

In the theatre proper, Selfridge, who had attended "more first nights than any man living" (Pound, p. 236) also saw that his interests were protected. In October 1910, four months after the closing of Frohman's Duke of York's season, he challenged Granville Barker's genial but cutting portrait by supporting the production, at the Savoy, of a one-act farce called *Selfrich's* [*sic*] *Annual Sale*. Constructed by Paul A. Rubens, the popular author of *Dear Little Denmark* (1909), the piece showed "Mr. Selfrich" and two assistants ("Miss Marshall and Miss Snelgrove") confronting a rush of seasonal shoppers. Timed to promote Selfridges actual sale, it portrayed "*a sort of burlesque department – where you can buy hats, cheese, gowns, toys, ribbons, and live animals*" (p. 4). After enduring a succession of indecisive buyers, Selfrich encounters Sadie Vandergilt, an emancipated woman, who orders, without hesitation "a shirt waist – white cachemire – two dollars." When she identifies herself as an American who knows "what she wants," Selfrich concludes the piece by replying "Thank God!" (p. 24). It was, by Selfridge's lights, didactic drama, instructing female playgoers in the art of efficient consumption.[28] Perhaps, though, Selfridge's views on shopping, fashion, and free womanhood are best summed up in "a new and original musical play" called *The Suffrage Girl*, produced at the Royal Court Theatre in the spring of 1911. Presented by the Arlington Social and

Athletic Association, a troupe of Selfridge employees, organized by Percy Nash, and operating under store auspices, the piece is a bizarre attempt to accommodate women's suffrage to the conventions of the shop-girl musical. Set in a utopian future in which women have already gained the vote, the play charts the fortunes of well-dressed "suffrage girl" Sybil Dewston, estranged from her aristocratic family over her love for a foundling turned department-store manager. The plot hinges on a contested by-election, in which Sybil's father is challenged by a Labour candidate who shamelessly panders to a female electorate he addresses as "my fellow sisters." In the final scene Sybil reconciles her family and future husband by casting what turns out to be the deciding vote for her own father. It is a benign vision of female enfranchisement consistent with family values, aristocratic patriarchy, and the defeat of an upstart Labour movement. As such *The Suffrage Girl* amounts to special pleading on behalf of a management using the stage to reduce the larger aspirations of Edwardian feminists to the self-serving cry of "let my shoppers vote!" A modest but lucrative attempt to return the theatre, after some two decades of dress debate, to the uncritical marketing of the pre-Wilde nineties, it would prove a harbinger of an era Granville Barker had cautioned against – a new age in which, Selfridge proclaimed, "the merchant, the man of business or affairs" would be "in the centre of the movement" (Selfridge, p. 385).

Notes

I THE GLASS OF FASHION

1 For the best recent accounts of the House of Worth and its influence see
   Diana de Marly, *Worth: Father of Haute Couture* and the same author's *The
   History of Haute Couture 1850–1950*. Also of value is Edith Saunders, *The
   Age of Worth* and Jean-Philippe Worth's posthumously published, and
   not always accurate, account of his father's regime in *A Century of Fashion*.
2 Throughout our study we have used "millinery" and "milliner" as the
   terms were often used in the period to refer generally to women's finery
   and its makers. When the more restricted sense of hats or hatmakers is
   intended, it will be made obvious by context.
3 For Worth's dressing of actresses for Dumas and Sardou, including his
   dispute with Sardou over the stage gowns of Mlle. Antoine, see de
   Marly, *Worth*, pp. 171–186.
4 Precise dates can be fixed by consulting Kelly's annual *Trades* and *Court
   Directories*. Marginal crosses, indicating orders for Drawing Room
   presentations, first appear for Mary Elizabeth Humble in 1892, Mrs.
   James Wallace (Lucile) in 1894, Madame Eroom, and Mesdames
   Savage and Purdue in 1895.
5 The type of "naive" merchandising Shaw condemns reached a *ne plus
   ultra* of sorts in Sydney Grundy's *Frocks and Frills*, an adaptation of Scribe
   and Legouvé's *Les doigts de fée* (1858) staged at the Haymarket in the
   winter of 1902. For each of the work's four acts, producers Cyril Maude
   and Frederick Harrison contracted separate couture firms. Fashion
   columnist Charlotte, writing for the *Daily Mail*, describes both the
   walking tour of West End showrooms that resulted in the engagement of
   Mrs. Nettleship (Act i), Maison Lucile (Act ii), Messrs. Jay (Act iii), and
   Madame Paquin (Act iv), and the consequent parade of "house styles"
   that transformed an evening's entertainment into an exercise in
   comparison shopping (6 January 1902, 7). The *Era*, in parallel dress and
   drama columns, predicted that the "'smarter' sections of the playgoing
   world ... [would] flock to the Haymarket to recognize ... their own
   friends and their own fashions" (4 January 1902, 15), while the *Sketch*
   enthusiastically proclaimed the play "a great advertisement for those

firms who have so 'regardlessly' gowned it" (22 January 1902, 37). The *Lady's Pictorial* praised the work in general terms, but restricted fashion coverage to the gowns of Messrs. Jay, the only one of Maude's costumiers to advertise in its January issues (4 January 1902, 14; 11 January 1902, 39). See also the *Queen*, 11 January 1902, 48, 70.

6 In registering such objections Wilde was echoing sentiments previously voiced in the French fashion press. Even his picture-frame metaphor is anticipated by a writer for the tailors' journal *Fashion-Théorie*, who complained in 1862 that "women admit us to their receptions ... only in the black suit, because rigged out this way, we are frankly ugly, and we serve as a foil to set off their beauty" (Steele, *Paris Fashion*, p. 93).

7 Wilde's most sustained discussion of stage dress, "The Truth of Masks" (1891), was first published as "Shakespeare and Stage Costume" in the *Nineteenth Century* in May 1885 (800–818). As John Stokes has demonstrated, the essay is in large part a tribute to the "creative archaeology" of designer-producer E. W. Godwin (*Resistible Theatres*, pp. 61–64). Written some half-decade before Wilde's first stage successes, the piece shows a keen and detailed awareness of what it calls the "picturesque" and "dramatic" uses of costume. Of particular interest for students of the society plays is Wilde's early acceptance of the limitations that social and stage conventions placed upon sartorial originality – his recognition of the fact that to be "read" by their viewers stage costumes had to speak a familiar language: "[to] invent an entirely new costume is almost impossible except in burlesque or extravaganza" (*Complete Works*, p. 1075).

8 The late revelation proved so distressing that Alexander entered into a "strictly private" correspondence with critic Clement Scott that resulted in the eventual shifting of the episode to Act II (Kaplan, "A Puppet's Power," 59–73).

9 It was an opportunity facilitated by Wilde's decision to set his play in mid-summer, with numerous references to the Season in its final phase. Lady Windermere's ball in Act II is probably "the last ... of the season" (pp. 29–30), Lady Agatha's match is "not love at first sight, but love at the end of the season" (p. 46), while the Windermeres, at the play's close, decide to return to their country estate as "the season is almost over" (p. 72).

10 The direction appears in two early typescript drafts of the play (now in the Clark Library), and the Lord Chamberlain's Licensing Copy, as well as in Elkins and Lane's first published edition (1893). See Small, ed., *Lady Windermere's Fan*, Appendix, "The Entry of Mrs. Erlynne," pp. 90–94. All references to Wilde's society plays are, unless otherwise specified, to the New Mermaid editions of Ian Small (*Lady Windermere's Fan*) and Ian Small and Russell Jackson (*Two Society Comedies: A Woman of No Importance and An Ideal Husband*).

11 In *Dorian Gray* Madame de Ferrol is said, "when she is in a very smart gown," to resemble "an *édition de luxe* of a bad French novel" (*Complete*

Works, p. 136). Mrs. Erlynne's appeal to a specifically "English market" rings a significant variation upon the jest.

12 When the cloak resurfaced in Charles Brookfield's parody of the play, *The Poet and the Puppets*, at the Comedy later that same season, the only way a disreputable past could be read into it was by covering the garment with a pattern of outsized question marks. For an illustration of Brookfield's "Mrs. Earlybird" in her "interrogatory" outfit (by costumier Nathan) see the *Players*, 10 June 1892, 104. For Thalia's rejection of the "short cape to the waist" which "has just reached us from Paris," see "Wardrobe Wrinkles" (*Players*, 8 March 1892, 268).

13 Raby also notes, with the arrival of Lord Darlington and his entourage, the manner in which the "dark formal clothes" of Wilde's men serve to isolate "the beautifully dressed Mrs. Erlynne" (p. 90). A similar point has been made by Katharine Worth, who suggests that Wilde's assembly of "tailcoats and stiff shirts" makes Mrs. Erlynne seem "especially vulnerable in her isolation and the fragility of her evening dress" (p. 92).

14 In her "Garden" column of 12 March 1892 (434), Flos of the *Queen* advises readers that green carnations are still available through Messrs. Reid and Co. of King Street. Those curious about the "tinting" process by which such effects were obtained are referred to the *Gardener's Chronicle* for 5 March 1892 (306). While Wilde claimed, in a letter to the *Pall Mall Gazette* (1 October 1894), to have "invented that magnificent flower," carnations dyed green, blue, and heliotrope were not uncommon in the period. The earliest attempt to identify the flower's "unnatural" color with "unnatural" sexual practices – proclaiming it, in effect, a "badge" of homosexuality – appears in Robert Hichens's 1894 satiric novel *The Green Carnation*.

15 See, for example, Katharine Worth, pp. 92–94, Gagnier, pp. 117–119, and Raby, p. 89.

16 The shop of Jules Duvelleroy at 167 Regent Street was Victorian London's largest and most prestigious fan emporium. Founded in 1847 as a branch of Duvelleroy's Parisian business, the premises included showrooms, workrooms, and a repair department. Individual fans were priced from 6d to £300 (Adburgham, pp. 109–111).

17 The practice, apparently, was restricted to plays of modern life. Costumes for many of Tree's and Waller's historical productions were designed and co-ordinated by theatrical costumier John Lewis Nathan of Panton Street. For *Hypatia*, staged at the Haymarket in January 1893, both "Karl" (Charles Karl), Nathan's ranking designer, and artist Lawrence Alma Tadema were prominently credited on Tree's program.

18 For Worth's stage compromises with period styles in the 1880s and 1890s see de Marly, *Worth*, pp. 176–186.

19 See also the *Star* (20 April 1895, 217): "the 1830s fashion[s] of [Wilde's] 1893 (or rather 1903 – for they are a good decade in advance of their time) are excessive."

20 For a consideration of the close relationship between the two roles and plays, see Powell, pp. 60–65.

21 The *Sporting Times* (23 April 1893) made a similar point, noting that "sermons and silk and satin gowns are incompatible" (Tree, Clipping Book 1893, p. 225).

22 A parody of Mrs. Arbuthnot's Act II entrance appears in the *Theatre*'s "Condensed Drama" for June 1893 (326–328): "*Mrs. Arbuthnot (enters unexpectedly through a window)*: I am a lady with a past tempered by repentance; that is why I am attired in black velveteen."

23 In BL MS Add. 37944 Mrs. Arbuthnot confesses to Hester that "we are very poor, poorer than Gerald thinks. I work for hire, sewing." Gerald himself comments upon the shabbiness of his mother's appearance ("You always wear black and buy the most unbecoming things you can find"), while Lord Illingworth pays Mrs. Arbuthnot a final backhanded compliment ("Hard but handsome... you would do one credit if you were better dressed"). All three passages were cancelled by Wilde before the play's Haymarket debut. In Jackson and Small, ed., *Two Society Comedies*, pp. 110n, 280, 284.

24 For Victorian mourning fashions see Lou Taylor, *Mourning Dress: A Costume and Social History*, pp. 120–163. On Baudelaire and the rise of "dandiacal black" see Steele, *Paris Fashion*, pp. 81–96 and Hollander, pp. 374–376. Wilde in "The Truth of Masks," citing both Baudelaire and Hamlet's "black suit," suggests that "in modern plays the black frock-coat of the hero becomes important in itself, and should be given a suitable background" (*Complete Works*, pp. 1062, 1076–77). Wilde's comic variation on the topos appears in Jack Worthing's long Act II entrance "*dressed in the deepest mourning, with crape hat-band and black gloves*" for the death of the non-existent Ernest. See Russell Jackson, ed., *The Importance of Being Earnest*, p. 50. The dangers, from a fashion point of view, of unrelieved black are suggested by reactions to Savage and Purdue's costumes for R. C. Carton's *Liberty Hall* (St. James's 1892): "There is not much scope for display in costume... since [all] the characters are in deep mourning in the first act, and in poverty for the remainder of the piece" (unidentified clipping, Mander and Mitchenson).

25 See Jackson and Small, *Two Society Comedies*, p. 212n.

26 Mabel's Act IV gown, illustrated in the *Queen* (12 January 1895, 61, fig. 3) may be compared with "A Beautiful Gown: Madame Humble," shown in the *Lady's Pictorial* three months earlier (6 October 1894, 451).

27 In early drafts Mrs. Cheveley's Act I gown is either "green" or "white satin and gold." Contemporary reviewers describe it as "dark emerald" – "a wickedly vivid green" according to the *Queen* (12 January 1895, 59). By the 1899 Smithers edition, keeping pace with current trends, it had become (and has remained) "heliotrope."

28 See, for example, Sambourne's "A Bird of Prey" (*Punch*, 14 May 1892, 231) and "The 'Extinction' of Species: or, The Fashion-Plate Lady

Without Mercy and the Egrets" (*Punch*, 6 September 1899, 110). For a full discussion of the anti-plumage campaign, in both Britain and North America, see Doughty, *Feather Fashions and Bird Preservation*.

29 See *Reviews by Oscar Wilde* in *Collected Works*, ed. Robert Ross, p. 238.

30 For Wyndham's management of the Criterion see Rowell, "Wyndham of Wyndham's" and the same author's "Criteria for Comedy," pp. 24–37.

31 Jay's (or Jay) of Regent Street, which had opened in 1841, was London's most prestigious mourning house. By the close of the century it had built upon its funeral trade, branching into other modes of fashionable attire. See Adburgham, pp. 65–67. Together with Reville and Busvine, Jay's became a favorite target of Lucile, who would later accuse all three houses of producing pale imitations of Worth and Doucet (Etherington-Smith, pp. 58, 75).

32 All references to *The Case of Rebellious Susan* and *The Liars* are to Russell Jackson's edition of *Plays by Henry Arthur Jones*.

33 Lucile's own claims, however, need to be viewed in the light of Elizabeth Ewing's more comprehensive *Dress and Undress*, especially pp. 106–107, 118. While Lucile was certainly a pioneer in the merchandising of "naughty underthings," the market was not exclusively hers.

2 DRESSING MRS. PAT

1 For the *mise-en-scène* of the original staging at the Royal Theatre, Copenhagen (21 December 1879) as well as details of the 1889 London première see Marker, pp. 46–59.

2 Indeed, at one point Robins had intended to produce *Hedda* on a drawing-room set borrowed from Tree's Haymarket Theatre. When its flats proved too high for the Vaudeville stage a stock set from the Opera Comique had to be substituted (Cima, 152).

3 See also Davis, 112 and Cima, 151–153.

4 See, for example, Clement Scott's condemnation of Robins for "inconsistency" when, two years later, she appeared in Henry Pettitt's Adelphi melodrama *A Woman's Revenge* (*Illustrated London News*, 15 July 1893, 67).

5 All references to *The Second Mrs. Tanqueray* are to George Rowell's edition of *Plays by A. W. Pinero*.

6 Graham Robertson had categorized Nethersole as "a rough, melodramatic actress who would make Paula into the ordinary stage adventuress" (p. 248). For Nethersole's experience as a "stage adventuress" see Reily (pp. 106–120). Nethersole did play in revivals of both *The Second Mrs. Tanqueray* and *The Notorious Mrs. Ebbsmith*, taking the latter role in May 1895 when previous commitments obliged Mrs. Pat to relinquish it. In her autobiography Mrs. Pat observes, with unseemly satisfaction, that the play "did not survive the change of cast" (Campbell, p. 100).

7 Robertson, again, is useful: "Miss Robins would bring power and

intelligence to the part, but could she suggest the less presentable
characteristics of Paula, for which there were then still in use a few good,
full-mouthed Elizabethan adjectives, but which are now, I think, called
'temperamental'?" (pp. 247–248). When, at one point, it appeared that
the Adelphi would hold Mrs. Pat to an earlier contract, Robins was
signed for the role. She relinquished it after Mrs. Pat was released and
the matter frankly put to her by Pinero and Alexander (Campbell,
pp. 64–65; Peters, pp. 72–73).

 8 For conflicting accounts of what piece was actually played see Peters
    (p. 480). Mrs. Pat's prompt book, now in the Theatre Museum, London,
    specifies only music in a minor key and for the left hand alone.

 9 Although Elliott elsewhere describes Beardsley's *Yellow Book* portraits of
    actresses as "unnaturally elongated" ("Sights of Pleasure," 95) neither
    his studies of Madame Réjane (1894), Winnifred Emery (1894), nor an
    unidentified Camille (1894) seems particularly "stretched." At the same
    time, many contemporary responses to Beardsley's *Tanqueray* image –
    too tall, too thin, too "giraffe-like" – might easily be applied to more
    traditional renderings of Mrs. Pat in Pinero's play. See, for example,
    André Sleigh's impression of Paula's Act IV confrontation with Ellean
    (*Black and White*, 10 June 1893, 689).

10 The effect is also caught in Solomon J. Solomon's ghostly portrait of *Mrs.
    Patrick Campbell as Paula Tanqueray* (1894) now at London's Arts Club.

11 There may have been an element of personal malice in the depiction, as
    Philip, nephew to Edward Burne-Jones, was widely rumored to be one
    of Mrs. Pat's disappointed lovers (Marston, 56–58). The image,
    unidentified as Mrs. Pat, is reproduced and briefly discussed by Dijkstra
    (pp. 350–351).

12 Indeed, Mrs. Pat's appearance in the three roles triggered an extended
    correspondence in the letters columns of *The Times* on the increasing
    "morbidity" of "the modern society play." Begun on 4 December 1894
    by an anonymous contributor ("X. Y. Z.") who may have been
    Clement Scott (p. 7), the controversy was declared closed by the editors
    on 12 December (p. 9). Among forty-odd participants who debated the
    issue were Jones, Tree, and Drury Lane theatre composer James Glover.

13 All references to *The Notorious Mrs. Ebbsmith* are to Heinemann's first
    edition of 1895.

14 In the *Sketch*, Florence suggested that the dresses worn in Grundy's
    comedy might reconcile her readers to the "new" woman "as far only
    as her gowns are concerned, be it distinctly understood" (12 September
    1894, 386). The avowedly feminine bent of Grundy's "look" can be seen
    in Albert George Morrow's 1897 poster for the play (Cirker, p. 46).

15 In the following decade Kato would become a favorite bogeyman for
    the suffragettes. In 1910 a participant attending an "At Home" held by
    the Actresses' Franchise League at the Criterion Restaurant "sat
    expecting that Sir Richard Kato would pop in from the theatre below

and would say what he is saying nightly to the bold Elaine: there is an immense future for women as wives and mothers, and a very limited future for them in any other capacity" (*Referee*, 5 June 1910; Arncliffe-Sennett Papers, vol. x).

16 For possible discrepancies between the performance and published texts of the Bible episode see Kaplan, "Mrs. Ebbsmith's Bible Burning."

17 Pinero did let Mrs. Pat's company tour with *The Thunderbolt* in 1908. This was, however, a provincial revival of a play that had been unsuccessful in London. Pinero, moreover, was not personally involved.

18 For a lively account of the play's rehearsal and first night see Huggett's *The Truth about "Pygmalion,"* which, however, must be read in the light of the typescript reminiscences of Harald Melvill, one of Huggett's sources (Theatre Museum). Dukore includes a brief but excellent discussion of Shaw's rehearsal notes, now at the Harry Ransom Humanities Research Center at the University of Texas at Austin (*Shaw*, pp. 155–162). See Dent and Peters for a full consideration of the Shaw–Campbell correspondence.

19 In a letter despatched to Terry on 20 August 1912, Shaw repeats the claim: "I wrote a play for Alexander which was really a play for Mrs. Patrick Campbell. It is almost as wonderful a fit as *Brassbound* [was for Henry Irving and Terry herself]; for I am a good ladies' tailor, whatever my shortcomings may be" (*Collected Letters*, iii, p. 110).

20 *Pygmalion* had begun as a piece for the same players, playhouse, and production team that had staged (and recently revived) *The Second Mrs. Tanqueray*.

21 In a manuscript letter appended to the play's licensing copy, G. S. Street notes that as the word was not "used in anger" there was no need "to be particular about it."

22 See, for example, the *Queen* review of 14 June 1914, which contrasts the "broader brush" used in 1893 with the "reserve" upon which Mrs. Pat's "world-tired" Paula of 1914 had been built (1095).

23 Even this did not satisfy some fashion writers, who complained that, in 1914, a flower-girl's Sunday best would not include such an item. The "*little sailor hat of black straw*" Shaw had finally settled upon for Eliza's initial entrance is illustrated in one of Charles Buchel's posters for the 1914 production. It is unclear, however, whether Mrs. Pat wore any headgear in Act i. None is mentioned by contemporary critics, nor does any appear in production photographs.

24 See Melvill for a personal account of Eliza Keefe ("Flora"), the flower-girl Tree had hired to "criticize" his production. A photograph of Keefe, with three companion flower-sellers, on the front page of the *Evening Standard* shows all four wearing the *de rigeur* straw sailor hats mentioned by contemporary critics (11 April 1914).

25 So central was the hat to Shaw's conception of the play that a card sent to artist Felix Topolski, commissioned to illustrate the play's 1940

revised text, suggests setting the work in "1913" to accommodate "Eliza's shawl and hat with three ostrich figures [*sic*], now quite vanished." The card includes a crude sketch of "LIZA" weighed down by an enormous broad-brimmed hat with three outsized feathers.

26 The problem became increasingly awkward. In a 1920 revival, Mrs. Pat protested to Shaw that she could not "run about" as directed, as "my kimono...shows my legs" (Dent, p. 209).

27 Higgins's claim ("I said I'd make a woman of you, and I have") is odd under the circumstances. Nowhere in the play does Higgins make such a promise. Shaw, however, in his 1913 correspondence with Mrs. Pat, had twice vowed to "make" her "a woman" (Dent, pp. 131, 134). See also Silver, p. 232. For Mrs. Pat's spirited reply, "I am the woman I am and not the woman you would have me be," see Dent, p. 132.

3 THE GHOST IN THE LOOKING-GLASS

1 The previous week the centenary of Richard Cobden's birth had been celebrated with much fanfare throughout Britain. On 4 June a "great meeting" to mark the event was held at Alexandra Palace, with speeches delivered by Sir Henry Campbell-Bannerman, David Lloyd-George, and Winston Churchill. Similar demonstrations were held at Birmingham, Manchester, Edinburgh, and Cobden's birthplace in Midhurst, Sussex.

2 The Souls were a small and self-selecting coterie consisting "of about three dozen members of the Wyndham, Talbot, Charteris, Curzon, Brodrick and Lyttelton families, with George Curzon, Alfred Lyttelton, A. J. Balfour and St. John Brodrick at their centre" (Jalland, p. 103). Connected by public school and Oxbridge ties, the male Souls were primarily from established landed families, their connections providing female members like Edith Lyttelton with entry into aristocratic circles. Insisting upon their own right-thinking, they set out to alter the course of society according to their own lights, championing patronage of the arts, political tolerance, and the cultivation of intelligent conversation (Lambert, p. 32). Alfred and Edith Lyttelton's support for women's enfranchisement (she was a vice-president of the London Society for Women's Suffrage) was not, however, an enthusiasm shared by the group as a whole.

3 See for instance Tuckwell's *Women in Industry* (1908), and Black's two studies, *Sweated Industry and the Minimum Wage* (1907) and (with Adele Meyer) *Makers of Our Clothes* (1909).

4 The image was originally the subject of a work Redgrave executed for the Etching Club. The 1846 painting illustrated here is Redgrave's copy of his 1844 Royal Academy work (Edelstein, 186).

5 See also "Lucy in the Dressmaker's Workroom, at the west-end of London" (1858), reproduced in Walkley (p. 30). The image contains in

addition to its clock, seamstresses, and female overseer, an ironically posted sheet of Factory Act regulations.

6 All references to *Warp and Woof*, unless otherwise specified, are to the 1908 Fisher Unwin edition.

7 The attack upon working conditions at "Madame Elsie'"'s, particularly the much publicized case of a seamstress who died on the premises, was the immediate impetus behind "The Haunted Lady" cartoon. "Madame Elsie," dressmaker to Queen Victoria, survived the consequent inquiry to become dressmaker to Princess Alexandra.

8 She inveighs, in vain, it turns out, against Wilson, "... drat his impudence. He thinks, because he writes for the papers, he can do everything – but I won't stand it – and then he brings his Lady Jenny here wanting a gown for to-night, and she's not the sort I care to work for. I'm not going to have my place turned into a teashop where ladies can meet their young men, I can tell you ..." (p. 53).

9 The theatre critic for the *Lady* observed that "Mrs. Patrick Campbell has seldom looked more attractive than she does in the sombre, simple garments of Theodosia Hemming, the dressmaker's drudge" (23 June 1904, 1058).

10 See for instance Inez Bensusan's *The Apple* (Royal Court 1909) and Gertrude Vaughan's *The Woman with the Pack* (Actresses' Franchise League 1911). For a discussion of these works, as well as Elizabeth Robins's *Votes for Women!*, Bessie Hatton's *Before Sunrise*, and Gertrude Jennings's *A Woman's Influence*, all considered in our chapter 5, see Stowell, *A Stage of Their Own*, pp. 9–39, 45–58.

11 This penchant for bestowing flowers upon working women was such that in 1906 hampers were placed at various locations in Beckenham Station to collect flower contributions from commuters proceeding to London. The bouquets so obtained were distributed to factory girls through the Season (*Daily News*, 25 May 1906, 9).

12 In 1904 Jones's Company was the second largest manufacturer of sewing machines in Britain.

13 The Princess of Wales had attended that particular performance (*Clarion*, 15 July 1904, 3).

14 According to Mary Hamilton, Macarthur's biographer, *Warp and Woof* "had helped [Macarthur] to get a society formed" among dressmakers (p. 55).

15 Ettie Grenfell, an active member of the Souls, hosted a comprehensive fancy-dress ball at Taplow every year from 1905 to 1914 (Lambert, p. 98).

16 The authors have been assured by Zita Viola, Otto's daughter-in-law and a fashion mannequin for the firm in the post-war period, that at no time did Mrs. Viola take any interest in her husband's fashion house. During Viola's pre-war days Otto was assisted by his son Jack, who assumed control of the business after his father's death in 1921.

17 The image is used in Tuckwell's lecture delivered at the Anti-Sweating Exhibition of 1906: "the very things they were wearing might be sweated, and surely if it was so, and they knew, the clothes would burn into them like the fabled shirt of Nessus. For the sweater…is the purchaser…" (*Daily News*, 4 May 1906, 7).

18 Holcombe notes that while some claimed that women preferred to be served by men, others pointed to "the employment of women assistants as one of the most important among the increasing temptations for the public to buy, for many claimed that women were more industrious and conscientious and quicker to appreciate their customers' needs than were men" (p. 107).

19 According to Bondfield, shop assistants "were generally despised by industrial workers, who used to say that 'counter-jumpers are paid by the year because their wages are too small to divide by the week.' We were mostly snobs, I am afraid, and deserved this contempt until we began to organize" (*A Life's Work*, pp. 62–63).

20 Later the National Amalgamated Union of Shop Assistants, Warehousemen and Clerks (NAUSA).

21 Bondfield pointed to one establishment which fined workers 5s for losing duplicates valued at 3d, another which levied a 6d fine for the loss of a 3d duster. More common was the practice of fining shop assistants, who often earned less than 3d per hour, 6d for being no more than six to eight minutes late for work (*A Life's Work*, p. 65).

22 See, for instance, William Paine's *Shop Slavery and Emancipation* (1912), H. G. Wells's *Kipps* (1905), and Clementina Black's *Sweated Industry* (1907).

23 In an interview, Dam had confessed that his stage shop had been modelled upon both Whiteleys and the Army and Navy Stores (*Sketch*, 28 November 1894, 216).

24 It was observed at the time that "whereas large numbers of factory girls cannot be prevailed upon to give up their factory work after marriage, the majority of shop assistants look upon marriage as their one hope of release, and would, as one girl expressed it, 'marry anybody to get out of the drapery business'" (Holcombe, p. 117).

25 Hamilton, on the strength of the play, was in turn invited to lecture at meetings of the Shop Assistants' Union. For a more general consideration of Hamilton as feminist theorist and playwright, see Stowell, *A Stage of Their Own*, pp. 71–99.

26 In fact the play proved a long-standing favorite in the repertoire of certain South London socialist theatre co-operatives (Raphael, p. 32).

4 MILLINERY STAGES

1 As a previously divorced woman Lucile could not be presented at Court, but otherwise enjoyed access to the very highest circles. In 1907 her daughter Esmé was married to Anthony Giffard, Viscount Tiverton, son of the first Earl of Halsbury.

2 For the creation of the so-called "Poiret figure" see Steele, *Fashion and Eroticism*, pp. 224ff. Poiret's early opposition to the S-bend corset or *Gache Sarraute* is conveniently summarized in Mackrell, pp. 19–22.

3 Among Lucile's principal models Diana stood 5′ 11″, Dolores 6′, and Gamela 6′ 1″. All, Lucile tells us, "were 'big girls' with 'fine figures'... Not one of them weighed much under eleven stone, and several of them were considerably more" (Duff Gordon, pp. 79–82). For a more general consideration of the "Lucile" figure see Steele, *Fashion and Eroticism*, pp. 218ff.

4 In 1908 Glyn had herself appeared in a dramatic adaptation of her most notorious novel, the infamous *Three Weeks* (1907). A tale of sexual intrigue, whose public performance was banned by the Lord Chamberlain, the play was presented for a single "private" matinée at the Adelphi (*Sketch*, 26 August 1908, 3).

5 Lucile, often careless with dates, states in her memoirs, that the pageant was staged "twenty-seven years ago" – i.e. 1915 (Duff Gordon, p. 82). Etherington-Smith, her most recent biographer, fixes the year as 1909 (p. 89).

6 Upon being complimented, Poiret continues, "she would palpitate and dilate for the whole day." By 1914 Andrée was modeling for Redfern and Boué. Three photographs of her appear in a special *Sketch Supplement* on Parisian mannequins for that season (1 April 1914, 8–9).

7 The responses of Lucile's "loafers" and Poiret's dukes are anticipated by the reactions of Count Joseph Primoli and Edmond de Goncourt to Worth's mannequins in the 1870s (de Marly, *Worth*, p. 140). Both viewers, however, were interlopers, attending private showings for female clients.

8 The play survives in two published and four typescript versions. Barker's earliest drafts, including interleaved stage directions for the 1911 Sidgwick and Jackson text, are now housed at London's Theatre Museum. The licensing copy (Lord Chamberlain's Plays) is an intermediary text that does not reflect all of the changes made for the play's 1910 run. The much altered 1925 version, also published by Sidgwick and Jackson, incorporates substantial revisions introduced for the play's revival that year at the Ambassadors Theatre. Unless otherwise stated, citations are to Margery Morgan's edition of the 1911 text.

9 The point is made explicit in Philip's comments to cousin Emma: "people have been worrying your father at the shop lately about the drawbacks of the living-in system. Why don't you ask him to look at home for them?" (p. 25).

10 Constantine's paternity does not appear in the play's licensing copy. This has led Ritchie to assume that the addition was made after the play's first run (157). Yet a number of contemporary reviews clearly identify Constantine as the father of Miss Yates's child. See, for example, *Punch*, 16 March 1910, 188.

11 Jessica's second gown (Act IV), an evening ensemble of embroidered tulle over satin, by Christine of George Street, is the only outfit from the play's 1910 production either illustrated or described in the fashion press (*Evening Standard*, 10 March 1910, 19). The mannequins in the Madras House rotunda, discussed below, appear only as broad caricatures in H. M. Bateman's *Bystander* sketch (23 March 1910, 595). See plate 18.

12 Heidi Holder finds a model for Constantine in Octave Mouret, the department store entrepreneur of Zola's *Au bonheur des dames*, published in London in 1883 as *The Ladies' Paradise* (286). There are striking similarities, including Mouret's "orientalism." Worth, however, seems to us a common source for both figures. Zola himself likened Mouret to Bon Marché founder Aristide Boucicault. See Kristin Ross's introduction to *The Ladies' Paradise* (pp. v–xxiii).

13 Charles Dickens, in *All the Year Round*, has left us a portrait of Worth as he appeared in 1867, "officiat[ing] with all the gravity of a diplomatist who holds the fate of the world locked up in the drawers of his brain" (June–December 1867, 9).

14 Reginald Pound, Selfridge's biographer, notes that Selfridge was, at the time, "certainly identified" as Barker's American businessman, contrasting Selfridge's indulgence towards that character with his irritation at his less generous representation in Somerset Maugham's *Our Betters* (Globe 1923) (p. 236). Selfridge had also been named, by St. John Ervine, as the model for Shaw's Tarleton in *Misalliance*, a play conceived as a direct response to Barker's *Madras House*. For an account of the tangled relationship of the two works, see Morgan, *The Shavian Playground*, pp. 187–199. For a more recent consideration of State and Selfridge, see Holder, 83–85.

15 So transparent was the ruse that the *Organizer*, a trade magazine, felt called upon to note how "the long arm of coincidence has strained its biceps" (Pound, p. 73).

16 The play's first act is set in "The Interior of the Maison Duval," whose proprietor Monsieur Duval draws explicit comparisons between himself and "ze Frenchman" who "open up Bon Marché" (LCP, p. 3).

17 In the play's licensing copy all references are to "Harrods." Some have been altered (in ink) to "Garrods." Among items enumerated in the play's opening stage direction are Harrods' Ladies' Club, Travel Bureau, Ticket Booth, and Post Office. Also specified is the store's distinctive "*Trottoir Roulant* or sliding stairway," a pioneer escalator installed by Burbidge in "a magnificent burst of publicity" (Adburgham, p. 234).

18 "Cryptos" consisted of lyricists Percy Greenbank and Adrian Ross, and composers Ivan Caryll and Lionel Monckton. James Tanner was responsible for overall construction. Members of the team had collaborated previously on *The Messenger Boy* (1900) and *The Orchid* (1903) which played at the Gaiety for, respectively, 429 and 559 nights. *Our Miss Gibbs* would surpass both with a run of 636 performances.

19 Our numbering of gowns corresponds to the order in which the outfits are shown, not the numbers used (in French) by Mr. Windlesham.

20 In the months preceding the play's run society and satiric publications were full of accounts of "extreme Directoire dresses" and foundation garments in which it was "absolutely impossible" to walk or sit down (*Sketch*, 15 July 1908, 30). *Punch* depicted queues of tightly wrapped women hopping after trains and omnibuses (20 April 1910, 280), while the *Sketch* documented the plight of furniture manufacturers forced to market new lines of chairs and couches with "specially high legs" to facilitate sitting (9 March 1910, 271). Even theatre managers were encouraged to rethink the practicalities of conventional stalls seating (*Sketch Supplement*, 29 June 1910, 9). If, however, H. M. Bateman's caricatures of three couture-house outfits from *The Madras House* are to be trusted, the first three of Madame Hayward's 1910 creations were worn with the older S-bend corset (*Bystander*, 23 March 1910, 595). See plate 18.

21 Windlesham's coy reference to a well-known buyer may be a veiled allusion to Lucile enthusiast and royal hostess Mrs. Willy James. In the spring of 1910, Mrs. James had been much in the society news, having produced and acted in charity entertainments at the Corn Exchange, Chichester (*Tatler*, 16 February 1910, 172). In March of that year she had, with much fanfare, been appointed a Lady of Grace to the Order of St. John of Jerusalem in England (*Tatler*, 16 March 1910, 283).

22 In licensing Barker's 1925 revised text for production at the Ambassadors Theatre, the Lord Chamberlain's Office observed that "the stage direction might if clumsily carried out result in something too free." While matters were ultimately left to "the discretion and good taste of the producers" it was felt necessary to review the episode "in actual performance" (LCP Correspondence, file 6470, 19 November 1925).

23 At 55 guineas the cost of the gown, defended by Knoblock's heroine, was indeed extravagant. For a prominent charity raffle held during the play's run, gowns, and fur-trimmed coats were valued between 20 and 40 guineas. Of the evening dresses donated by major couture houses like Paquin, Hayward, and Reville and Rossiter, none were appraised at more than 50 guineas (*Ladies' Supplement, Illustrated London News*, 20 June 1914, iii).

24 Although Knoblock denied Poiret was his target, citing as evidence the six changes of make-up Eadie devised in creating his character (*Vanity Fair*, 7 May 1914, 46), a number of publications, including the *Stage* (23 April 1914, 22) and *Play Pictorial* (1914, 24: 145, 78) talked about the identity of "this eminent man." The *Sketch* hedged its bets by proposing a composite portrait of easily recognizable targets, none of whom could be named for fear of a libel suit (10 June 1914, 298).

25 With the exception of Marjorie Hume in the role of Trottinette, none of

Knoblock's mannequins had any stage experience. Gladys Barnett, who first took the part of Messaline, had been a "Miss *Vanity Fair*" covergirl.

26 The garment is now on permanent exhibition in the Costume Court of the Victoria and Albert Museum.

27 The play's recommendation for licensing, dated 17 March 1914, cautions that "care must be taken not to add indecency to the painfulness of the whole episode" by showing, as Knoblock intended, Jacquelin's mannequins behind their curtain "in various stages of undress." The play's printed text specifies that Psyche's bodice "*is still unbuttoned,*" while an unspecified mannequin is reduced to "*the satin slip over which she has worn her model*" (pp. 342–343).

5 THE SUFFRAGE RESPONSE

1 Formed in 1897 under the leadership of Millicent Garrett Fawcett, the National Union of Women's Suffrage Societies (NUWSS), initially an amalgam of sixteen pre-existing societies, was the best known and largest suffrage organization.

2 If it was considered appropriately manly to be indifferent to dress or appearance – so that the dandy was criticized by Carlyle and Thackeray, among others, as "a mere 'Clothes-wearing Man'" (Steele, *Fashion and Eroticism*, p. 92) – the reverse could be said to define women. Dress and appearance determined a woman, her preoccupation and successful manipulation of her look the mark of her "womanliness." "We should doubt" stressed the *Quarterly Review* in 1847, "whether the woman who is indifferent to her appearance be a woman at all" (March 1847, 379). We can see in such analysis that the concepts of "masculinity" and "femininity" are symbiotically linked, each defined in terms of the other, each becoming what the other is not.

3 The argument is graphically put in E. Crawley's anti-suffrage farce, *The Suffragette*, licensed for performance at the Metropole, Birmingham, in April 1908. The play's very slight action consists of the efforts of a Miss Catawall to confront and convert the Home Secretary. It ends as Catawall, dressed in the Home Secretary's clothes, orders him – by this time reduced to wearing a bath towel – to be taken away by the police.

4 That said, Emmeline Pethick-Lawrence observed in a speech delivered after her release from prison in 1909 that although initially she would have claimed that prison garb was "the very hardest thing to bear in prison" she came to "love those prison clothes" because with every prisoner dressed alike "gone was every mark of distinction, between one person and another. No class left, no sign of education left, no distinction of any kind – everything swept away, except humanity and womanhood. And it wasn't until you saw all those details swept away, it wasn't until you realised all that was gone, that you knew how much those great things were worth that were left. It wasn't until then that you realised

what your humanity or what your womanhood meant" (*Votes for Women*, 23 April 1909, 568).

5 Similarly a 1913 anti-suffrage newsreel, "Milling the Militants," depicted, as part of a dreaming man's fantasy, the shame of militant suffragettes forced to parade through the streets dressed in men's trousers.

6 Anticipating sales of more than 100 hats, obviously well-to-do WSPU members were urged to "obtain contributions to the millinery stall from their milliners. Many of our members must have accounts with the big hat shops" (*Votes for Women*, 11 February 1909, 330). This request produced a flurry of letters "pleading for the birds" and requesting that the stall refuse to accept any "murderous millinery" (18 February 1909, 352; 26 February 1909, 377; 12 March 1909, 425). There was no response from the stall's organizers, which included Emmeline Pankhurst.

7 The difficulty of women's position with regard to dress is underscored by the appearance of a poem in the following week's edition of *Punch* which satirizes "ethical dress": "And O my sisters, unto you / Let me address one word of warning: / Bid fashion's giddy modes adieu, / Let Ethics govern your adorning. / Take, in regard to hats and shoes, / Marcella as your guide, not Becky; / And study, ere your frocks you choose, / The works of Betham, Mill, and Lecky" (7 February 1906, 100).

8 Held on the occasion of George V's ascent to the throne, the Coronation Procession was organized by the WSPU with the co-operation of the NUWSS and took the Empire as its organizing theme. The largest of the suffrage demonstrations, it out-spectacled other spectacles at the same time that it high-lighted suffrage supporters' unease "with the status quo and the strains of their position with regard to the state" (Tickner, p. 57).

9 In Jerome K. Jerome's *Stage-land*, George is the generic name assigned to "the hero" of contemporary melodrama. From George Talboys in stage adaptations of Mary Braddon's *Lady Audley's Secret* (1863) through George Armitage in George Sims's *Lights o' London* (1881) the name does seem to have had "manly" associations. Even Wilfred Denver, the hero of Jones's persistently popular *Silver King* (1882), was "George" in the author's earliest drafts.

10 McKinnel's Pioneers should not be confused with Edith Craig's Pioneer Players. The latter organization was founded in March 1911 and offered annual seasons of subscription performances until 1921.

11 All references to *Clothes and the Woman* are, unless otherwise specified, to French's edition of 1922.

12 In the 1922 published version of the play, Robina wears instead a more currently fashionable "pretty little grey frock" (p. 61).

13 The stigma of the housemaid's cap, here rejected by Tilda, was so marked during the period that maids claimed that "owing to their hated

headdress they cannot put their head out of doors without being called 'skivvy' by passing workmen or errand boys" (Butler, p. 62).

14 White was explained as representing "purity," green "hope," or alternatively "regeneration," and purple "dignity" or sometimes "loyalty" or "courage." It is important to remember, however, that "so long as the concepts were positive the exact niceties of the symbolism were less important than the decorative impact of the colours and their effect in unifying the march[es] and evoking the cause" (Tickner, p. 294).

15 The AFL banner, made of "cotton sateen with appliqued pink silk embroidery and green and gold paint" and measuring 2,000 mm × 1,022 mm is now in the collection of the Museum of London (Atkinson, p. 109).

16 In the fall of 1912, finding themselves unable to support the new militant policy proposed by Emmeline and Christabel Pankhurst, Emmeline and Frederick Pethick-Lawrence agreed to leave the WSPU, taking with them *Votes for Women*, which they had edited since its inception. The couple went on to form a centrist splinter group called the Votes for Women Fellowship.

17 A notice in an earlier edition of the *Vote* advised that "a charming hat for members of the Women's Freedom League has been specially designed by Mrs. Thomson-Price, and is now being produced by Louise" (25 March 1911, 260).

18 The only exception is a brief notice in an early issue of *Votes for Women* (18 June 1908) that comments favorably upon a window display incorporating WSPU colors at the drapery establishment of Messrs. Nicolson, a firm that never advertised in the paper.

19 According to Andrew Rosen, the attacks upon the *Suffragette* may have been prompted by a letter from anti-suffrage Postmaster General, Herbert Samuel, to the Home Secretary, Reginald McKenna, in which he urged that the paper's publishers and printers, among others, be charged with illegal conspiracy: "If printers were deterred from publishing incitements to violence, the movement itself would be hampered not a little" (Rosen, p. 194). In the event, the manager of the Victoria House Press was released on an undertaking to cease printing the *Suffragette*. The others charged were found guilty and received sentences of from six to twenty-one months.

20 Although Rosen (p. 241) and Atkinson (p. 28) have observed that generally the number of advertisers declined in the *Suffragette* as a result of the WSPU's militancy and police harassment, as far as fashion advertising is concerned, if seasonal vagaries are taken into account and the period immediately following press shut-downs is ignored, there was no significant reduction.

21 With police in possession of their offices at Lincoln's Inn, the WSPU moved to new premises in Tothill Street, Westminster. These were in turn raided by the police on 8 June 1914, at which point the WSPU

relocated to Campden Hill Square. Those offices were raided on 12 June 1914. By July 1914 the government tried to prevent distribution of the *Suffragette* by threatening to charge anyone publishing or distributing the paper.

22 Marshall and Snelgrove's first advertisements in *Votes for Women* and the *Suffragette* date from April 1913 and contain notices requesting readers to inform sales staff that purchases were prompted by such advertising. Presumably the testimonials were effective because advertising continued after demands for proof of its efficacy ceased. While Marshall and Snelgrove's decision to buy space first in the more radical papers might confirm the WSPU's more affluent membership, the store found its initial investment so profitable that it began to advertise in both the *Common Cause* and the *Vote* the following year.

23 Bondfield praised Debenhams and Derry and Toms (another regular suffrage advertiser) for their enlightened labor practices. Both firms opposed "living-in" and would, according to Bondfield, go down "in history as citizens first and drapers in the second place" (*Socialism for Shop Assistants*, p. 7).

24 In addition, suffrage societies actively recruited shop assistants to the movement. A columnist for *The Shop Assistant*, a union publication, praised their activism, noting that during a four-day period in May 1910 suffrage meetings, with "music and recitations," were hosted for employees of Peter Robinson's, Marshall and Snelgrove, Debenhams and Selfridges. The column ends with a plea to union organizers to "go ye and do likewise" (4 June 1910).

25 Rolley describes a similar scene in "The Masque of Women" published in *Votes for Women* (8 September 1911, 778) in which "a chorus of antis dance around 'a doll clothed with jewels and gold chains, symbolic of Woman beneath Man's chivalrous treatment'" (57).

26 The NUWSS's Active Service League was one of the outcomes of that organization's 1913 cross-Britain Pilgrimage.

27 Selfridge's views on commerce, suffrage, and related issues may be sampled in a series of opinion columns that began to appear in a variety of papers in 1909. After 25 January 1912, Selfridge wrote most pieces under the pseudonym "Callisthenes," described as "press agent" to Alexander the Great. Each column is prefaced by a heading that identifies it as "an article reflecting the policies, principles, and opinions of this House of Business upon various points of public interest." As no single paper contains a complete run of columns, we have used the "Callisthenes" clipping books now housed at Selfridges' Oxford Street Archive. See also Honeycomb, pp. 171–174.

28 Indeed, it was a piece of puffery so blatant that the Lord Chamberlain's Examiner of Plays observed that any fuss his office made over the use of the Selfridge name would only increase the play's value as an advertisement.

Works cited

NEWSPAPERS AND MAGAZINES

All the Year Round
Anglo-Continental
Athenaeum
Bioscope
Black and White
Bystander
Clarion
Common Cause
Daily Graphic
Daily Mail
Daily News
Daily Telegraph
Dramatic Review
Echo
Era
Evening News
Evening Standard
Fashion Théorie
Fun
Gardener's Chronicle
Gentleman's Magazine
Graphic
Illustrated Church News
Illustrated London News
Illustrated Sporting and Dramatic News
Lady
Lady's Pictorial
Lady's World
Leicester Daily Post
Manchester Guardian
Modern Society

Morning Post
New York Herald
Observer
Organizer
Pall Mall Gazette
Play Pictorial
Players
Punch
Quarterly Review
Queen
Referee
Reynolds
Saint Paul's
Saturday Review
Sheffield Daily Telegraph
Shop Assistant
Sketch
Sporting Times
Star
Suffragette
The Sunday Times
Tatler
Theatre
The Times
Vanity Fair
Vote
Votes for Women
Westminster Gazette
Woman's World
World
Yellow Book

BOOKS AND ARTICLES

Adburgham, Alison. *Shops and Shopping: 1800–1914*. London: Unwin, 1964.
Allen, Inglis. *The Suffragette's Redemption*. Lord Chamberlain's Plays, British Library.
Archer, William. *The Theatrical World of 1894*. London: Walter Scott, 1895. *The Theatrical World of 1895*. London: Walter Scott, 1896.
Arncliffe-Sennett Papers. Compiled and annotated by Maud Arncliffe-Sennett. 37 vols. 1906–1936. London: British Library.
Ashwell, Lena. *Myself a Player*. London: Michael Joseph, 1936.
Atkinson, Diane. *The Purple, White & Green: Suffragettes in London 1906–14*. London: Museum of London, 1992.
Auerbach, Nina. *Woman and the Demon*. Cambridge: Harvard University Press, 1982.
Baker, Elizabeth. *Chains. Contemporary Plays*, ed. Thomas H. Dickinson. Boston: Houghton Mifflin, 1925, pp. 209–243.
Edith. London: Sidgwick & Jackson, 1927.
Miss Tassey. London: Sidgwick & Jackson, 1913.
Bantock, Leedham, *et al*. *The Girl Behind the Counter*. Lord Chamberlain's Plays, British Library.
Barthes, Roland. "The Diseases of Costume." *Critical Essays*, trans. R. Howard. Evanston: Northwestern University Press, 1972.
Beaton, Cecil. *The Glass of Fashion*. London: Weidenfeld & Nicolson, 1954.
Beckett, Jane and Deborah Cherry. *The Edwardian Era*. Oxford: Phaidon & Barbican Art Gallery, 1987.
Bensusan, Inez. *The Apple. Sketches from the Actresses' Franchise League*, ed. Viv Gardner. Nottingham: Nottingham Drama Texts, 1985, pp. 29–39.
Black, Clementina. *Sweated Industry and the Minimum Wage*. London: Duckworth, 1907.
Black, Clementina and Adele Meyer. *Makers of our Clothes*. London: Duckworth, 1909.
Bondfield, Margaret. *A Life's Work*. London: Hutchinson & Co., 1948. *Socialism for Shop Assistants*. London: Clarion, 1909.
Booth, Michael. *Victorian Spectacular Theatre: 1850–1910*. London: Routledge, 1981.
Braddon, Mary Elizabeth. *Lady Audley's Secret. Nineteenth Century Plays*, ed. George Rowell. Oxford University Press, 1953.
Brookfield, Charles. *The Poet and the Puppets*. Lord Chamberlain's Plays, British Library.
Random Reminiscences. London: Nelson, 1911.
Butler, Christine. *Domestic Service*. London: Women's Industrial Council, 1912.
Cadbury, Edward *et al*. *Women's Work and Wages*. Chicago: University of Chicago Press, 1912.

"Callisthenes" [H. Gordon Selfridge]. Clipping Books, Selfridge Archive, London.
Campbell, Mrs. Patrick. *My Life and Some Letters.* London: Hutchinson, 1922.
Carton, R. C. *The Home Secretary.* Lord Chamberlain's Plays, British Library.
Liberty Hall. London: French, 1900.
Chambers, C. Haddon. *John a' Dreams.* Lord Chamberlain's Plays, British Library.
Chapman, Alice. *At the Gates.* Lord Chamberlain's Plays, British Library.
Cima, Gay. "Elizabeth Robins: The Genesis of an Independent Manageress." *Theatre Survey,* 22.2 (November 1980): 145–163.
Cirker, Hayward and Blanche. *The Golden Age of the Poster.* New York: Dover, 1971.
Clark, Barrett H. *A Study of the Modern Drama.* New York: D. Appleton & Co., 1928.
Cordell, Richard. *Henry Arthur Jones and the Modern Drama.* New York: Long, 1932.
Corelli, Marie. *Woman or Suffragette?* London: C. Arthur Pearson, 1907.
Coward, Noël. *Hayfever.* London: French, 1927.
Crawley, E. *The Suffragette.* Lord Chamberlain's Plays, British Library.
"Cryptos" [Ross *et al.*]. *Our Miss Gibbs.* Lord Chamberlain's Plays, British Library.
Dam, H. J. W., Ivan Caryll, *et al. The Shop Girl.* Lord Chamberlain's Plays, British Library.
Dance, George. *The Suffragette.* Lord Chamberlain's Plays, British Library.
Davidoff, Leonore. *The Best Circles: Society, Etiquette and the Season.* London: Croom Helm, 1973.
Davidson, John. *For the Crown.* Lord Chamberlain's Plays, British Library.
Davis, Tracy. "Acting in Ibsen." *Theatre Notebook,* 39.3 (1985): 113–123.
Dawick, John. "The 'First' Mrs. Tanqueray: Pinero's Scandalous Play in Rehearsal and Production." *Theatre Quarterly,* 9.35 (Autumn 1979): 77–93.
de Marly, Diana. *The History of Haute Couture 1850–1950.* London: Batsford, 1980.
Worth: Father of Haute Couture. London: Elm Tree, 1980.
Dent, Alan, ed. *Bernard Shaw and Mrs. Patrick Campbell: Their Correspondence.* London: Victor Gollancz, 1952.
Dijkstra, Bram. *Idols of Perversity: Fantasies of a Feminine Evil in Fin de Siècle Culture.* Oxford University Press, 1986.
Doughty, Robin W. *Feather Fashions and Bird Preservation.* Berkeley: University of California Press, 1975.
The Dramatic Peerage: Personal Notes and Professional Sketches of the Actors and Actresses of the London Stage, ed. Erskine Reid and Herbert Compton. London: Raithby, 1892.

Duff Gordon, Lady (Lucile). *Discretions and Indiscretions*. New York, Frederick A. Stokes Company, 1932.

Dukore, Bernard. *Bernard Shaw, Director*. London: Allen & Unwin, 1971.

"*The Madras House* Prefinished." *Educational Theatre Journal*, 24 (1972): 135–138.

Edelstein, T. J. "They Sang 'The Song of the Shirt': The Visual Iconology of the Seamstress." *Victorian Studies* (Winter 1980): 183–210.

Elliott, Bridget. "New and Not so 'New Women' on the London Stage: Aubrey Beardsley's *Yellow Book* Images of Mrs. Patrick Campbell and Réjane." *Victorian Studies* (Autumn 1987): 33–57.

"Sights of Pleasure: Beardsley's Images of Actresses and the New Journalism of the Nineties." *Reconsidering Aubrey Beardsley*, ed. Robert Langenfeld. Ann Arbor: UMI Research Press, 1989.

Ellmann, Richard. *Oscar Wilde*. London: Hamish Hamilton, 1987.

Etherington-Smith, Meredith and Jeremy Pilcher. *The It Girls*. London: Hamish Hamilton, 1986.

Ewing, Elizabeth. *Dress and Undress: A History of Women's Underwear*. London: Batsford, 1978.

Fyfe, Hamilton. *Sir Arthur Pinero's Plays and Players*. London: Ernest Benn, 1930.

Gagnier, Regenia. *Idylls of the Marketplace: Oscar Wilde and the Victorian Public*. Stanford University Press, 1986.

Galsworthy, John. *Justice. The Plays of John Galsworthy*. London: Duckworth, 1929, pp. 217–274.

The Pigeon. London: Duckworth, 1912.

Gates, Eleanor. *Poor Little Rich Girl*. London: Hodder & Stoughton, 1913.

Gernsheim, Alison. *Fashion and Reality: 1840–1914*. London: Faber & Faber, 1963.

Gielgud, John. *An Actor and His Time*. London: Sidgwick, 1979.

Gielgud, Kate Terry. *A Victorian Playgoer*, ed. Muriel St. Clare Byrne. London: Heinemann, 1980.

Glyn, Elinor. *Three Weeks*. London: Duckworth, 1907.

Granville Barker, Harley. "The Coming of Ibsen." *The Eighteen-Eighties: Essays by Fellows of the Royal Society of Literature*, ed. Walter de la Mare. Cambridge University Press, 1930, pp. 159–196.

The Madras House (1) ed. Margery Morgan. London: Methuen, 1977; (2) Typescript drafts with authorial corrections. Theatre Museum, London; (3) Lord Chamberlain's Plays, British Library.

Plays by Harley Granville Barker: The Marrying of Ann Leete, The Voysey Inheritance, Waste, ed. Dennis Kennedy. Cambridge University Press, 1987.

Grundy, Sydney. *Frocks and Frills*. Lord Chamberlain's Plays, British Library.

The New Woman. London: Chiswick, 1894.

Hamilton, Cicely. *Diana of Dobson's*. London: French, 1925.
Life Errant. London: J. M. Dent, 1935.
Marriage as a Trade. 1909. London: Women's Press, 1981.
Hamilton, Cicely and Christopher St. John [Christabel Marshall]. *How the Vote was Won*. *How the Vote was Won and Other Suffragette Plays*, ed. Dale Spender and Carole Hayman. London: Methuen, 1985, pp. 17–33.
Hamilton, Mary Agnes. *Mary Macarthur*. New York: Thomas Seltzer, 1926.
Hankin, St. John. *The Dramatic Works of St. John Hankin*, 3 vols. London: Secker, 1912.
Mr. Punch's Dramatic Sequels. London: Bradbury, Agnew & Co., 1901.
Harris, Frank. *Mr. and Mrs. Daventry*. London: Richards Press, 1956.
Hatton, Bessie. *Before Sunrise*. *Sketches from the Actresses' Franchise League*, ed. Viv Gardner. Nottingham: Nottingham Drama Texts, 1985, pp. 59–65.
Hichens, Robert. *Bella Donna*. London: Heinemann, 1909.
The Green Carnation. London: Heinemann, 1894.
Hicks, Seymour *et al*. *Captain Kidd*. Lord Chamberlain's Plays, British Library.
Hoffe, Monckton. *The Little Damozel*. London: French, 1912.
Holcombe, Lee. *Victorian Ladies at Work: Middle-Class Working Women in England and Wales 1850–1914*. Newton Abbot: David & Charles, 1973.
Holder, Heidi. "'The Drama Discouraged': Judgment and Ambivalence in *The Madras House*." *University of Toronto Quarterly*, 58.2 (Winter 1988/9): 275–294.
Hollander, Anne. *Seeing Through Clothes*. New York: Viking Press, 1978.
Holt, Adern. *Fancy Dresses Described*. London: Debenham & Freebody, 1896.
Honeycombe, Gordon. *Selfridges: Seventy-Five Years, the Story of the Store, 1909–1984*. London: Selfridges, 1984.
Huggett, Richard. *The Truth about "Pygmalion."* London: Heinemann, 1969.
Ibsen, Henrik. *A Doll's House*, trans. Michael Meyers, 1965. London: Methuen, 1985.
Ghosts, trans. Michael Meyer. London: Methuen, 1985.
Hedda Gabler, trans. Michael Meyer. 2nd rev. ed. London: Methuen, 1974.
Little Eyolf, trans. William Archer. London: Heinemann, 1895.
Jalland, Pat. *Women, Marriage and Politics 1860–1914*. Oxford: Clarendon, 1986.
Jennings, Gertrude. *A Woman's Influence*. *Sketches from the Actresses' Franchise League*, ed. Viv Gardner. Nottingham: Nottingham Drama Texts, 1985, pp. 67–74.
Jerome, Jerome K. *Stage-land: Curious Habits and Customs of its Inhabitants*. London: Chatto & Windus, 1893.

Jones, Doris Arthur. *The Life and Letters of Henry Arthur Jones*. London: Victor Gollancz, 1930.

Jones, Henry Arthur. *Plays by Henry Arthur Jones: The Silver King, The Case of Rebellious Susan, The Liars*, ed. Russell Jackson. Cambridge University Press, 1982.

The Dancing Girl. London: French, 1907.

The Heroic Stubbs. London: Chiswick, 1906.

The Masqueraders. London: French, 1909.

Mrs. Dane's Defence. *English Plays of the Nineteenth Century*, vol. II (*Drama 1850–1900*), ed. M. R. Booth. Oxford: Clarendon, 1969, pp. 341-427.

The Physician. London: Macmillan, 1899.

Representative Plays of Henry Arthur Jones, 4 vols., ed. Clayton Hamilton. London: Macmillan, 1926.

"The Theatre and the Mob." *Nineteenth Century*, 14 (July–December 1883): 441–456.

Kaplan, Joel H. "Mrs. Ebbsmith's Bible Burning: Page vs Stage." *Theatre Notebook*, 44.3 (1990): 99–101.

"A Puppet's Power: George Alexander, Clement Scott, and the Re-plotting of *Lady Windermere's Fan*." *Theatre Notebook*, 46.2 (1992): 59–73.

Keating, P. J. *Into Unknown England 1866–1913*. Manchester University Press, 1976.

Kennedy, Dennis. *Granville Barker and the Dream of Theatre*. Cambridge University Press, 1985.

Knoblock [Knoblauch], Edward. *Kismet and Other Plays: Kismet, The Faun, Milestones, My Lady's Dress*. London: Chapman & Hall, 1957.

Lambert, Angela. *Unquiet Souls*. London: Macmillan, 1984.

Leclerq, Pierre. *Illusion*. Lord Chamberlain's Plays, British Library.

Leese, Elizabeth. *Couture on the Screen*. Bembridge: BCW Publishing Limited, 1976.

Lemon, Mark. *The Sempstress*. London: Dick's Standard Plays, 1886.

Lyttelton, Edith. *The Macleans of Bairness*. Lord Chamberlain's Plays, British Library.

Peter's Chance. London: Duckworth, 1912.

St. Ursula's Pilgrimage. London: Vacher & Sons, 1909.

Warp and Woof. London: Fisher Unwin, 1908.

Warp and Woof. Lord Chamberlain's Plays, British Library.

McDonald, Jan. *The 'New Drama' 1900–1914*. London: Macmillan, 1986.

McKinnel, Norman. Clipping Books. University of Glasgow, Special Collections.

Mackrell, Alice. *Paul Poiret*. London: Batsford, 1990.

MacQueen-Pope, W. *The Gaiety: Theatre of Enchantment*. London: W. H. Allen, 1949.

Mander, Raymond and Joe Mitchenson. *Musical Comedy*. London: Peter Davies, 1969.

Marker, Frederick J. and Lise-Lone. *Ibsen's Lively Art: A Performance Study of the Major Plays*. Cambridge University Press, 1989.

Marston, Henry P. "An Artist's Revenge: The Romance of the Famous Vampire." *New England Home Magazine* (October 1898): 56–58.

Mason, A. E. W. *Sir George Alexander and the St. James' Theatre*. London: Macmillan, 1935.

Maugham, Somerset. *Our Betters*. London: Heinemann, 1923.

Meacham, Standish. *A Life Apart: The English Working Class 1890–1914*. London: Thames and Hudson, 1977.

Melvill, Harald. "I Was There (A Personal Reminiscence of the 'First Night' of Shaw's *Pygmalion*)." Typescript, Theatre Museum, London, 1982.

Melville, Frederick. *The Bad Girl of the Family*. Lord Chamberlain's Plays, British Library.

Moore, Mary. *Charles Wyndham and Mary Moore*. Edinburgh: privately printed, 1925.

Morgan, Margery. *The Shavian Playground*. London: Methuen, 1972.

Morley, Sheridan. *Gladys Cooper*. London: Heinemann, 1979.

Morton, Edward *et al*. *The Merry Widow*. Lord Chamberlain's Plays, British Library.

Murray, Gilbert. *The Trojan Women*. London: George Allen, 1905.

Nash, Percy and Frank Armstrong. *The Suffrage Girl*. Lord Chamberlain's Plays, British Library.

Nathan, Archie. *Costumes by Nathan*. London: Newnes, 1960.

Neilson, Julia. *This for Remembrance*. London: Hurst & Blackett, 1940.

Paine, William. *Shop Slavery and Emancipation*. London: P. S. King & Son, 1912.

Peters, Margot. *Mrs. Pat: The Life of Mrs. Patrick Campbell*. London: Hamish Hamilton, 1985.

Pettitt, Henry. *A Woman's Revenge*. Lord Chamberlain's Plays, British Library.

Pinero, Arthur Wing. *The Amazons*. London: Heinemann, 1894.

　　The Notorious Mrs. Ebbsmith. London: Heinemann, 1895.

　　Plays by A. W. Pinero: The Schoolmistress, The Second Mrs. Tanqueray, Trelawny of the 'Wells', The Thunderbolt, ed. George Rowell. Cambridge University Press, 1986.

　　The Profligate. London: Heinemann, 1891.

　　The Second Mrs. Tanqueray. London: Heinemann, 1895.

　　The Social Plays of Arthur Wing Pinero, vol. 1, ed. Clayton Hamilton. New York: Dutton, 1917.

　　The Weaker Sex. London: Heinemann, 1894.

Pogson, Rex. *Miss Horniman and the Gaiety*. London: Rockliff, 1952.

Poiret, Paul. *My First Fifty Years*, trans. Stephen Haden Guest. London: Victor Gollancz, 1931.

Post Office London Directories: Trades and Court; Streets and Commercial. London: Kelly.

Postlewait, Thomas. *Prophet of the New Drama: William Archer and the Ibsen Campaign.* Westport: Greenwood Press, 1986.

Pound, Reginald. *Selfridge.* London: Heinemann, 1960.

Powell, Kerry. *Oscar Wilde and the Theatre of the 1890s.* Cambridge University Press, 1990.

Purdom, C. B. *Harley Granville Barker.* London: Barrie & Rockliff, 1955.

Quigley, Austin E. *The Modern Stage and Other Worlds.* New York: Methuen, 1985.

Raby, Peter. *Oscar Wilde.* Cambridge University Press, 1988.

Raphael, Samuel *et al. Theatres of the Left, 1880–1935: Workers' Theatre Movements in Britain and America.* London: Routledge & Kegan Paul, 1985.

Reily, Joy Harriman. "A Forgotten 'Fallen Woman': Olga Nethersole's *Sappho.*" *When They Weren't Doing Shakespeare,* ed. Judith L. Fisher and Stephen Watt. Athens, Ga.: Georgia University Press, 1989, pp. 106–120.

Richardson, Mary. *Laugh a Defiance.* London: Weidenfeld & Nicolson, 1953.

Ritchie, Harry M. "Harley Granville Barker's *The Madras House* and the Sexual Revolution." *Modern Drama,* 15 (September 1972): 150–158.

Robertson, W. Graham. *Time Was.* London: Hamish Hamilton, 1931.

Robertson, Tom. *School.* London: French, 1890.

Robins, Elizabeth. *Ibsen and the Actress.* London: Hogarth Press, 1928.

Votes for Women! London: Mills & Boon, 1909.

Rolley, Katrina. "Fashion, Femininity and the Fight for the Vote." *Art History,* 13.1 (March 1990): 47–71.

Rosen, Andrew. *Rise Up, Women!* London: Routledge, 1974.

Rowell, George. "Criteria for Comedy: Charles Wyndham at the Criterion Theatre." *British Theatre in the 1890s,* ed. Richard Foulkes. Cambridge University Press, 1992, pp. 24–37.

"Wyndham of Wyndham's." *The Theatre Manager in England and America,* ed. J. Donohue. Princeton University Press, 1971, pp. 189–213.

Royle, Edwin. *A White Man.* Lord Chamberlain's Plays, British Library.

Rubens, Paul A. *Dear Little Denmark.* Lord Chamberlain's Plays, British Library.

Selfrich's Annual Sale. Lord Chamberlain's Plays, British Library.

Rubinstein, David. *Before the Suffragettes.* Brighton: Harvester, 1986.

Salmon, Eric, ed. *Granville Barker and His Correspondents.* Detroit: Wayne State University Press, 1986.

Saunders, Edith. *The Age of Worth.* London: Longmans, 1954.

Selfridge, H. Gordon. *The Romance of Commerce.* London: Bodley Head, 1918.

Shaw, Bernard. *The Bodley Head Bernard Shaw Collected Plays with their Prefaces*, 7 vols. ed. Dan H. Laurence. London: Reinhardt, 1970–1974.

Collected Letters I 1874–1897, ed. Dan H. Laurence. New York: Dodd, Mead & Company, 1965.

Collected Letters II 1898–1910, ed. Dan H. Laurence. New York: Dodd, Mead & Company, 1972.

Our Theatres in the Nineties, 3 vols. London: Constable, 1931.

Pygmalion (1) London: Constable, 1913; (2) Printer's copy with author's notes and extensive authorial revisions, 10 June 1912, HRHRC; (3) Lord Chamberlain's Plays, British Library; (4) Annotated acting copy belonging to Mrs. Patrick Campbell, 1914, Theatre Museum, London; (5) Shaw's rehearsal notes, author's manuscript, 3 February–2 October 1914, HRHRC.

Three Plays for Puritans. London: Grant Richards, 1901.

Showalter, Elaine. *A Literature of Their Own*. Princeton University Press, 1977.

Silver, Arnold. *Bernard Shaw: The Darker Side*. Stanford University Press, 1982.

Sims, George. *The Black Domino*. Lord Chamberlain's Plays, British Library.

The Lights o' London. Lord Chamberlain's Plays, British Library.

The Trumpet Call. Lord Chamberlain's Plays, British Library.

States, Bert O. *Great Reckonings in Little Rooms*. Berkeley: University of California Press, 1985.

Steele, Valerie. *Fashion and Eroticism*. Oxford University Press, 1985.

Paris Fashion: A Cultural Study. Oxford University Press, 1988.

Stokes, John. *Resistible Theatres*. London: Elek, 1972.

Stowell, Sheila. *A Stage of Their Own: Feminist Playwrights of the Suffrage Era*. Manchester University Press, 1992.

Suffrage Annual and Women's Who's Who, ed. "A. J. R." London: Paul, 1913.

Swift, Deborah. "The Tyranny of Fashion." *The Englishwoman*, 4.11 (1909): 135–143.

Symonds, Emily Morse [George Paston]. *The Career of Candida*. New York: D. Appleton & Co., 1892.

Clothes and the Woman. Lord Chamberlain's Plays, British Library.

Clothes and the Woman. London: French, 1922.

A Modern Amazon. London: Osgood, 1894.

The Pharisee's Wife. 1904. [Restaged as *The Conynghams*. Lord Chamberlain's Plays, British Library.]

Tilda's New Hat. London: French, 1909.

Tanner, James T. *et al. The Messenger Boy*. Lord Chamberlain's Plays, British Library.

The Orchid. Lord Chamberlain's Plays, British Library.

Taylor, Lou. *Mourning Dress: A Costume and Social History*. London: Allen and Unwin, 1983.

Taylor, Tom. *The Bottle.* Lord Chamberlain's Plays, British Library.

Terris, Ellaline. *Just a Little Bit of String.* London: Hutchinson, 1955.

Thompson, Paul. *The Edwardians: the Remaking of British Society.* London: Weidenfeld & Nicolson, 1975.

Thompson, Paul and Eileen Yeo, ed. *Unknown Mayhew: Selections from the Morning Chronicle 1849–50.* Harmondsworth: Penguin, 1984.

Tickner, Lisa. *The Spectacle of Women.* London: Chatto & Windus, 1987.

Toulmin, Camilla. "The Orphan Milliners: A Story of the West End." *Illuminated Magazine*, 2 (1845): 279–285.

Tree, Herbert Beerbohm. Clipping Books. University of Bristol, Theatre Collection.

Trewin, J. C. "Cicely Hamilton." *Dictionary of Literary Biography*, vol. x. *Modern British Dramatists, 1900–1945*, ed. Stanley Weintraub. Detroit: Gale, 1982, pp. 212–215.

Tuckwell, Gertrude, ed. *Women in Industry from Seven Points of View.* London: Duckworth, 1908.

Valverde, Mariana. "Love of Finery: Fashion and the Fallen Woman in Nineteenth-Century Social Discourse." *Victorian Studies*, 32:2 (1989): 169–188.

Vanbrugh, Irene. *To Tell My Story.* London: Hutchinson, [1948].

Vaughan, Gertrude. *The Woman with the Pack.* London: Ham-Smith, 1912.

Veblen, Thorstein. *The Theory of the Leisure Class.* 1899. Harmondsworth: Penguin, 1979.

Vicinus, Martha. *Independent Women: Work and Community for Single Women 1850–1920.* University of Chicago Press, 1985.

Walkley, Christina. *The Ghost in the Looking Glass.* London: Peter Owen, 1981.

Wearing, J. P., ed. *The Collected Letters of Sir Arthur Pinero.* Minneapolis: University of Minnesota Press, 1974.

Webster, Margaret. *The Same Only Different.* London: Victor Gollancz, 1969.

Wells, H. G. *Kipps.* London: Macmillan, 1905.

Wentworth, Vera. *An Allegory. Sketches from the Actresses' Franchise League*, ed. Viv Gardner. Nottingham: Nottingham Drama Texts, 1985, pp. 91–96.

Whitaker, Wilfred. *Victorian and Edwardian Shopworkers.* Newton Abbot: David and Charles, 1973.

Wilde, Oscar. *Collected Works*, 15 vols, ed. Robert Ross. London: Methuen, 1908–1922.
    Complete Works ed. J. B. Foreman. London: Collins, 1966.
    The Importance of Being Earnest, ed. Russell Jackson. London: Ernest Benn, 1980.
    Lady Windermere's Fan, ed. Ian Small. London: Ernest Benn, 1983.
    Lady Windermere's Fan. London: Elkins and Lane, 1893.
    More Letters of Oscar Wilde, ed. Rupert Hart-Davis. Oxford University Press, 1987.

Selected Letters of Oscar Wilde, ed. Rupert Hart-Davis. Oxford University Press, 1979.

"Shakespeare and Stage Costume." *Nineteenth Century*, May 1885: 800–818.

Two Society Comedies: A Woman of No Importance and An Ideal Husband, ed. Ian Small and Russell Jackson. London: Ernest Benn, 1983.

Willner, A. M. *et al. The Dollar Princess*. Lord Chamberlain's Plays, British Library.

A Woman's Vote. Lord Chamberlain's Plays, British Library.

Worth, Jean-Philippe. *A Century of Fashion*, trans. Ruth Scott Miller. Boston: Little, 1928.

Worth, Katharine. *Oscar Wilde*. London: Macmillan, 1983.

Zola, Emile. *The Ladies' Paradise (Au bonheur des dames)*, intro. Kristin Ross. Berkeley: University of California Press, 1992.

Index

Note: page numbers in *italic* refer to illustrations.

213